Pirandello's Major Plays

LUIGI PIRANDELLO

Pirandello's Major Plays

Right You Are
Six Characters in Search of an Author
Emperor Henry
The Man with the Flower in His Mouth

English Versions by Eric Bentley
With a Foreword by Albert Bermel

Northwestern University Press   Evanston, Illinois

Northwestern University Press
625 Colfax
Evanston Illinois 60201

Printed in the United States of America
First published 1991 by Northwestern University Press

95 94 93 92 91   5 4 3 2 1

Library of Congress Cataloging-in-Publication Data

Pirandello, Luigi, 1867–1936.
  [Plays. English. Selections]
  Pirandello's major plays / Luigi Pirandello ; English versions by
Eric Bentley ; with a foreword by Albert Bermel.
    p.   cm.
  Includes bibliographical references.
  Contents: Right you are —Six characters in search of an author —
—Emperor Henry —The man with the flower in his mouth.
  ISBN 0-8101-0866-6 (alk. paper). —ISBN 0-8101-0867-4 (pbk. :
alk. paper)
  1. Pirandello, Luigi, 1867–1936—Translations into English.
 I. Bentley, Eric, 1916–   . II. Title. III. Title: Major plays.
PQ4835.I7A23   1991
852'.912—dc20
                                                        90-25529
                                                          CIP

The paper used in this publication meets the minimum requirements of American National Standard for Information Sciences—Permanence of Paper for
Printed Library Materials, ANSI Z39.48-1984

Contents

The Comic Agony in Pirandello

> . . . I love
> The sight of agony, and the sense of joy,
> When this shall be another's, and that mine . . .
>
> —Count Cenci in Shelley's *The Cenci*

At the close of the overnight conversation reported in *The Symposium* Socrates, stimulated rather than blunted by his intake of wine and by the onset of dawn, is addressing himself to Agathon the tragedian and Aristophanes, the supreme creator of farcical comedy, insisting that "the man who knew how to write a comedy could also write a tragedy, and [that] a skillful tragic writer was capable of being also a comic writer." [1] The two poets do not dispute his claim, very likely because the wine and the hour have hit them harder and they are on the brink of sleep. In Plato's account (taken from Apollodorus, who had it from Aristodemus) Socrates doesn't go on to propose that a comic or a tragic playwright might concoct a drama that would be at the same time comic *and* tragic; and neither of his groggy listeners, from what we know of their work, would later attempt such an experiment in dramatic miscegenation.

But tragedies that are also comedies strike us today as being anything but startling, for they have become the dominant mode in twentieth-century writing, not only of plays but also of prose fiction and poetry. They differ from the Italian and French Renaissance and early Baroque tragicomedy, in which a "serious" action slides away from a tragic ending or a comic action turns unexpectedly sour; in either case, the prevailing tone, the tragic or comic mood, switches into its opposite, and unless the playwright transposes with uncommon discretion, the result may appear awkward, as if the last part of the work has been tacked on. From much of Shakespeare and subsequent drama the term tragicomedy acquired another connotation: that a play given this label *keeps* switching direction. A funny scene or moment precedes a dismal or disastrous one, which in turn leads to more merriment. This process needs not happen with mechanical precision. A final tally may show two comic scenes for every four "straight" ones. But the switching from mood to mood or tone to tone, back and forth, persists through the action.

Samuel Johnson had something like this switching in mind when he defended the art of Shakespeare, who "has united the powers of exciting laughter and sorrow not only in one mind but in one composition. Almost all his plays are divided between serious and ludicrous characters, and, in the successive evolutions of the design, sometimes produce seriousness and sorrow, and sometimes levity and laughter."[2] Johnson added that "this is a practice contrary to the rules of criticism," but he approved of such a practice if it led to Shakespearean theatre. Nearly two centuries later George Bernard Shaw, in a letter to his biographer, went further in elucidating Shakespeare's art. In *King Lear*, he says, "we find the alternation of tragic and funny dropped for an actual interweaving of the two; so that we have the tragic and the comic simultaneously, each heightening the other with a poignancy otherwise unattainable."[3] In separating "alternation" from "interweaving" Shaw catches an essential distinction between tragicomedy and what I would call "the comic agony" in plays, between what Johnson means by "successive evolutions in the design" and what Shaw calls simultaneous interweaving of comic and tragic threads in a fabric that is iridescent, indebted to both their colorings yet unlike either one. In his essay, "Tragi-Comedy," Eric Bentley adverts to more or less the same mix when he refers to "that comedy which is infused with gloom and ends badly, that tragedy which is shot through with a comedy that only makes the outlook still bleaker."[4]

In the modern era Pirandello did not initiate the comic agony. Ibsen, Shaw, Wedekind, Chekhov, and others had already employed it on the stage. But he became its most dogged and influential practitioner, mostly because he encased a tragic or melodramatic inner play performed only in fragments, within a comic or farcical outer play, and showed it striving to break out. *Emperor Henry* has an unusual pattern. As visitors to the villa and as observers, Countess Matilda and Baron Belcredi occupy the outer drama. But they both belonged to the original triangle, with "Henry," before and during the incidents at the carnival. When the quarrel erupts in the third act, culminating in the killing of the Baron, the inner drama implicates the two of them as it explodes into the outer one. In *Right You Are* and *Six Characters* the "outer" players form a distinct and impressionable onstage audience for those trapped in the inner one. Some of them make it difficult for us, as a second tier of spectators, to appreciate the agony of the inner play without *at the same time* being amused by their inappropriate responses and interpretations, their opaquely comic filterings.

The incomplete inner drama of *Right You Are,* the tragic knot that binds that black-clad Ponza and his wife (who might be awaiting their own funeral, which is also the partial enactment of their lives) to Signora Frola, is, in effect, demeaned by the inquisitiveness of the onstage audience, that twentieth-century school for scandal, the Agazzis and their guests; and it is further disfigured by Laudisi's interfering comments and his chortling, which the playwright exactly repeats with four snorts of laughter at the end of each act. In *Six Characters,* as we witness the tragic plight of the six unfortunates, two of them also garbed in black, we find that plight similarly tamed and given a comic gloss by the actors who mimic it and the director who would reshape it for popular consumption. "Henry," seething with the anguished memories of his past, has willfully imprisoned himself in the fate of a medieval ruler and forfeited his identity; but he plays games with his four "knights" and becomes, in his turn, the plaything of a psychiatric terror (with the first name of Dionysos and "a fine, satyr's face"), whose shock treatment has a calamitous outcome. The offhanded and metaphorical farewell bidden by the Man with the Flower in His Mouth, as he finishes talking, talking, talking through his instrument of doom and takes care to dodge his too-loving wife (another figure in black), has a grotesquely comic flavor that may evoke nervous laughs as he bitterly makes light of his condition—of the pathos of his one-character inner drama.[5]

Pirandello, though, seldom receives the tribute he merits as a comic writer. I would put forward four principal reasons for the neglect. First, much criticism dwells on his training and doctorate in German philosophy and on his remark that he had "the misfortune to belong" in the ranks of "philosophical writers."[6] On the assumption that philosophers, in their search for eternal verities, or even a nugget or two of stopgap wisdom, shed their sense of humor—the examples of Socrates, Nietzsche, and scores of others notwithstanding—the criticism in question shies away from this author's structural comedy. Second, the characters from the inner dramas portray themselves with such passion that their tragic intensity may overpower the comic infusions of the outer drama, especially when the inner roles are performed with the Sicilian vehemence that marks their dialogue and the directives from the author. Third, the later moments of each of these plays incorporate an act or revelation that leaves both audiences, onstage and off, stunned and apprehensive. After the speech of Signora

Ponza in *Right You Are* and after the deaths (one a presumed suicide) in *Six Characters* and the murder in *Emperor Henry,* the agony prevails: we'd feel almost profane if we released a smile or a laugh. Fourth, a traditional comedy or farce ends in a resolution of sorts; the dramatist leaves us with the conviction that there is nothing further to say. But a tragedy generally ends as a gaping wound; far from having resolved itself, the conclusion provokes questions; the action remains disturbingly incomplete. Each of these three plays even leaves both audiences—us and the one onstage, our distorting mirror—wondering what actually happened in the inner drama. Some secret that might reconcile the conflicts hangs in the air like a challenge.

In any event, the comedy will make itself felt. Pirandello's plays deal in large part with the refusal of some characters—some human beings— to comprehend the sufferings of others; and while the sufferings will be blatantly visible and audible, so will the incomprehension which, as it arises from time to time, puts the suffering at a remove and confers on it a layer of comic callousness. Lamberto Laudisi personifies this callousness. He remains onstage more persistently than any of the other characters. He starts out as a humanitarian, who sympathizes with Ponza and makes fun of the chorus of observers in the Agazzi household as they pursue their quest for an elusive, possibly unknowable truth; but he also revels in their perplexity, entertaining us when he chastises their altogether natural curiosity over the curious inner drama. He even prolongs the ordeal of Ponza and Signora Frola by coming up with the idea of interrogating Ponza's wife. Laudisi, who admits that he himself enjoys listening to gossip, is a spirit of mischief; he puckishly delights in playing up to an audience, even when he stands alone in front of a mirror and, for the benefit of the auditorium alone, asks his reflection which of the two of them is mad. For him, acting is being.

Here we run into another paradoxical matter in Pirandello's theater. The tragic characters wear masks of one kind or another which would seem to fix or "type" them; the comic characters (with a few exceptions, such as Laudisi) do not; yet, the former are more pliable and richer as roles. Pirandello suggests actual masks for the Six Characters—a suggestion rarely followed in practice—and specifies a "fundamental sentiment" for each of the four adult masks, but as the action continues the wearers do not conform to the restrictions of those masked expressions, while the unmasked members of the acting troupe behave conventionally, if not predictably. Neither "Henry" nor Matilda sports a literal mask, but he has applied "very obvious" makeup to his cheeks and has dyed his hair at the front and sides in a futile effort to preserve the illusion that he is still only twenty-six, and she uses "violent" cosmetics that give her "the haughty head of a Valkyrie." The text offers no clear signal of how she now feels about "the Emperor," except that she was fascinated enough by her remembrance of him to have come back to see him again, and her motives remain clouded throughout. He, volatile in the extreme, rocks between past and present, Germany and Italy, monarch and commoner, raving and oratorical lucidity. We cannot be sure that he did recover his sanity, as he alleges, twelve years after his accident, but nor can we know that he was ever certifiably insane. Has he persisted *consciously* with performance after performance, drawn out a twenty-year run of his bravura act, "perpetuating," as Belcredi says, "the unhappy joke of a carnival day"? "Henry"'s instability, his array of feelings (his multiplicity of "masks") during any one scene, constitutes the kernel of the play's inner drama. To hold the role together, to find a sort of architecture for it, means coping with one of the trickiest characterizations in the modern theatre.

Signora Frola, another "mask" at first, if we judge her by the "sweet smile that is constantly on her lips," also explores a range of emotions. Ponza, introduced as "almost fierce-looking," fluctuates from deference to defiance, from rage at being spied upon to extravagant tenderness toward his mother-in-law. His wife, the most masked of all Pirandello's characters, the apex of the tragic triangle in *Right You Are,* enters wearing a "thick veil, black, impenetrable," and does not lift it; yet, in her brief appearance, from her opening silence to her ten or so lines, she embodies the imponderable. We learn nothing from her or about her. She is "no one . . . To myself—I am the one that each of you thinks I am," utterly indeterminate, a creature of infinite latency.

Because of the fluidity of their roles, the "inner" characters not only change *as we perceive them* but also take part in shifting interactions. We cannot gauge with any confidence how they feel about one another from one instant to the next, much less how they will feel in their encounters to come. Spectators at the initial performances in Italy and elsewhere didn't hesitate to vent their bafflement over these uncertainties. They wanted readily identifiable characters engaged in relationships that were recognizable, clearcut. Pirandello, however, had put before them figures who floated free of definition, ambiguous entities in comparison with the meticulously planned, almost compartmentalized, roles they had grown accustomed to.[7]

An attentive theatergoer is bound to entertain further doubts—about the background material, the part of the unenacted story that precedes the action and is reported *during* the action. Some of this material involves clashes of information that help to impel the drama, such as the dispute over whether Lina/Julia is the first or second wife of Ponza. Other batches of material seem designed to withhold or suppress or disguise information, to tease us by omission. How did the trio manage to survive the selective earthquake that destroyed the village in which they were living, all the buildings, all the records, all their relatives? Were they away from home at the time? In an earthquake shelter? We are not told that they so much as suffered minor injuries or inhaled quantities of dust. Afterward, if Ponza wished to protect his privacy, why did he place his mother-in-law in the apartment next to Agazzi, his employer and interlocutor?

The Countess has been a widow "for many years," but we are never told whom she married after she refused "Henry," perhaps a count from whom she takes her title, though his name is never mentioned. Does "Henry," who has not seen her for twenty years, think she married the Baron, whom she keeps in tow as a lover and also as a butt for her mockery? Did the Baron cause the accident with the horse? "Henry" says so—nobody else confirms it—and he has evidently nursed his revenge for twenty years, but is it revenge for his fall and derangement or for having lost the Countess to this rival? Or both?

Signora Ponza declares that "the truth" is "simply this. I am Signora Frola's daughter . . . And I am Signor Ponza's second wife . . . And to myself I am no one." Do we understand her to be saying (not at all "simply") that she *chooses* to call herself one person to the husband and another to the mother, relinquishing her innateness in order to sustain a precarious harmony in the three-way relationship; or that she, or two of the three, or all of them, are insane; or that she cannot tell an unmentionable secret? One secret that would lend an evasive truth to her words is that she and Ponza are sister and brother and the children of Signora Frola.

Nor is it easy to take at face value the relationships among the family in *Six Characters,* especially the parentage of the four children.[8] In this play, too, Pirandello supplies hints but not quite enough information to suggest incest, the taboo that arouses the ghosts of Greek tragedy. A comparable secret that lurks behind the striking physical likeness implied in *Emperor Henry* between the protagonist and his nephew, "the young marquis" Carlo di Nolli, so that the presence of the one in a frame can be mistaken for the portrait of the other. Such a resemblance of nephew to uncle, though it does not unduly strain belief, would become even more telling if the Marquis were the *son* of "Henry," the counterpart of Frida, who, in the matching frame, plays her mother, the Countess. But "Henry's" siring of the Marquis denotes incest between "Henry" and his dead sister. That rich and inordinately selfless lady, who appears only in the exposition, transformed her Umbrian villa into an eleventh-century German palace to allow him to live on in his state of royal exaltation. On her deathbed, she begged her son to take care of him and bring people to see him, convinced that "her beloved brother's recovery was imminent," not long after he'd said "certain strange things to her" and "shown her a most unusual tenderness," as a result of which she grew "extremely upset." And are we to deduce any significance from the age of Frida, nineteen, in conjunction with the carnival's having taken place twenty years earlier, and "Henry's" clasping of her in the last act as he shouts, "You are mine, mine, mine! And by right!"? If he and the Countess were once lovers, and not only riding partners in the cavalcade; if he therefore sees Frida, rightly or wrongly, as his daughter, and not simply as a rejuvenated image of the Countess; and if the Marquis's likeness to him is more than coincidence, incest again rears its insidious head in the prospective marriage of the two young people.

Among the Six Characters, some accuse others of lying: conflicting evidence once more. The Mother begs that the story not be played out, even though she cannot come to stage life unless it *is* played out. She may feel her part in it has been shameful in having given herself to the Father, after he sent her to his former Secretary, and in not acknowledging the true parentage of the four children. Withheld information again. So is the absence of the Secretary, already conveniently dead, like "Henry's" sister, and unable to contribute his story, in order that a family secret may be safeguarded.

Suppositions like these can plunge us into deep, turbulent waters. We may avoid them and stay on the plays' surface by arguing that Pirandello wrote hurriedly, carelessly, but such an assumption is always risky with a writer of his rare caliber. In all likelihood he would have removed any material he considered blemishes, undesirably misleading, or superfluous, when he revised his work for the edition from which Eric Bentley, our most enlightened theater scholar,[9] has made these versions of four of Pirandello's most celebrated plays. How far, then, should the troubling ambiguities, which sharpen the agony of the characters' interplay, be taken into account when it comes to a staging? If many of the lines in each play are double-edged, one of the edges has an innocence to it that permits them to go almost unnoticed. Should they slip past in performance or receive sufficient weight—but not too much!—to permit insinuations of hidden, forbidden depths? There is no point in prescribing one or another approach; each decision will rest with a director and actors. But they should be aware of the choices open to them, their prerogatives, and the likely consequences of those choices. Trying to sound the depths will push a production in the direction of tragedy fostered by unconfessed guilt; trying to avoid them will give the production a lighter tone and a more rapid narrative flow that is not necessarily nearer to comedy. I believe that each company should allow for the darker, secret possibilities without sacrificing the comic overlay and yet without traducing a literal reading of each inner and outer drama. Such playing will call for a complicated interlocking of forcefulness and subtlety. But who ever claimed that capturing the majestic, immensely rewarding theater of Pirandello was easy?

ALBERT BERMEL

NOTES

1. Translation by Walter Hamilton in *Plato: The Symposium* (New York: Viking-Penguin, 1951), 113.

2. Preface to Johnson's edition of *The Plays of Shakespeare* (1765). See W. K. Wimsatt, Jr., *Samuel Johnson on Shakespeare* (New York: Hill and Wang, 1960), 23–69.

3. Archibald Henderson, *George Bernard Shaw: Man of the Century* (New York: Appleton-Century-Crofts, 1956), 471.

4. Chapter 10 of *The Life of the Drama* (New York: Atheneum, 1964), 353.

5. The agony of the Man with the Flower in His Mouth is no less affecting for being pathetic, rather than tragic. Tragedy implies responsibility for one's plight and suffering; but he did not cause the cancer, did not will it to appear and to grow. If anything, he communicates that agony to us all the more powerfully because of his attempt to put himself at a distance from it.

6. See Bentley's translation of the Preface to *Six Characters* in *Naked Masks* (New York: Dutton, 1952), 364–65.

7. The openness of Pirandello's characters and dramatic situations makes us look back suspiciously at the life-versus-form antithesis propounded by Pirandello and developed by Adriano Tilgher, the most methodical Pirandello critic among the playwright's contemporaries. In *Pirandello: A Biography* (London and New York: Oxford, 1975, translated and severely cut by Alastair Hamilton), Gaspare Giudice points out that Tilgher's theories impressed Pirandello himself for a time and even influenced his later writings.

Tilgher probably owed his theory to Pirandello's most strenuous allusion to form in opposition to life, the statements in *Six Characters* of the Father, who says that the writer will die but his characters will live on because they are fixed. Yes, on paper they *look* fixed, but Pirandello's and all other characters will spring to life in the theatre unforeseeably, according to the whims of casting. As for the fixed word in print, critics have continued to disagree about the nature of the characters as written, i.e., to unfix them by raising questions about their "form."

8. In *Contradictory Characters: An Interpretation of the Modern Theatre* (New York: Dutton, 1973) I have pursued this question of parentage at more length. See "The Living Statues," 122–43.

9. His book *The Pirandello Commentaries* (Evanston: Northwestern University Press, 1986) collects Bentley's Pirandello criticism, which, apart from its intrinsic and indispensable value, has inspired much writing by subsequent critics, including this introduction.

Right You Are

CHARACTERS

The Governor *of the Province*
Centuri *Police Commissioner*
Councillor Agazzi
Dina, *his daughter*
Amalia, *his wife*
Lamberto Laudisi, *her brother*
Signor Ponza, *an executive secretary under Agazzi*
Signora Ponza, *his wife*
Signora Frola, *his mother-in-law*

Signor Sirelli ⎫
Signora Sirelli ⎬ *friends of the Agazzis*
Signora Cini, *a friend of Signora Sirelli*
Signora Nenni, *a friend of Signora Cini*
Butler
A Man
A Second Man
Other Citizens

The Place: A province in central Italy
The Time: The present

Act I   Scene 1

The curtain rises on the home of Councillor Agazzi.[1] In the drawing room are
AMALIA, DINA, *and* LAUDISI. LAUDISI *is walking across the room, irritated.*
A man of about forty, quick and lithe, he dresses well without overdoing it; he
has on a violet-colored smoking jacket with black lapels and braid.

LAUDISI. Aha! So he's gone to take the matter up with the Governor?

AMALIA [*about forty-five, gray hair. Makes a great show of importance because*
of her husband's place in society, at the same time giving us to understand
that she could play the part all by herself and on many occasions would take
quite a different line from his.]. Heavens, Lamberto, just for a member
of his staff?

LAUDISI. Member of his staff? In the Government Building, yes. But not
at home!

DINA [*nineteen years old. Has a certain air of understanding everything better*
than her mother or her father. But this air is softened by considerable youth-
ful charm]. But he's come here and put his mother-in-law in an apartment right next to ours—on our floor!

LAUDISI. Wasn't he entitled to? There was an apartment for rent, so he
rented it for his mother-in-law. [*Petulant, laying it on thick*] Or do you
think the old lady should have asked your permission? Just because
your father is above her son-in-law at the office?

AMALIA. What do you mean? As a matter of fact, Dina and I took the
initiative and went to visit her first. [*With emphasis*] She didn't receive
us.

LAUDISI. And now what's your husband gone running to the Governor
for? Is he appealing to the authorities? To *force* them into an act of
courtesy?

AMALIA. Into an act of just reparation anyway! You don't leave two ladies
standing at the door like a couple of posts.

LAUDISI. What a pompous attitude! Aren't people allowed to stay home
and enjoy a little privacy?

AMALIA. All right, if you don't wish to realize that we were the ones who
tried to be courteous to a stranger. We went to her first.

DINA. Now really, Uncle, be sensible! If you like we'll be frank and admit
it: we were courteous out of curiosity. But, come, isn't that natural?

3

LAUDISI. Natural, by all means: you've all got nothing to do.

DINA. Now, look, Uncle. There you stand minding your own business. Taking no notice of what other people are doing. Good. I come into the room. And there—on the little table just in front of you—cool as a cucumber, or rather with a long face like that jailbird we were talking about—I set down—well, what?—let's say a pair of the cook's shoes.

LAUDISI [*impatiently*]. What have the cook's shoes to do with it?

DINA [*quickly*]. Ha, you see? You're amazed. You find it queer and at once ask the why and wherefore.

LAUDISI [*pauses, smiles coldly, speedily recovers*]. What a girl! Pretty bright, aren't you? But you're talking with me, don't forget. You come and put the cook's shoes on the table just to awaken my curiosity. Obviously—since you did it with this in mind—you can't reproach me if I ask: "But *why* are the cook's shoes here on the table, my dear?" Just as you have to show me that this Signor Ponza—rascal and boor as your father calls him—*intentionally* found an apartment for his mother-in-law here in this house.

DINA. All right. Let's suppose it wasn't intentional. You can't deny that the strange way the man lives would be bound to arouse the curiosity of the whole town, it's only natural. Think. He arrives. He finds a place to live on the top floor of that murky tenement, the one on the edge of town, looking out on the orchards . . . Have you seen it? Inside, I mean?

LAUDISI. You've been to see it?

DINA. Yes, Uncle. With Mother. And we're not the only ones either. Everybody's been to see it. There's a courtyard, and is it dark! Like a well. Way up on the top floor there's a balcony with an iron railing. They let baskets down from it on ropes.

LAUDISI. What of it?

DINA [*with amazement and indignation*]. That's where he's put his wife: up there.

AMALIA. While he puts his mother-in-law here—next door to us.

LAUDISI. In a nice apartment with a central location. Lucky mother-in-law!

AMALIA. Lucky? He's just compelling her to live apart from her daughter!

LAUDISI. Who told you? Couldn't it be her own idea? She may want more freedom.

DINA. What nonsense, Uncle! Everyone knows it's his idea.

AMALIA. Now look. Everyone understands a daughter leaving her mother's house when she gets married—and going to live with her husband—in another city, if necessary. But you don't mean to say you understand it if a mother—unable to bear being away from the daughter—follows her and then is compelled to live apart from her in a city where after all *she's* a stranger too?

LAUDISI. Why not? Have you no imagination? Is it so hard to suppose that through her fault, or his, or nobody's, there might be some . . . incompatibility of character through which, even in those conditions . . .

DINA [*interrupting, amazed*]. What, Uncle? Between mother and daughter?

LAUDISI. Why between mother and daughter?

AMALIA. Because it couldn't be the other two, they're always together.

DINA. It's true. To everyone's astonishment, husband and mother-in-law are always together.

AMALIA. He comes here every evening—to keep her company.

DINA. Even in the day he usually comes over a couple of times.

LAUDISI. You suspect they make love maybe—husband and mother-in-law?

DINA. Uncle! How can you speak so of a poor old lady?

AMALIA. He never brings her daughter. Never, never, never does he bring his wife to her own mother!

LAUDISI. She must be sick, poor girl, and can't go out of doors . . .

DINA. Nonsense. The mother goes there . . .

AMALIA. She goes, yes, just to look on from a distance! Everyone knows the poor mother isn't allowed to go up to the daughter's apartment.

DINA. She can only talk to her from the courtyard below.

AMALIA. From the courtyard, understand?

DINA. While her daughter is up there on the balcony—in the sky practically! The poor old thing enters the courtyard, pulls the rope, the bell rings up above, the daughter comes out on the balcony, and the old lady talks to her, from the bottom of that well, stretching her neck back like this. Imagine! She doesn't even see her, she's blinded by the sunlight pouring down from above.

[*There is a knock at the door and the* BUTLER *appears.*]

Scene 2

The same, the BUTLER, *then* SIGNORA SIRELLI, SIGNOR SIRELLI, SIGNORA CINI

BUTLER. Are you at home, Signora?

AMALIA. Who is it?

BUTLER. Signor Sirelli, Signora Sirelli, and another lady, Signora.

AMALIA. Very well, show them in.

[*The* BUTLER *bows and leaves.*]

AMALIA [*to* SIGNORA SIRELLI]. How are you, my dear?

SIGNORA SIRELLI [*fattish, red-faced, still young, dressed with exaggerated provincial elegance, burning with restless curiosity; harsh to her husband*]. I've ventured to bring my good friend Signora Cini who *so* much wanted to meet you!

AMALIA. How are you, Signora? Do sit down, everybody. [*Making the introductions*] This is my daughter, Dina. My brother, Lamberto Laudisi.

SIRELLI [*bald, around forty, fat, with oiled hair and much pretense of elegant dress, squeaking, shiny shoes. Bowing*]. Signora! Signorina! [*Shaking* LAUDISI's *hand*]

SIGNORA SIRELLI. Ah, dear Signora, we come here as to the fountain, two poor women *athirst* for news!

AMALIA. News of what, ladies?

SIGNORA SIRELLI. Why, of this blessed new secretary in the Government Building. No one in town talks of anything else!

SIGNORA CINI [*an old fool, full of greedy malice veiled beneath an air of naïveté*]. We feel such curiosity about it, such curiosity!

AMALIA. But we don't know any more about it than you, believe me, Signora!

SIRELLI [*to his wife, as if scoring a triumph*]. What did I tell you? They don't know any more than me, maybe less. [*Turning to the others*] The reason why this poor mother can't go and visit her daughter, for example—do you know what it really is?

AMALIA. I was just speaking of it with my brother.

LAUDISI. In whose opinion you've all gone mad!

DINA [*quickly, so as to ignore* LAUDISI]. Because the husband—so they say—forbids her to.

SIGNORA CINI [*in a tone of lamentation*]. Not enough of a reason, Signorina.

SIGNORA SIRELLI. [*pressing the issue*]. Not nearly enough, there's more to it!

SIRELLI [*with a gesture to attract attention*]. A piece of news for you, hot off the griddle. [*Emphasizing every syllable*] He keeps her under lock and key!

AMALIA. Whom? His mother-in-law?

SIRELLI. No, Signora. His wife!

SIGNORA SIRELLI. His wife, his wife!

SIGNORA CINI [*in a tone of lamentation*]. Under lock and key!

DINA. You understand, Uncle? You who wish to excuse—

SIRELLI [*astonished*]. What? You'd want to excuse this monster?

LAUDISI. But I don't wish to excuse him in the least! I say that your curiosity—begging all your pardons—is insufferable—if only because it is useless.

SIRELLI. Useless?

LAUDISI. Useless! Useless, good ladies!

SIGNORA CINI. Useless? To try and find out?

LAUDISI. Find out what, if I may ask? What can we really know of other people, who they are, what they are, what they are doing, why they are doing it—

SIGNORA SIRELLI. By demanding news, information—

LAUDISI. If anyone should be abreast of all the news, that person is you, Signora—with a husband like yours, always informed of everything!

SIRELLI [*trying to interrupt*]. Excuse me—

SIGNORA SIRELLI. No, no, my dear: I admit it's the truth! [*Turning to* AMALIA] The truth, my dear, is that, with a husband who always claims to know *every*thing, I never manage to know *any*thing!

SIRELLI. No wonder! She's never satisfied with what I tell her. Always suspects that a thing is not as I have said. Maintains, as a matter of fact, that it *can't* be as I have said. And in the end decides it must be exactly the opposite.

SIGNORA SIRELLI. Now just a minute, if you come and tell me—

LAUDISI [*laughs aloud*]. May I say something, Signora? I will answer your husband. My dear man, how do you expect your wife to be satisfied with the things you tell her if you—as is natural—present them as they are to you?

SIGNORA SIRELLI. As they absolutely cannot be!

LAUDISI. Ah no, Signora, permit me to say that now *you* are in the wrong! To your husband, rest assured, things are as he tells you they are!

SIRELLI. They are what they *really* are, what they *really* are!

SIGNORA SIRELLI. Not in the least. You are always wrong!

SIRELLI. *You* are wrong, I beg you to believe. *I* am right!

LAUDISI. No, no, my dear friends. Neither of you is wrong. May I explain? I'll prove it to you. [*He rises and goes to the middle of the room.*] Both of you see me? You do see me, don't you?

SIRELLI. Why, of course.

LAUDISI. No, no, don't speak too quickly, my friend. Come here!

SIRELLI [*looks at him, smiles, perplexed and a little disconcerted, not wishing to lend himself to a joke he doesn't understand*]. What for?

SIGNORA SIRELLI [*pushing him. Her voice is irritable*]. Go on.

LAUDISI [*to* SIRELLI *who has now approached, trembling*]. You see me? Take a better look. Touch me.

SIGNORA SIRELLI [*to her husband, who still hesitates to touch him*]. Touch him!

LAUDISI [*to* SIRELLI, *who has raised one hand with which he gingerly touches his shoulder*]. That's it, well done. You're sure you touch me—just as you see me—isn't that so?

SIRELLI. I'd say so.

LAUDISI. You can't doubt it, of course. Go back to your seat.

SIGNORA SIRELLI [*to her husband who has remained in front of* LAUDISI, *stupefied*]. It's no use standing there blinking, go and sit down!

LAUDISI [*to* SIGNORA SIRELLI, *now that her husband has gone back, still in a stupor, to his seat*]. Now would *you* like to come, Signora? [*Quickly, before she can move*] No, no, I'll come to you. [*He is now before her, down on one knee.*] You see me, don't you? Raise one little hand, touch me. [*And as* SIGNORA SIRELLI, *still seated, places one hand on his shoulder, bending down to kiss it*] Dear little hand!

SIRELLI [*warningly*]. Uh, uh.

LAUDISI. Take no notice of him. Are you, too, certain that you touch me just as you see me? You can't doubt it, can you? But I beg you, don't tell your husband, or my sister, or my niece, or this lady here, Signora—

SIGNORA CINI [*prompting*]. Cini.

LAUDISI. Cini. Don't tell them *what* you see in me, because all four will tell you you are wrong, whereas you are not wrong in the least: I really am as you see me. But, dear lady, that doesn't stop me really being as your husband sees me, as my sister sees me, as my niece sees me, as this lady here, Signora—

SIGNORA CINI [*prompting*]. Cini.

LAUDISI. Cini sees me—for they aren't wrong either.

SIGNORA SIRELLI. How's that? You're a different person for each one of us?

LAUDISI. Certainly I am, dear lady, aren't you?

SIGNORA SIRELLI [*in a rush*]. No, no, no, no, no! As I see it, I'm myself and that's that.

LAUDISI. As *I* see it, I'm *my*self and that's that. And if you people don't see
me as I see myself, I say you're wrong—but this is all so much presumption—in me or in you, dear lady.

SIRELLI. May I ask what you hope to conclude with all this hocus-pocus?

LAUDISI. You think there's no conclusion to be drawn? Well, well. You're
all so anxious to find out who other people are and what things
are like, almost as if people and things were simply this way or that
way.

SIGNORA SIRELLI. According to you, then, one can never know the truth?

SIGNORA CINI. Why, if seeing and touching aren't believing . . .

LAUDISI. But they are, dear lady, rest assured! All I'm saying is: respect
what other people see and touch even if it's the opposite of what *you*
see and touch!

SIGNORA SIRELLI. Listen to him! I turn my back on you, I won't talk with
you any more. I don't want to go mad.

LAUDISI. Well, that's enough then. Go on talking of Signora Frola and
Signor Ponza, her son-in-law. I won't interrupt again.

AMALIA. God be praised! You'd do even better, my dear Lamberto, if you
would leave us.

DINA. Yes, leave us, Uncle, do, do!

LAUDISI. Why should I? It amuses me to hear you talk. I'll keep my mouth
shut, don't worry. At the most I'll permit myself a quiet smile—and if
I actually burst out laughing you'll just have to excuse me.

SIGNORA SIRELLI. And to think that we had come to find out . . . ! Now,
Signora, isn't your husband above this Signor Ponza in the office?

AMALIA. The office is one thing, the home another, Signora.

SIGNORA SIRELLI. That's right, I understand! But haven't you even tried
to see his mother-in-law who lives here?

DINA. Oh yes, Signora. Twice.

SIGNORA CINI [*with a start; then, with greedy, intent concentration*]. Ah! So
you *have* talked to her?

AMALIA. She didn't receive us, my dear.

SIRELLI, SIGNORA SIRELLI, SIGNORA CINI. Oh!!! How is that possible?

DINA. We went there this morning for the second time—

AMALIA. The first time we waited more than a quarter of an hour at the
door. Nobody came to open it, we couldn't so much as leave a visiting
card. Today we tried again—

DINA [*with a gesture of horror*]. And *he* came to the door!

SIGNORA SIRELLI. That face of his! There's something *bad* in it. It's a public menace, the whole town is affected. Then the way he dresses, al-

ways in black . . . All three of them wear black, his wife too—the old lady's daughter—isn't that so?

SIRELLI [*with annoyance*]. You know that no one has even seen the old lady's daughter! I've told you a thousand times. One *supposes* she wears black . . . They're from a village in Marsica—

AMALIA. Yes, totally destroyed, it seems—

SIRELLI. Razed to the ground in the last earthquake.

DINA. I heard they lost all their relatives.

SIGNORA CINI [*anxious to take up the interrupted discussion*]. Yes, yes—so, *he* came to the door?

AMALIA. The moment I saw him in front of me with that face of his I was struck dumb. I couldn't even find the words to say we'd come to call on his mother-in-law. He said nothing either! Didn't even thank me.

DINA. Oh, well, he did bow!

AMALIA. Only just: he nodded his head like this.

DINA. His eyes spoke, though, didn't they? They're a wild beast's eyes, not a man's.

SIGNORA CINI [*as above*]. What next? What did he say next?

DINA. He was very embarrassed—

AMALIA. And very disheveled. He told us his mother-in-law was not well, that he wanted to thank us for our courtesy, then he just stood there in the doorway waiting for us to go!

DINA. What a humiliation!

SIRELLI. He's a boor. Oho, you can be sure *he's* at the bottom of the whole thing. Maybe he has his mother-in-law under lock and key too!

SIGNORA SIRELLI. The nerve of the man! To behave like that to a lady— the wife of a superior!

AMALIA. This time my husband really got indignant. He said the fellow was gravely lacking in respect and off he's gone to make a strong protest to the Governor and demand satisfaction.

DINA. Oh good, here *is* Father!

Scene 3

The same, COUNCILLOR AGAZZI

AGAZZI [*fifty, red hair, untidy, with beard, gold-rimmed glasses; an air of authority and malevolence*]. My dear Sirelli. [*He approaches, bows, and shakes hands with* SIGNORA SIRELLI.] Signora.

AMALIA [*introducing him to* SIGNORA CINI]. My husband—Signora Cini.

AGAZZI [*bows, shakes hands*]. Delighted. [*He then turns, almost solemnly, to his wife and daughter.*] I have to report that Signora Frola will be here at any moment.

SIGNORA SIRELLI [*clapping her hands, exultant*]. Really? She'll be here?

AGAZZI. It had to be done. Could I tolerate such a glaring misdemeanor toward my home, toward my womenfolk?

SIRELLI. Quite so. Just what we were saying.

SIGNORA SIRELLI. And it would be good to take this opportunity—

AGAZZI [*anticipating*]. To notify the Governor of everything the town is saying in regard to this gentleman? Don't worry, I've done so!

SIRELLI. Oh, good, good!

SIGNORA CINI. Such *inexplicable* things! Absolutely *inconceivable!*

AMALIA. Positively *wild!* Do you know he keeps them under lock and key—both of them!

DINA. Well, Mother, we don't know about the mother-in-law yet.

SIGNORA SIRELLI. It's certain about his wife, though!

SIRELLI. What about the Governor?

AGAZZI. Yes, the Governor . . . well . . . it made a profound impression on him . . .

SIRELLI. That's good.

AGAZZI. Something had got through to him too, of course, and now, like the rest of us, he sees how advisable it is to clear up this mystery. To find out the truth.

[LAUDISI *laughs aloud.*]

AMALIA.The only thing missing in the picture: Lamberto laughing!

AGAZZI. What's he found to laugh at this time?

SIGNORA SIRELLI. He says it's not possible to discover the truth!

Scene 4

The same, the BUTLER, *then* SIGNORA FROLA

BUTLER [*comes to the doorway and announces*]. A visitor, Signora. Signora Frola.

SIRELLI. Ah! Here she is.

AGAZZI. We'll soon see if it's possible to discover the truth, my dear Lamberto.

SIGNORA SIRELLI. Wonderful! Oh, I'm so glad!

AMALIA [*rising, to* AGAZZI]. Shall we have her come in?

AGAZZI. Yes, yes, show her in. But let's set the stage. Move your chairs back a little, will you?[2] That's it. Now sit down, I beg you. Wait till she arrives. We should all be seated. Seated. [*The* BUTLER *withdraws. After a brief pause* SIGNORA FROLA *enters and all rise.* SIGNORA FROLA *is an old lady, neat, unpretentious, very affable; with a great sadness in her eyes, softened by the sweet smile that is constantly on her lips.* AMALIA *goes forward and extends her hand.*]

AMALIA. Come in, Signora. [*Holding her hand, she introduces her.*] Signora Cini, Signora Sirelli, my good friend. Signor Sirelli. My husband. My daughter, Dina. My brother, Lamberto Laudisi. Please sit down, Signora.

SIGNORA FROLA. I'm most distressed. I've come to beg pardon for having neglected my duty till today. It was so gracious of you, Signora, to honor me with a visit when it was for me to be the first to come.

AMALIA. Among neighbors, Signora, we take no notice whose turn comes first. Especially since you're alone here and strange to the neighborhood, we thought you might be in need . . .

SIGNORA FROLA. Thank you, thank you . . . you are too kind . . .

SIGNORA SIRELLI. You are alone in our town, Signora?

SIGNORA FROLA. No, I have a married daughter. She came here too not long ago.

SIRELLI. The Signora's son-in-law is a secretary in the Government Building—Signor Ponza—isn't that so?

SIGNORA FROLA. That's right, yes. And I do hope Councillor Agazzi will excuse me . . . and my son-in-law too . . .

AGAZZI. To tell you the truth, Signora, I did take it rather ill—

SIGNORA FROLA [*interrupting*]. You were right, quite right! But you must excuse him! Believe me when I say we are still overwhelmed by . . . what happened.

AMALIA. Of course, you were in that terrible disaster!

SIGNORA SIRELLI. You lost relatives?

SIGNORA FROLA. All of them—all, Signora. There isn't a trace of our village left. Just a heap of ruins with fields all round. Deserted.

SIRELLI. Just what we heard.

SIGNORA FROLA. I only had a sister—and her daughter, unmarried luckily . . . But it was a much harder blow for my poor son-in-law: mother, two brothers, a sister, the brothers' wives, the sister's husband, two nephews . . .

SIRELLI. A massacre!

SIGNORA FROLA. Blows you can never recover from. It's like being—stunned.

AMALIA. It certainly is.

SIGNORA SIRELLI. And all from one moment to the next. It's enough to drive people mad.

SIGNORA FROLA. Your mind doesn't work, you forget and overlook things without in the least meaning to, Councillor.

AGAZZI. Please, Signora, not a word of excuse!

AMALIA. This terrible . . . blow was one of the reasons my daughter and I came to see you . . . first.

SIGNORA SIRELLI [*writhing with curiosity*]. That's right. They knew how alone you were! Though . . . excuse me, Signora, for wondering how it is . . . with your daughter here. . . . after such a blow . . . that . . . [*After this enterprising start she is suddenly bashful.*] . . . it seems to me that survivors would feel the need to stand together—

SIGNORA FROLA [*continuing, to save her from embarrassment*]. How it is that I am quite alone?

SIRELLI. Exactly! It does seem strange—to be frank with you.

SIGNORA FROLA [*distressed*]. Yes, I understand. [*Then, trying a possible way out*] But—when your son or your daughter gets married, it's my opinion they should be left to themselves—to make their own life, that's all.

LAUDISI. How right you are! And this life must be a new life, revealing itself in the new relationship with wife or husband.

SIGNORA SIRELLI. But not to the extent, my dear Laudisi, of excluding the mother's life from her own!

LAUDISI. Who talked of exclusion? We are talking now, if I understand the matter, of a mother who sees that her daughter neither can nor should stay tied to her as she was before—because now she has a life of her own.

SIGNORA FROLA [*with keen gratitude*]. That's it, that's how it is, ladies! Thank you, that's exactly what I was trying to say.

SIGNORA CINI. But I'm sure your daughter *does* come quite often—to keep you company?

SIGNORA FROLA [*uncomfortable*]. Surely . . . of course . . . we see each other, naturally . . .

SIRELLI [*promptly*]. Yet your daughter never goes out—at any rate no one has ever seen her!

SIGNORA CINI. Perhaps she has children to look after?

SIGNORA FROLA [*promptly*]. No. There are no children yet. And maybe she
will never have any—now. She's been married seven years. She has
things to do in the house, of course. But that isn't it. [*She smiles in her
distress, adding, as another possible way of escape*] In small towns we're
used to staying home all the time, we women are used to it.

AGAZZI. Even when there's a mother for us to go and see? A mother who
doesn't live with us any more?

AMALIA. But the Signora does go to see her daughter, doesn't she?

SIGNORA FROLA [*promptly*]. Certainly. Oh, yes! I go once or twice a day.

SIRELLI. You climb all those stairs twice a day—to the top floor of that
tenement?

SIGNORA FROLA [*growing pale, still trying to turn the torture of this question-
ing into a smile*]. No, it's true I don't go up, you're right, ladies, they'd
be too many for me, the stairs. I don't go up. My daughter comes to
the balcony in the courtyard and—we see each other, we talk.

SIGNORA SIRELLI. Only that way? You never see her close up?

DINA [*with her arm around her mother's neck*]. As a daughter, I don't claim
my mother would climb ninety or a hundred stairs for me, but I
wouldn't be satisfied with seeing her, with talking to her from a distance, without embracing her, without feeling her near me.

SIGNORA FROLA [*keenly disturbed, embarrassed*]. You are right. Oh, well, I
see I have to speak out. I wouldn't like you to think something of my
daughter that is not the case—that she isn't fond of me, isn't considerate toward me. As for myself—I'm her mother—ninety or a hundred stairs wouldn't keep a mother away, even if she *is* old and tired,
when such a prize awaits her at the top, and she can press her daughter
to her heart.

SIGNORA SIRELLI [*triumphant*]. Aha! Just what we said, Signora! There
must be a reason!!

AMALIA [*pointedly*]. You see, Lamberto: there *is* a reason!

SIRELLI [*promptly*]. Your son-in-law, eh?

SIGNORA FROLA. Oh dear, please, please, don't think ill of him! He's such
a fine young fellow. You can't imagine how kind he is—what tender
and delicate affection he shows me—how much attention he pays me!
To say nothing of the loving care he lavishes on my daughter! Believe
me, I couldn't have wished her a better husband!

SIGNORA SIRELLI. But . . . in that case . . .

SIGNORA CINI. *He* can't be the reason!

AGAZZI. Of course not. It doesn't seem to me *possible* he should forbid his wife to go and see her mother—or her mother to come and be with *her* a little!

SIGNORA FROLA. Forbid? But I never said he forbade it. It's ourselves, Councillor, my daughter and I: we do without each other's company—of our own accord, believe me—for his sake.

AGAZZI. But how, pray, could he take offense? I don't see it.

SIGNORA FROLA. It's not a matter of offense, Councillor. It's a feeling . . . a feeling, ladies, rather hard to understand. But when you do understand it, it's not hard—to sympathize—although it may mean we have to make a real sacrifice, my daughter and I.

AGAZZI. At least you must admit it's *strange,* what you have to tell us, Signora.

SIRELLI. It certainly is. It arouses, and justifies, curiosity.

AGAZZI. Curiosity—and suspicion.

SIGNORA FROLA. Against him? Please, please don't say that! *What* could anyone suspect, Councillor?

AGAZZI. Nothing at all. Don't be disturbed. I'm saying that suspicion *could* arise.

SIGNORA FROLA. Oh no, no! *What* can they suspect, if we are in perfect agreement? My daughter and I are satisfied, completely satisfied!

SIGNORA SIRELLI. He's jealous, perhaps?

SIGNORA FROLA. Jealous of her mother? I don't think you could call it that. Though, of course, I can't claim to know. Look, he wants his wife's heart all to himself. He admits my daughter loves me too, must love me, he fully and gladly admits it, but he wants her love to come to me through him, *he* wants to bring it to me.

AGAZZI. No, I don't see. If you'll forgive me, I consider it the purest cruelty, behavior like that.

SIGNORA FROLA. Cruelty!! No, NO!! Don't call it cruelty, Councillor, it's something else, believe me. I don't know how to put it into words. . . . His *nature,* that's it. Or—maybe—maybe it's a kind of—illness, call it that. It's—it's the fullness of his love, a love entire, exclusive. She must live shut up in it. With no doors: she mustn't go out and no one else must come in.

DINA. Not even her mother?

SIRELLI. Sheer selfishness I call that!

SIGNORA FROLA. Perhaps. But a selfishness that gives itself utterly and provides a world to live in—for his own wife. After all it would be selfishness on my part, were I to force my way into this closed world of love—when my daughter is happy within it. Happy and adored. To a mother, ladies, that should be enough, shouldn't it? For the rest, if I see her, if I talk to my daughter . . . [*With a graceful, confidential movement*] The little basket in the courtyard carries a few words up to her, and a few words back to me . . . our letters give the day's news. I'm satisfied with that. And by this time I'm used to it—I'm resigned, you might say. It doesn't hurt me now.

AMALIA. Well, of course, if you're both satisfied, you and your daughter . . .

SIGNORA FROLA [*rising*]. We are, we are! Because he's so kind, believe me! He couldn't be more so. We all have our weaknesses, don't we? and we need each other's sympathy. [*Taking her leave of* AMALIA] Signora. [*Taking her leave first of* SIGNORA CINI, SIGNORA SIRELLI, SIRELLI, *then turning to* COUNCILLOR AGAZZI] You will excuse me, won't you?

AGAZZI. Don't mention it, my dear Signora. We are most grateful for your visit.

SIGNORA FROLA [*nods to* DINA *and* LAUDISI, *then turns to* AMALIA]. Please don't—just stay here—please don't come to the door.

AMALIA. Why, of course I will, it's my duty, Signora.

[SIGNORA FROLA *leaves the room with* AMALIA, *who returns a moment later.*]

SIRELLI.Well, well, well! Are you satisfied with the explanation?

AGAZZI. What explanation? It seems to me everything is still shrouded in mystery.

SIGNORA SIRELLI. And who knows how much this poor soul of a mother must suffer!

DINA. Her daughter too, poor thing.

[*Pause*]

SIGNORA CINI [*from the corner of the room whither she has retired to hide her tears, with a strident explosion*]. She was nearly crying, the whole time!

AMALIA. I noticed it when she said she'd climb far more than a hundred stairs just to press her daughter to her heart!

LAUDISI. *I* thought she was trying to protect her son-in-law from suspicion. That seemed to be the whole aim of her visit.

SIGNORA SIRELLI. Not at all. Why, heavens, she had no idea how to excuse what he has done!

SIRELLI. Excuse? Excuse violence? Excuse downright barbarism?

Scene 5

The same, the BUTLER, *then* PONZA

BUTLER [*coming to the doorway*]. Signor Agazzi, Signor Ponza is here. He wishes to be received.

SIGNORA SIRELLI. Ah! That man!!

[*General surprise. A movement of anxious curiosity, almost of dismay*]

AGAZZI. He wants *me* to receive him?

BUTLER. Yes, Signore, that's what he says.

SIGNORA SIRELLI. Oh please, Councillor, receive him, receive him *here!* I'm almost afraid, but I'm so curious to see him close up! The monster!!

AMALIA. What does he want?

AGAZZI. Let's find out. Show him in. Be seated, everybody. We must all be seated!

[*The* BUTLER *bows and withdraws. A moment's pause. Enter* PONZA. *Thickset, dark, almost fierce-looking, clad all in black, thick black hair, low forehead, big black mustache. He keeps clenching his fists, speaks with an effort, with barely suppressed violence. From time to time he wipes his sweat off with a black-bordered handkerchief. When he speaks his eyes stay hard, fixed, dismal.*]

Come in, come right in, Signor Ponza. [*Introducing him*] The new executive secretary: Signor Ponza. My wife—Signora Sirelli—Signora Cini—my daughter—Signor Sirelli—my brother-in-law, Laudisi. Please sit down

PONZA. Thank you. I'll only be troubling you for a moment.

AGAZZI. Would you like to speak with me in private?

PONZA. No, I can—I can speak in front of everybody. It's better that way. The declaration I have to make is a matter of duty—*my* duty—

AGAZZI. You mean about your mother-in-law's not visiting us? You really needn't bother, because—

PONZA. It's not that, Councillor. I feel I must tell you my mother-in-law, Signora Frola, would undoubtedly have come to visit you before your wife and daughter had the goodness to come to her, had I not done all I could to prevent her doing so. I couldn't permit her either to pay visits or to receive them.

AGAZZI [*with pride and resentment*]. And why not, may I ask?

PONZA [*getting more excited all the time despite his efforts to control himself*]. I suppose my mother-in-law has been talking to you all? Has told you I forbid her to enter my home and see her daughter?

AMALIA. No, no! She was full of consideration and kindness toward you.

DINA. She had nothing but good to say of you.

AGAZZI. She said she refrains from entering her daughter's home of her own accord, out of respect for a feeling of yours which we frankly admit we don't understand.

SIGNORA SIRELLI. In fact if we were to say what we really think of it . . .

AGAZZI. Yes. It seemed to us a piece of cruelty. Real cruelty.

PONZA. I came here expressly to clear this up, Councillor. This lady's condition is a pitiful one, but my own is scarcely less pitiful. For I see I am obliged to beg pardon, I am obliged to tell you all about a misfortune which—which only such violence as this could compel me to reveal. [*He stops a moment to look at everyone. Then, in a slow and staccato voice*] Signora Frola is mad.

EVERYONE [*jumping out of his skin*]. Mad?

PONZA. She's been mad for four years.

SIGNORA SIRELLI [*with a cry*]. Heavens, she doesn't *seem* mad!

AGAZZI [*stunned*]. What? Mad?

PONZA. She doesn't *seem* mad, but she *is* mad. And her madness consists precisely in believing that I don't wish her to see her daughter. [*With terrible excitement, almost ferocious perturbation*] And what daughter, in heaven's name? Her daughter died four years ago.

EVERYONE [*flabbergasted*]. Died? Oh! What? Died?

PONZA. Four years ago. That's what drove her mad.

SIRELLI. Then, the lady who is your wife today?

PONZA. I married again. Two years ago.

AMALIA. And the old lady thinks your present wife is her daughter?

PONZA. Such has been her good fortune, one might almost say. She was under surveillance, not allowed to go out. But one day, through her window, she saw me in the street with my second wife. She thought it was her daughter, still alive. She started laughing, trembling all over. At a single blow she was free of the dark desperation she had fallen into—only to find herself in another insanity. At first she was exultant, ecstatic. Then, bit by bit, she grew calmer and, despite the anguish in her heart, managed to subside into an attitude of resignation. She is satisfied, as you could see. She persists in believing that her daughter is not dead but that I want to keep her all to myself and not let anyone see her. She seems quite cured. So much so that, to hear her talk, you wouldn't think she was mad in the least.

AMALIA. Not in the least!

SIGNORA SIRELLI. It's true, she does say she's satisfied now.

PONZA. She tells everyone that. And is grateful and affectionate to me. Because I try to back her up in every possible way, even if it means heavy sacrifices. I have to maintain two households. I oblige my wife—who, luckily, complies in the spirit of charity—to confirm the illusion of being her daughter. She comes to the window, talks to her, writes to her. But—well, my friends, there are human limits to charity, to duty. I can't compel my wife to live with her. In the meanwhile she lives in a prison, poor woman, I have to lock her up—for fear *she* might one day climb those stairs and knock on our door. Yes, she is peaceful now, and of a gentle disposition in any case, but you will understand how my wife would feel were the old lady to shower motherly caresses on her. She'd shudder from head to foot.

AMALIA [*with a start: horror and pity mixed*]. Oh, of course! Poor lady, just imagine!

SIGNORA SIRELLI [*to her husband and* SIGNORA CINI]. Ah, so she *wishes* to be under lock and key, did you hear?

PONZA [*cutting her short*]. Councillor Agazzi, you will understand that I couldn't have permitted this visit of my mother-in-law's—except that I had to.

AGAZZI. I understand perfectly. Yes, it's clear to me now.

PONZA. I know people should keep their misfortunes to themselves. But I was compelled to have my mother-in-law come here. And I was obliged to make this declaration of my own. With a position like mine to keep up. We can't have the people in town believing a public official would do such things. Believing he would keep a poor mother from seeing her daughter. Out of jealousy or anything else. [*Rises*] Councillor Agazzi. [*He bows. Then passing* LAUDISI *and* SIRELLI, *he nods to them.*] Gentlemen. [*He leaves.*]

AMALIA [*in astonishment*]. Oh!! So she's mad!!!

SIGNORA SIRELLI. Poor lady: mad!

DINA. So that's it; she thinks herself still a mother, but that woman isn't her daughter! [*Horrified, she buries her face in her hands.*] Heavens!

SIGNORA CINI. Who could ever have guessed such a thing?

AGAZZI. Well, I don't know . . . from the way she talked—

LAUDISI. You knew all along?

AGAZZI. Not exactly . . . but it *is* true she—didn't quite know what to say.

SIGNORA SIRELLI. But that's only natural. She's lost her reason.

SIRELLI. I wonder, though. It's strange—for a mad woman. She wasn't very reasonable, certainly. But all this trying to explain why her son-in-law doesn't want to let her see her daughter. All this excusing of him and quickly adapting herself to her own improvisations of the moment . . .

AGAZZI. Gracious! That's precisely the proof that she's mad—the fact that she seeks excuses for her son-in-law without finding a single one that's halfway convincing.

AMALIA. Yes, yes. She was always saying things and then taking them back again.

AGAZZI [*to* SIRELLI]. D'you think anyone who wasn't mad could accept such conditions? To see her daughter only at the window—with the excuse she gives about the morbid love of the husband who wants his wife all to himself?

SIRELLI. I don't know. *Would* a madwoman accept such conditions? And resign herself to them? I find it strange, very strange. [*To* LAUDISI] What do you say?

LAUDISI. Me? Why, nothing.

Scene 6

The same, the BUTLER, then SIGNORA FROLA

BUTLER [*knocking, then appearing in the doorway, excited*]. Excuse me, sir. Signora Frola is here again.

AMALIA [*upset*]. Heavens, what now? Shall we never be rid of her?

SIGNORA SIRELLI. Never be rid of her? Oh, you mean because she's mad— I see.

SIGNORA CINI. Lord, Lord, who knows what she'll say this time? Still, I'd like to hear it.

SIRELLI. I'm curious about it too. I'm not at all convinced she *is* mad.

DINA. Look, Mother, there's nothing to be afraid of. She's so calm.

AGAZZI. We must receive her, of course. Let's hear what it is she wants. If there's trouble, we can take care of it. But let's set the stage. And be seated, everybody. We must all be seated. [*To the* BUTLER] Show her in.

[*The* BUTLER *withdraws.*]

AMALIA.Help me, all of you, please! I don't know how to talk to her now.

[SIGNORA FROLA *re-enters.* AMALIA *rises and comes toward her, frightened. The others look on in dismay.*]

SIGNORA FROLA.Excuse me.

AMALIA. Come in, come right in, Signora. My friends are still here, as you see—

SIGNORA FROLA [*with very mournful affability, smiling*]. The look you all give me . . . you too, dear Signora, you think I'm a poor madwoman, don't you?

AMALIA. Why, no, Signora, what are you saying?

SIGNORA FROLA [*with profound sorrow*]. The first time you came I didn't even go to the door, it was better that way. I never thought you'd come again. My son-in-law opened the door without thinking. So you had called, and I had to return the visit. Alas, I knew what the consequences would be!

AMALIA. Not at all, believe me. We're very pleased to see you again.

SIRELLI. The Signora is troubled . . . we don't know why: let her speak.

SIGNORA FROLA. Wasn't it my son-in-law who just left?

AGAZZI. Well, yes. He came—he came, Signora, to talk with me about—office business, that's all.

SIGNORA FROLA [*wounded, with great consternation*]. That's a little white lie—you're saying it just to soothe me down . . .

AGAZZI. No, no, Signora, be assured, I'm telling the truth.

SIGNORA FROLA [*as above*]. At least he was calm? He talked calmly?

AGAZZI. Yes, yes, completely calm, wasn't he?

[*Everyone assents, confirms.*]

SIGNORA FROLA.Oh dear, you all think *you're* reassuring *me* whereas what I want is to reassure you about him!

SIGNORA SIRELLI. On what score, Signora? If we repeat that—

AGAZZI. He spoke with me about some office business—

SIGNORA FROLA. I see how you all look at me! But wait. It's not a matter of me at all. From the way you look at me I see that his coming here has proved what I should never have revealed for all the gold in the world. You can all bear witness that not long ago I didn't know what to reply to your questions. Believe me, they hurt, they hurt very much. And I gave you an explanation of this strange way of living— an explanation that could satisfy no one, I see that. But could I tell

you the real reason? Could I tell you the story he tells—that my
daughter died four years ago and that I'm a poor madwoman who
believes she's still alive and that he doesn't want me to see her?

AGAZZI [*stunned by the profound note of sincerity in* SIGNORA FROLA]. Ah!
What's this? Your daughter?

SIGNORA FROLA [*quickly, anxiously*]. You know it's true. Why try to hide
it? That's what he told you . . .

SIRELLI [*hesitating, but scrutinizing her*]. Yes . . . in fact . . . he did say . . .

SIGNORA FROLA. I know. And unhappily I know how it will stir him up to
feel compelled to say it of me. Our situation, Councillor, is one we've
been able to handle—by ceaseless effort, in the face of great suffering—but only this way: by living as we are living. I quite understand
how it attracts attention, provokes scandal, arouses suspicion. On the
other hand, he's a good worker, scrupulous, conscientious—you must
have tried him out already.

AGAZZI. Well, actually, I haven't had the chance to discover.

SIGNORA FROLA. Please don't judge from the way it looks now! He's
good—everyone he's ever worked for said so. So why should he be
tormented with an investigation of his family life? I told you, Councillor: you're investigating a situation which is under control. To
bring it out in the open is simply to hurt him in his career.

AGAZZI. Signora, please don't distress yourself in this way! No one wishes
to torment him.

SIGNORA FROLA. Oh dear, how can I help being distressed when I see him
compelled to give everybody an absurd explanation, a horrible explanation. Can you seriously believe that my daughter is dead? That I am
mad? That his present wife is his second? But for him, it's a *necessity* to
say it is so. Only in this way could he find peace and self-respect. Yet
he himself admits the enormity of what he says. Whenever he's compelled to say it, he gets terribly excited, he's quite overcome—you
must have noticed!

AGAZZI. Yes . . . in fact, he was . . . he was rather excited.

SIGNORA SIRELLI. Oh dear, what are we to make of it now? It's him?

SIRELLI. Of course. It must be. [*Triumphant*] My friends, I told you so!

AGAZZI. My God, is it possible?

[*Much agitation all round*]

SIGNORA FROLA [*quickly, joining her hands*]. Please, please, good people!
What are you thinking? It's only . . . he has one sore spot that mustn't
be touched. Be reasonable: would I leave my daughter alone with him

if he were really mad? No! You can test what I say at any time at the office, Councillor; you'll find he performs his duties to perfection!

AGAZZI. Well, Signora, you owe us an explanation—a clear explanation. Is it possible that your son-in-law came here and *invented* the whole story?

SIGNORA FROLA. Yes, Signore, it is. Let me explain it to you. But you must sympathize with him, Councillor.

AGAZZI. What? Then it isn't true that your daughter is dead?

SIGNORA FROLA [*horrified*]. Why no, heaven forbid!

AGAZZI [*very annoyed, shouting*]. Then it's he that's mad!

SIGNORA FROLA [*supplicating*]. No, no . . . look . . .

SIRELLI [*triumphant*]. But it must be, it must be!

SIGNORA FROLA. No, no, look! He's not mad. Let me speak. You've seen him: he has a strong constitution, he's violent. When he got married he was seized with a veritable frenzy of love. My daughter is so delicate, he came near to destroying her—with the force of his passion. On the advice of the doctors and all the relations—even his (dead now, poor things!)—my daughter was taken off in secret and shut up in a sanitorium. He was already quite—exalted with excess of love, so when he couldn't find her in the house, oh! my friends, he fell into such a desperate state of mind. He *really* believed she was dead. Would hear of nothing else. Wanted to wear black. Did all sorts of crazy things. And wouldn't budge from his idea. A year later, when my daughter was well again, and blooming, and was brought back to him, he said no, it wasn't she, no, no, he looked and looked: it wasn't she. What torture, my friends! He would go up to her, seem to recognize her, and then—no, no! To induce him to take her, I got together with his friends and we went through the pretense of a second wedding.

SIGNORA SIRELLI. Ah! So that's why he says . . .

SIGNORA FROLA. Yes, but for some time now he hasn't believed it himself. That's why he has to convince other people, he can't help it. To relieve his own insecurity, you understand? For maybe, from time to time, the fear flashes across his mind that his wife might be taken from him again. [*In a lower tone, taking them into her confidence with a smile*] That's why he keeps her under lock and key, keeps her all to himself. But he adores her. I am sure of it. And my daughter is satisfied. [*Rising*] Now I must be going. I mustn't be here if he comes back again in that excited state. [*She sighs sweetly, with a movement of her joined hands.*] We must be patient. That poor girl must pretend she's not herself but someone else, and I—I must pretend I'm mad, my friends!

What of it? As long as *he's* at peace. Please don't come to the door. I know the way. Good-bye, good-bye!

[*Bowing and nodding to everyone, she hurriedly withdraws. They all remain standing, looking at each other, astounded, dumbfounded. Silence*]

LAUDISI [*coming center*]. You're looking each other over? The truth, hm?

[*He bursts out laughing.*]

ACT II   Scene 1

When the curtain rises, AMALIA, DINA, *and* SIGNORA SIRELLI *are talking in the music room. In the drawing room are* AGAZZI, LAUDISI, *and* SIRELLI. AGAZZI *is on the phone, standing by his desk.* LAUDISI *and* SIRELLI, *seated, are looking in his direction, waiting.*[3]

AGAZZI. Hello. Yes. Is that Police Commissioner Centuri? Well? Yes, fine. [*After listening for some time*] But really, how is that possible? [*Another long wait*] I quite understand, but if we could keep at it . . . [*Another wait*] It's really very strange we can't . . . [*Pause*] I see, yes, I see. [*Pause*] That'll do for now then, we'll have to see . . . Good-bye. [*He puts down the receiver and walks forward.*]

SIRELLI [*anxiously*]. Well?

AGAZZI. Nothing.

SIRELLI. They can't find anything at all?

AGAZZI. Everything's either dispersed or destroyed: the city hall, the municipal archives, all records of births, deaths, and marriages.

SIRELLI. But aren't there survivors who could give testimony?

AGAZZI. We've no news of any. And if there *are* some, it's going to be damned hard to find them at this point.

SIRELLI. So there's nothing for it but believing one or other of the two of them? Just that: no proofs, nothing.

AGAZZI. Unfortunately.

LAUDISI [*rising and drawing the curtains between the two rooms*]. Would you like to take *my* advice? Believe them both.

AGAZZI. Very well, and what if—

SIRELLI. What if one says black and the other says white?

LAUDISI. In that case, believe neither.

SIRELLI. You're trying to be funny. There may be no precise facts, the proofs may be missing, but the truth—the truth must be on one side or the other.

LAUDISI. Precise facts. Hm. What would you deduce from precise facts?

AGAZZI. Now, really. Take the daughter's death certificate—I mean if it's Signora Frola that's mad. It's true we can't find it, but then we can't find anything—yet it must have existed—and it might turn up tomorrow—and if it did—why, it'd be clear that *he's* in the right—the husband.

SIRELLI. Would you deny the validity of the evidence if you were given this certificate?

LAUDISI. I? I'm not denying anything. I'm very careful not to. It's you who feel the need of precise facts, documents and so forth. So you can affirm or deny. I wouldn't know what to do with them. For me reality isn't in *them*—it's in the two people, in the hearts of the two people. And how could *I* get into *their* hearts? All I know is what they tell me.

SIRELLI. Exactly. And doesn't each of them tell you the other is mad? Either *she's* mad or *he's* mad, there's no getting away from it. Well, which?

AGAZZI. That is the question.

LAUDISI. In the first place, it's not true each says the other is mad. Signor Ponza says Signora Frola is mad. She not only denies this, she denies that *he* is mad too. At worst, she says, he was . . . "exalted with excess of love" but that now he's completely well.

SIRELLI. Then you incline, as I do, toward *her* version of the story?

AGAZZI. It's clear the whole thing can be satisfactorily explained on the basis of her statement.

LAUDISI. The whole thing can be satisfactorily explained on the basis of his statement too.

SIRELLI. Then—neither of them is mad? But, damn it, one of them *must* be!

LAUDISI. Then, which? You can't say. Nor can anyone else. And this isn't just because your precise facts have been wiped out—dispersed or destroyed—in some accident, a fire or an earthquake. No, it's because they have wiped them out in themselves, in their hearts. Do you see that? She has created for him, or he for her, a fantasy. This fantasy is as real as reality. And they're living inside it now, with perfect harmony. They have found peace there. They breathe and see and hear and touch there. It is their reality, and no document could conceivably destroy it. At best a document might do *you* some good, it could satisfy your foolish curiosity. But no document has turned up, so here you are faced by two things—fantasy and reality—and you can't tell the one from the other. That is your punishment. Marvelous, isn't it?

AGAZZI. That's just philosophy, my dear fellow. Wait. We'll see if we can't get to the bottom of this.

SIRELLI. We've listened to him and we've listened to her. We now put both stories together—confront one version with the other—and figure out where fantasy begins, where reality leaves off. Don't you think we'll succeed?

LAUDISI. All I ask is that you let me go on laughing when you've finished.

AGAZZI. Well, well, we'll see who'll be laughing when we've finished. Now let's lose no time. I have an idea! [*He goes toward the music room and calls*] Amalia, Signora Sirelli, will you come in here now?

Scene 2

The same, AMALIA, SIGNORA SIRELLI, DINA

SIGNORA SIRELLI [*to* LAUDISI, *threatening him with one finger*]. Still at it, you naughty man!

SIRELLI. He's incorrigible.

SIGNORA SIRELLI. Here we all are—in the grip of a mighty passion—determined to get to the heart of the mystery if we go mad in the process—I didn't sleep a wink last night, myself—and *you,* you are cold and indifferent?

AGAZZI. Please, Signora, simply ignore him. Just sit down all of you and pay attention to me.

LAUDISI. Yes, just pay attention to my brother-in-law. He's preparing you the best of sleeping pills for tonight.

AGAZZI. Well now, where were we? Oh, yes, my idea! You ladies will go to Signora Frola's . . .

AMALIA. But will she receive us?

AGAZZI. Oh yes, I think so.

DINA. It's our duty to return the visit.

AMALIA. But if he doesn't want to allow her to pay visits or receive them?

SIRELLI. That was before. When no one knew anything yet. But now she's been forced to speak and in her own way she's explained her reason for being so reserved . . .

SIGNORA SIRELLI. She may even enjoy speaking to us of her daughter.

DINA. She's so good-natured! *I* haven't a doubt in the world—he's the one that's mad.

AGAZZI. Let's not rush the verdict. Now, er, listen to me a moment. [*He looks at the clock.*] Don't stay there long—a quarter of an hour, not more.

SIRELLI [*to his wife*]. Make a note of it.

SIGNORA SIRELLI [*an angry outburst*]. May I ask *why* you say that to *me*?

SIRELLI. Why, because once you start talking—

DINA [*preventing a quarrel*]. A quarter of an hour: *I'll* make a note of it.

AGAZZI. I must go to the Government Building. I'll be back here at eleven. That's not more than twenty minutes or so from now.

SIRELLI [*fretting*]. What about me?

AGAZZI. Wait. [*To the women*] A little before eleven use some pretext to get Signora Frola to come here.

AMALIA. Pretext—what pretext?

AGAZZI. Any pretext. You'll find one in the normal course of conversation, won't you? Or are you women for nothing? You have Dina and Signora Sirelli to help you . . . You'll bring her into the music room, of course. [*He goes to the threshold of the music room.*] Now, let's set the stage! These doors must be left open—wide open like this—so we can hear you talking from in here. On my desk I leave these papers, which I should be taking with me. Office business—a brief specially prepared for Signor Ponza. I pretend to forget it and so find an excuse to bring Ponza here.

SIRELLI [*as above*]. What about me? Where do I come in? And when?

AGAZZI. When? Several minutes past eleven. When the ladies are in the music room and I am here with him. You come for your wife. Through that door. [*Pointing stage left*] I introduce you to Ponza as you're passing through this room. Then I ask you to invite the ladies to join us in here. When they all come in, Ponza will be sitting here. I then put Signora Frola here. [*He indicates the two ends of a little sofa.*] So they'll be side by side and—

LAUDISI. We discover the truth!

DINA. Now really, Uncle, when the two of them meet face to face—

AGAZZI. Take no notice of him, for heaven's sake! Go on, go on, there isn't a moment to lose!

SIGNORA SIRELLI. Yes, let's be going, let's be going. [*To* LAUDISI] I won't shake hands with you!

LAUDISI. Then I'll do it for you, Signora. [*He shakes one hand with the other.*] Good luck!

[AMALIA, DINA, *and* SIGNORA SIRELLI *leave.*]

AGAZZI [*to* SIRELLI]. Shall we be going too, hm? Let's go.
SIRELLI. Yes, let's. Goodbye, Lamberto.
LAUDISI. Goodgye, goodbye.

[AGAZZI *and* SIRELLI *leave.*]

Scene 3

LAUDISI, *then the* BUTLER

LAUDISI [*walks round the room a bit, grinning to himself, and nodding. Then he stops before the large mirror*[4] *on the mantelpiece, looks at his own reflection, and talks to it.*]. Ah, so there you are! [*He waves at it with two fingers, winks wickedly, and laughs sarcastically.*] Well, old boy, which of us two is the madman? [*He raises one hand and levels the index finger at his reflection which in turn levels its index finger at him. Again the sarcastic laugh*] Yes, I know: I say *you* and you point your finger at *me.* Come now, between ourselves, we know each other pretty well, the two of us. The only trouble is, I see you one way and other people see you another way. So what becomes of you, my dear fellow? Here am I. I can touch myself. I can see myself. But what can I make of you—the you that other people see, I mean—what is it to me? I can't touch it. I can't see it. In short, you're a creature of fantasy, a phantom, a ghost! Well, you see *these* madmen? They're ghosts too. But do they know it? Not in the least. "Let's set the stage. Signor Ponza will be sitting here. I'll put Signora Frola here . . . " Driven by curiosity, they go running after other ghosts—the Ponza *they* take him to be, the Frola *they* take her to be—*other* ghosts are something else again—

[*The* BUTLER *enters but stops in his tracks, astounded, to hear* LAUDISI's *last words. He then announces*]

BUTLER.Signor Lamberto.
LAUDISI. Uh?
BUTLER. There are two ladies here. Signora Cini and another.
LAUDISI. Do they want me?
BUTLER. They asked for the mistress, Signore. I said she'd gone to visit Signora Frola next door and so . . .

LAUDISI. And so?

BUTLER. They looked at each other. Then they slapped their little hands with their gloves. "Really?" they said, "Really?" Then they asked very anxiously if there was no one at all at home.

LAUDISI. And you said no one at all.

BUTLER. No, I said there was you, Signore.

LAUDISI. Me? Oh, no, only the fellow they take me for.

BUTLER [*more astonished than ever*]. What do you say, Signore?

LAUDISI. You really think they're the same man?

BUTLER [*as above, miserably attempting a smile, his mouth open*]. I don't understand.

LAUDISI. Who are you talking to?

BUTLER [*dumbfounded*]. What?!Who am I talking to? You, Signore!!!!

LAUDISI. And you're quite sure I'm the same man those ladies are asking for?

BUTLER. Well, Signore . . . I wouldn't know . . . They said the mistress's brother . . .

LAUDISI. Oh, I see . . . in that case, it *is* me, isn't it? . . . show them in, show them in . . .

[*The* BUTLER *withdraws but turns several times to look at* LAUDISI. *He hardly believes his own eyes.*]

Scene 4

The same, SIGNORA CINI, SIGNORA NENNI

SIGNORA CINI. May we come in?

LAUDISI. Please do, Signora.

SIGNORA CINI. They told me Signora Agazzi isn't here. I have brought my friend Signora Nenni with me. [*She introduces* SIGNORA NENNI,[5] *an old woman even more foolish and affected than herself. She too is full of greedy curiosity but is wary, upset.*] She *so* much wished to meet the Signora—

LAUDISI. Signora Frola?

SIGNORA CINI. No, no, Signora Agazzi, your sister.

LAUDISI. Oh, she'll be coming, she'll be here soon. Signora Frola too. Please be seated. [*He invites them to sit on the little sofa. Then deftly inserting himself between them*] May I? Three can sit on it quite comfortably. Signora Sirelli is with them.

SIGNORA CINI. Yes. The butler told us.

LAUDISI. It's all arranged, you know. Oh, it'll be such a scene, such a scene! Soon. At eleven o'clock. Here.

SIGNORA CINI [*dizzy*]. Arranged? What's arranged?

LAUDISI [*mysteriously, first with a gesture—that of joining the tips of his forefingers—then with his voice*]. The meeting. [*A gesture of admiration*] A great idea!

SIGNORA CINI. What—what meeting?

LAUDISI. A meeting of those two. First, *he* will come in *here*. [*He points toward the door on the left.*]

SIGNORA CINI. Signor Ponza?

LAUDISI. Yes. And *she* will be brought in *there*. [*He points toward the music room.*]

SIGNORA CINI. Signora Frola?

LAUDISI. Precisely. [*Again, with an expressive gesture first, then with his voice*] Can't you see it? Both of them here on this sofa, the one confronting the other, and the rest of us all around watching and listening? A great idea!

SIGNORA CINI. In order to find out—

LAUDISI. The truth! But we know it already. Nothing remains but to unmask it.

SIGNORA CINI. [*With surprise and the keenest anxiety*] Ah! We know it already? Who is it then? Which of the two? Which is it?

LAUDISI. Let's see. Guess. Which would you say?

SIGNORA CINI [*hesitant*]. Well . . . I . . . look…

LAUDISI. He or she? Let's see . . . Guess . . . Come on!

SIGNORA CINI. I . . . I guess . . . him!

LAUDISI [*looks at her for a moment*]. He it is!

SIGNORA CINI [*tickled*]. It is? Ah, so that's it. Of course! It *had* to be him!

SIGNORA NENNI [*tickled*]. Him! We said so. We women said so.

SIGNORA CINI. And how did it come to light? Are there proofs? Documents?

SIGNORA NENNI. The police department found them, I suppose? We said so. With the Governor's authority behind us, we couldn't fail!

LAUDISI [*motions them to come closer, and then speaks quietly to them, mysteriously, weighing each syllable*]. The license of the second marriage!

SIGNORA CINI [*taking it like a blow on the nose*]. Second?

SIGNORA NENNI [*bewildered*]. What's that? The *second* marriage?

SIGNORA CINI [*reviving, but put out*]. Then . . . then *he* was right!

LAUDISI. Facts are facts, dear ladies. The license of the second marriage—
so it seems—is pretty clear.

SIGNORA NENNI [*almost weeping*]. Then *she* is the mad one!

LAUDISI. Yes, it does seem to be she.

SIGNORA CINI. What's this? Before, you said him, now you say her?

LAUDISI. Yes, dear lady, because the license—this license of the second
marriage—could quite well have been gotten up with the help of
friends to strengthen his delusion that his present wife is his second.
A forged document, understand? In line with Signora Frola's explanation.

SIGNORA CINI. Ah! A document—without validity?

LAUDISI. That is, that is to say . . . with whatever validity, dear ladies, with
whatever value anyone wants to give it. Remember, there are also the
messages Signora Frola says she received every day from her daughter.
Let down into the courtyard in a basket. There are those messages,
aren't there?

SIGNORA CINI. What if there are?

LAUDISI. More documents, Signora! Even these written messages are documents, with whatever value you wish to give them. Signor Ponza
comes along and says they're forged—just done to strengthen Signora Frola's delusion.

SIGNORA CINI. Oh dear, then we know nothing for certain?

LAUDISI. Nothing, how do you mean, nothing? Let's not exaggerate. Tell
me, how many days are there in the week?

SIGNORA CINI. Why, seven.

LAUDISI. Monday, Tuesday, Wednesday . . .

SIGNORA CINI [*feeling invited to continue*]. Thursday, Friday, Saturday–

LAUDISI. Sunday! [*Turning to the other woman*] And months in the year?

SIGNORA NENNI. Twelve!

LAUDISI. January, February, March . . .

SIGNORA CINI [*struck with a bright idea*]. We've got it: you want to make
fun of us!!

Scene 5

The same, DINA

DINA [*suddenly comes running in*]. Uncle, please . . . [*Seeing* SIGNORA CINI,
she stops.] Oh, Signora, you here?

SIGNORA CINI. Yes, I came with Signora Nenni—

LAUDISI. Who *so* much wanted to meet Signora Frola.

SIGNORA NENNI. No, no, please . . .

SIGNORA CINI. Go on teasing us! Oh, Dina dear, he's been getting us all mixed up! I feel like a train entering a station: poum, poum, poum, poum, all the time switching from one track to another! We're dizzy!

DINA. Oh, he's being so naughty. With all of us. But wait. We have all the proof we need now—I'll just tell Mother you're here, and we'll drop the whole thing. Oh, Uncle, if you only heard her! What a wonderful old lady she is! How she talks! How good she is! Her apartment is so neat, so elegant, everything in order, white covers on the furniture . . . She showed us all her daughter's letters.

SIGNORA CINI. Very well . . . but if . . . as Signor Laudisi was saying . . .

DINA. What does *he* know about it? He hasn't read them!

SIGNORA NENNI. Couldn't they be forged?

DINA. Forged, what *do* you mean? Could a mother mistake her daughter's way of saying things? The last letter, yesterday . . . [*She stops—hearing the sound of voices from the music room.*] Ah, there they are, they must be back already. [*She goes to the curtains to look.*]

SIGNORA CINI [*following her at a run*]. With her? With Signora Frola?

DINA. Yes, you two come with me. We all have to be in the music room. Is it eleven yet, Uncle?

Scene 6

The same, AMALIA

AMALIA [*suddenly coming in from the music room. She too is agitated.*]. We can do without now: there's no further need of proof!

DINA. Quite right. Just what I think.

AMALIA [*hastily acknowledging* SIGNORA CINI's *presence, sad and anxious*]. How are you, Signora?

SIGNORA CINI [*introducing* SIGNORA NENNI]. This is Signora Nenni. She came with me to—

AMALIA [*hurriedly greeting* SIGNORA NENNI *too*]. A pleasure, I'm sure. [*Pause*] There's no further doubt. It's *he!*

SIGNORA CINI. It's *he?* You're sure it's *he?*

DINA. Let's not go on deceiving the old lady this way, let's tell Father it's all off.

AMALIA. Oh, this bringing her over to our apartment, it's a betrayal!

LAUDISI. Oh, an outrage, an outrage, you're right! It's even becoming clear to me that she's the one. She must be, she *is!*

AMALIA. She's the one? What? What do you say?

LAUDISI. I say it's she, she, she!

AMALIA. Oh, stop it!

DINA. *We're* quite sure the opposite is the case!

SIGNORA CINI AND SIGNORA NENNI [*overjoyed, to* LAUDISI]. Really? You really mean it's she?

LAUDISI. Sure, I mean it. You're all very certain—and *I'm* all very certain!

DINA. Oh, come on, let's get out of here. Don't you see he's doing it on purpose?

AMALIA. Yes. Let's get out, ladies. [*In the doorway*] Please excuse us.

[*Exeunt* SIGNORA CINI, SIGNORA NENNI, AMALIA. DINA *starts to go.*]

LAUDISI [*calling her to him*]. Dina!

DINA. I don't want to listen to you. Leave me alone.

LAUDISI. Let's close these doors—if there's no further need of proof.

DINA. What about Father? It's he that's left them open. He'll be here any moment with that man.[6] If he found them closed . . . You know Father.

LAUDISI. But you'd all explain—*you* would, especially—that there was no need to keep them open. Aren't you convinced?

DINA. Utterly.

LAUDISI [*with a challenging smile*]. Then close them.

DINA. You want the pleasure of seeing I still haven't decided. I won't close the doors—but only because of Father.

LAUDISI [*as above*]. Shall *I* close them then?

DINA. That's entirely your affair.

LAUDISI. Unlike you, I can't claim to be sure it's he that's mad.

DINA. Just come into the music room and listen to the old lady for a minute as we have. You'll not have a doubt in the world. Will you come?

LAUDISI. Yes, I'll come. And I can close the doors? Since it's entirely my affair?

DINA. I see. Even before you hear her talk . . .

LAUDISI. No, my dear. It's because I'm sure that by this time your father agrees that there's no need of proof.

DINA. Father agrees?

LAUDISI. Of course. He's talking with *him*. There can, therefore, be no doubt: by this time he's certain it's *she* that's mad. [*He approaches the folding doors with decision.*] I'll close the doors.

DINA [*suddenly restraining him*]. No. [*Then, correcting herself*] I'm sorry . . . but if that's what you think . . . we'd better leave them open . . . [LAUDISI *bursts into his usual laugh.*] I mean because of Father.

LAUDISI. Your father will say because of the rest of you. But we can leave them open.

[*From the music room comes the sound of the piano. It is an old melody, full of sweet and mournful grace, "Il mio ben, quando verrà?" from the opera* Nina Mad Through Love *by Paisiello.*⁷]

DINA. Ah! It's she, do you hear? It's *she,* playing!

LAUDISI. The old lady?

DINA. Yes. She told us her daughter was always playing that tune. In the old days. Do you hear how sweetly she plays? Let's go in.

Scene 7

AGAZZI, PONZA, *then* SIRELLI

After LAUDISI *and* DINA *have left, the stage is empty for a while. The sound of the piano from the next room continues. Then* PONZA *comes in by the door on the left with* AGAZZI. *Hearing the music, he is profoundly disturbed; he becomes more and more so, as the present scene progresses.*

AGAZZI [*in the doorway*]. After you, after you, please. [*He has* PONZA *enter, then he himself enters, and goes toward the desk to take the papers that he has pretended to forget.*] Here's where I must have left them. Please be seated. [PONZA *remains standing. He looks agitatedly toward the music room whence the sound of the music is still pouring.*] And here they are, in fact! [*He takes the papers and approaches* PONZA, *leafing through them.*] It's a suit that's been dragging on for years, as I was telling you, a mess of complications! [*He too turns toward the music room, irritated by the piano.*] This music! At such a moment! [*Turning he makes a gesture of contempt, as if to say: "These women!"*] Who is playing? [*He goes to look into the music room through the open door, sees* SIGNORA FROLA *at the piano. Gesture of amazement*] Ah! Look!!

PONZA [*coming over to him, convulsed*]. In God's name, is it she? Is *she* playing?

AGAZZI. Yes. It's your mother-in-law! How well she plays!

PONZA. But what *is* this? They've brought her here—again? And they make her play?

AGAZZI. Well, I don't see any harm in that.

PONZA. But, please, not *that,* not *that* tune! It's the one her daughter used to play.

AGAZZI. Oh dear, it hurts you to hear her play it?

PONZA. It's not me. It hurts *her.* It does her incalculable harm. I told you, Councillor, I told the ladies what the condition of poor Signora Frola is—

AGAZZI [*endeavoring to calm him in his ever increasing agitation*]. Yes, yes . . . but . . .

PONZA [*continuing*]. And that she must be left in peace! That she can't receive visits—or pay them! I'm the only one—the only one—who knows how to look after her. You are ruining her, ruining her!

AGAZZI. Not at all. How so? Our women folk know perfectly well . . .

[*The music suddenly stops, and so does* AGAZZI. *A chorus of approval is heard from the music room.*]

You see? . . . Just listen . . .

[*From the music room the two following speeches are heard:*]

DINA. You still play wonderfully, Signora!

SIGNORA FROLA. *I* play wonderfully? What about Lina? You should hear my daughter Lina. How *she* plays!

PONZA [*fretting, digging his nails into his hands*]. Do you hear?! She says, "my daughter Lina"?!

AGAZZI. Yes, of course, her daughter.

[*Again from the music room:*]

SIGNORA FROLA. No, it's true, she's not been able to play. Since that time. That's maybe what gives her most pain, poor child!

AGAZZI. It seems natural enough . . . she thinks her still alive . . .

PONZA. But you mustn't make her say these things. She mustn't say them. Did you hear? "Since that time." She said "since that time." Because it's the old piano. You don't know. It's the piano my first wife played.

[*At this point* SIRELLI *comes in by the door on the left. When he hears* PONZA's *last words and notes his extreme exasperation, he stops in his tracks, dumbfounded.* AGAZZI *is also dismayed but signals to him to come over.*]

AGAZZI. Ask the ladies to come in here, will you? [*Giving the two men a wide berth,* SIRELLI *goes to the music room and calls the ladies.*]

PONZA. The ladies? Here?! No, no! Better . . .

Scene 8

The same, SIGNORA FROLA, AMALIA, SIGNORA SIRELLI, DINA, SIGNORA CINI, SIGNORA NENNI, LAUDISI

Having seen SIRELLI's *dismay, the ladies and* LAUDISI *are quite upset as they come in.* SIGNORA FROLA, *seeing her son-in-law's extreme excitement—he is shaking all over, like an animal in pain—is panic-stricken. When he rails against her in the following scene with the utmost violence, from time to time she gives the company significant looks. The scene is swift and tense.*

PONZA. You—here? Here—again? What have you come for?

SIGNORA FROLA. Well, I came . . . don't be impatient . . .

PONZA. You came here to repeat . . . What have you been saying, what have you been saying to these ladies?

SIGNORA FROLA. Nothing, I swear, nothing!

PONZA. Nothing? What do you mean, nothing? I heard! This gentleman heard too! [*He points at* AGAZZI.] You said "she plays." *Who* plays? Lina? You know perfectly well your daughter has been dead for four years.

SIGNORA FROLA. Of course she has, my dear. Please be calm!

PONZA. You said "she hasn't been able to play any more—since that time." How right you are: she hasn't been able to play since that time— because she's *dead!*

SIGNORA FROLA. Yes, yes, quite. Didn't I say so myself, ladies? Didn't I say she hasn't been able to play since that time? She's dead!

PONZA. Then why do you still think about the piano?

SIGNORA FROLA. I don't, I honestly don't, I never think of it!

PONZA. I smashed it. As you well know. I smashed it when your daughter died. So that this—other—wife couldn't touch it—and in any case she can't play! You know she doesn't play!

SIGNORA FROLA. Certainly she can't play, certainly!

PONZA. And what was her name? She was called Lina, wasn't she—your daughter? Now tell these people what my second wife is called. Just tell them. You know well enough: what's her name?

SIGNORA FROLA. Julia. Her name is Julia. But it *is*, I tell you: it's Julia!

PONZA. Julia, then. Not Lina. And this winking at people—when you tell them her name's Julia—don't do it!

SIGNORA FROLA. Winking? I wasn't winking!

PONZA. Yes, you were, I saw you, you were winking at them all, you want to ruin me, you want these people to believe I still wish to keep your daughter all to myself as if she weren't dead at all. [*He breaks down in terrible sobs.*] As if she weren't dead at all!

SIGNORA FROLA [*quickly, with infinite tenderness and humility, running to him*]. *I* want that? No, *no*, NO, dearest! Please be calm now. I never said such things—did I, did I, ladies?

AMALIA AND SIGNORA SIRELLI. No, no, she never said anything of the sort. She always said she was dead!

SIGNORA FROLA. Yes, didn't I? I said she's dead. Of course. And that you're so kind to me. [*To the ladies*] I did, didn't I? Ruin you? Hurt you? I?

PONZA [*rising, terrible*]. All the same you go around in other people's houses looking for a piano. Then you play the sonatinas she used to play—and tell them "Lina plays them like this, Lina plays them better!"

SIGNORA FROLA. No, it was . . . just . . . to show . . .

PONZA. But you can't! You mustn't! Playing the pieces your dead daughter used to play—how can you possibly think of such a thing?

SIGNORA FROLA. You're right, poor boy—poor boy! [*She is deeply touched and weeps.*] I'll never do it again, never, never again!

PONZA [*coming close to her, with terrible violence*]. Go! Get out! Get out!

SIGNORA FROLA. Yes, yes . . . I'm going, I'm going . . . Oh, dear! [*Backing out, she sends beseeching looks to the company, as if asking that they be considerate to her son-in-law. Weeping, she withdraws.*]

Scene 9

The same, minus SIGNORA FROLA

Overcome with pity and terror, they look at PONZA. *But he, as soon as his mother-in-law has left, completely changes his mood. He is calm. He re-assumes his normal manner, and says simply:*

PONZA. I must ask you all to forgive me for the scene I had to make. It was a necessary remedy for the harm you had done her, with your compassion. Of course you didn't intend it. You didn't even know.

AGAZZI [*astounded, like all the others*]. What? You were just pretending?

PONZA. I had to, I'm afraid. It's the only way, don't you see, to hold her to her illusion—my shouting out the truth like that—as if it were madness? You will forgive me, won't you? And I must beg to be excused; *she* needs me. [*He leaves, hurriedly. Once more they are all astounded, silent, looking each other over.*]

LAUDISI [*coming center*]. So this, my friends, is the truth! [*He bursts out laughing.*[8]]

Act III   Scene 1

LAUDISI *is lounging in an armchair, reading. Through the folding doors that lead to the music room comes the confused noise of many voices. The* BUTLER *brings in* POLICE COMMISSIONER CENTURI *through the door on the left.*

BUTLER. Will you come in here, please? I'll go and tell the Councillor.

LAUDISI [*turns and notices* CENTURI]. Oh, Commissioner Centuri! [*He rises hurriedly and recalls the* BUTLER.] *Wait a moment!* [*To* CENTURI] Any news?

CENTURI [*tall, stiff, frowning, about forty*]. Well yes, we *have* heard something.

LAUDISI. Oh, good. [*To the* BUTLER] You may go. I'll call my brother-in-law myself, when the time comes. [*He indicates the folding doors with a nod. The* BUTLER *bows and goes out.*] So you've performed the miracle. You're saving a city. You hear? You hear the noise they're making? Well, is the news definite?

CENTURI. We *have* managed to track down a few people—

LAUDISI. From Ponza's village? They know about him?

CENTURI. Yes—up to a point. The few facts we have seem certain.

LAUDISI. Oh, good, good. What, for example?

CENTURI. Well, here are the papers I've been sent. [*He takes an open yellow envelope with a document in it out of the inside pocket of his coat and hands it to* LAUDISI.]

LAUDISI. Let's see, let's see. [*He takes the document out of the envelope and reads it to himself, from time to time interjecting an oh! or an ah!—his tone changing from satisfaction to doubt, then to something like commiser-*

ation, and finally to complete disenchantment.] No, no, no! This amounts to absolutely nothing, there's nothing definite in this, Commissioner.

CENTURI. That's all we could find out.

LAUDISI. But not one of the doubtful points is cleared up. [*Looks at him, then with sudden resolution*] Do you want to do a good deed, Commissioner? Perform a distinguished service to the community and earn the gratitude of God Almighty?

CENTURI [*looking at him, perplexed*]. What service do you mean, exactly?

LAUDISI. Well, look. Sit down there. [*He points to the desk.*] Tear up this half-page of information, it doesn't get us any further. And on the other half of the page write something precise and certain.

CENTURI [*astonished*]. Me? What do you mean? What sort of thing?

LAUDISI. Anything. Whatever you like. In the name of his two fellow townsmen, the ones you tracked down. For the general good! To restore peace and quiet to our town! They want something *true*—it doesn't matter *what*—so long as it's good and factual, categorical, specific. You give it to them!

CENTURI [*with emphasis, getting heated, and more or less offended*]. How can I give it to them if I don't have it? Do you wish me to commit forgery? I'm amazed you dare propose such a thing to me. I'm more than amazed, in fact. Now that's enough: please present me to Councillor Agazzi at once!

LAUDISI [*opens his arms in a gesture of surrender*]. At once.

[*He goes over to the folding doors and opens them. Immediately the noise of all the people in the music room is louder. But as soon as* LAUDISI *steps through the doorway the shouting stops. From the music room one hears* LAUDISI'S *voice announcing:* "Commissioner Centuri has arrived. He has definite news from people who know!" *Applause and cries of* "Hurrah!" *greet the announcement.* COMMISSIONER CENTURI *gets disturbed because he knows the information he brings will not suffice to satisfy so much expectation.*]

Scene 2

The same, AGAZZI, SIRELLI, LAUDISI, AMALIA, DINA, SIGNORA SIRELLI, SIGNORA CINI, SIGNORA NENNI, *and many other men and women*

They all rush in with AGAZZI *at their head, inflamed, exultant, clapping their hands and shouting.*[9]

ALL. Good work, Centuri!

AGAZZI [*with arms outstretched*]. My dear Centuri, I was sure of it: you couldn't miss!

ALL. Good work, good work! Let's see, let's see the proofs! Right now! Who is it? Which is the one?

CENTURI [*astonished, uncomprehending, lost*]. There's some mistake . . . I, er . . . well, Councillor . . .

AGAZZI. Please, ladies and gentlemen, quiet, please!

CENTURI. It's true, I . . . er, left no stone unturned, but if Signor Laudisi says I also—

AGAZZI. That you also bring definite news!

SIRELLI. Precise facts!

LAUDISI [*loudly, decisively, warningly*]. Not many facts but precise ones! From people he managed to track down. In Signor Ponza's own village. People who know.

ALL. At last! Oh, at last, at last!

CENTURI [*shrugging, presenting the document to* AGAZZI]. Here you are, Councillor.

AGAZZI [*opening it up amid the press of all the people who are milling around*]. Now let's see, let's see.

CENTURI [*resentful, approaching* LAUDISI]. Now really, Signor Laudisi . . .

LAUDISI [*quickly, loudly*]. Let him read it, for heaven's sake, let him read it!

AGAZZI. Just be patient one moment longer, ladies and gentlemen. And don't press so close, I can't read! *That's* better.

[*There is a moment's pause. Then, into the silence, is projected the precise, firm voice of* LAUDISI.]

LAUDISI. I've already read it!

ALL [*leaving* AGAZZI *and rushing noisily over to* LAUDISI]. You have? Well? What does it say? They know the answer?

LAUDISI [*very formally*]. It is certain, it is irrefutable, we have the testimony of a fellow townsman of Signor Ponza's—that Signora Frola has been in a sanatorium!

ALL [*disappointed, crestfallen*]. Oh!

SIGNORA SIRELLI. Signora Frola?

DINA. Was it definitely she?

AGAZZI [*who has read the document in the meantime, waves it, and shouts*]. No, no, no! There's nothing of the sort here at all!

ALL [*leaving* LAUDISI, *they rush back to* AGAZZI, *shouting*]. What's this? What do you say, what do you say?

LAUDISI [*loudly, to* AGAZZI]. But there is! It says "the lady." It specifically says "the lady"!

AGAZZI [*louder*]. Not at all! This man only says he "thinks" so, he isn't even sure. In any event he doesn't profess to know if it was mother or daughter!

ALL [*satisfied*]. Ah!

LAUDISI [*insisting*]. But it must be the mother, it must be!

SIRELLI. Not in the least, it's the daughter, it's the daughter!

SIGNORA SIRELLI. Besides the old lady told us so herself!

AMALIA. Exactly—that's right—when they took the poor girl from her husband secretly—

DINA. —and shut her up in a sanatorium!

AGAZZI. Besides, this informant isn't even from the same village. He says he "often went there," that he "doesn't quite recall," that "he thinks he heard it said" . . .

SIRELLI. Oh, just hearsay!

LAUDISI. Excuse me for saying so, but if you're all so convinced that Signora Frola is right, what more do you want? Have done with the whole thing once and for all! It's he that's mad, and that's all there is to say.

SIRELLI. That's all very well, my dear man, if we could ignore the Governor's opinion.[10] But he believes just the opposite. He makes a great show of the confidence he feels in Signor Ponza and *his* version of the story.

CENTURI. That's very true. The Governor believes in Signor Ponza, he told *me* so too!

AGAZZI. But this is because the Governor hasn't talked with the old lady next door.

SIGNORA SIRELLI. Exactly! He's only talked with *him!*

SIRELLI. But there are others who agree with the Governor!

A MAN. I do, for instance! I do! Because I know a similar case: a mother who's gone mad at the death of her daughter and believes her son-in-law is refusing to let her see the girl. The same thing!

SECOND MAN. Oh no, because *that* son-in-law has remained a widower and lives alone, whereas Signor Ponza is not alone, he—

LAUDISI [*as an idea dawns on him*]. Good heavens, do you hear that? Now we have the answer. For heaven's sake—Columbus's egg![11] [*Clapping the* SECOND MAN *on the shoulder*] Good work, my dear fellow! Did you all hear what he said?

ALL [*perplexed, not comprehending*]. What's this? *What* did he say?

SECOND MAN [*amazed*]. What did I say? I've no idea . . .

LAUDISI. What did he say? But he's solved the whole question. Hold on a minute, everybody! [*To* AGAZZI] The Governor is to come here?

AGAZZI. Yes, we're expecting him . . . But why? Explain.

LAUDISI. It's no use his coming here to talk with Signora Frola. Up to now he believes in her son-in-law. When he's talked with the old lady he won't know himself which of the two to believe. No, that won't do. It's something else that the Governor must do here. One thing in particular.

ALL. And what's that?

LAUDISI [*with an air of triumph*]. What is it? Didn't you hear what our friend said? "Signor Ponza is not alone." In other words, he has a wife!

SIRELLI. You mean, we could get his *wife* to talk?! I see, I see.

DINA. But he keeps her locked up, doesn't he?

SIRELLI. The Governor would have to use his authority and *order* her to speak!

AMALIA. Certainly, she's the one to tell us the truth!

SIGNORA SIRELLI. How so? She'd say whatever her husband wants.

LAUDISI. Yes—*if* she had to talk with him present.

SIRELLI. Then she should talk with the Governor in private!

AGAZZI. Surely. The authority of the Governor will do the trick. When she's alone with him she'll undoubtedly explain just how things really are, of course she will, don't you agree, Centuri?

CENTURI. Not a doubt of it—if the Governor is interested!

AGAZZI. It's the only way. We must tell him about it and spare him the trouble of coming over. Would you mind looking after it, Centuri?

CENTURI. Not a bit. I'll go at once. Good day, everyone. [*He bows and leaves.*]

SIGNORA SIRELLI [*clapping her hands*]. At last! Good for Laudisi!

DINA. Good old uncle, what a clever idea!

ALL. Good work, good work! Yes, it's the only way, the only way!

AGAZZI. Of course. Why didn't we think of it before?

SIRELLI. Think of it. No one's ever seen her. It's as if the poor woman didn't exist!

LAUDISI [*struck with another bright idea*]. Oh! By the way, you're all sure she exists?

AMALIA. Now really, Lamberto!

SIRELLI [*pretending to laugh*]. You want us to doubt her very existence?

LAUDISI. Just a minute. You say yourselves no one has ever seen her!

DINA. Not at all. There's the old lady who sees her and talks to her every day.

SIGNORA SIRELLI. What's more, her husband admits it.

LAUDISI. Very good. But reflect a moment. To be strictly logical, all you'd expect to find in that apartment is a phantom. A ghost.

ALL. A ghost?

AGAZZI. Oh come on, drop it for once.

LAUDISI. Let me finish. The ghost of a second wife, if Signora Frola is right. The ghost of her daughter, if Signor Ponza is right.[12] It remains to be seen, my friends, if what is a ghost to husband or mother, is also a real person—to herself. Having come so far, we can permit ourselves to doubt it.

AMALIA. Run along with you. You just want everyone to be as mad as you.

SIGNORA NENNI. Good heavens, it gives me the creeps!

SIGNORA CINI. I don't know what pleasure it can give you to frighten us this way!

ALL. Nothing of the sort! He's joking!

SIRELLI. She's a woman of flesh and blood, there's no reason to doubt it. And we'll get her to talk, we'll get her to talk!

AGAZZI. It was you yourself that proposed to have her talk with the Governor—just a minute ago!

LAUDISI. Why, yes, if it's really a woman that's up in that apartment—a woman in the ordinary sense of the word. But think it over, ladies and gentlemen, how *can* it be a woman in the ordinary sense of the word? It can't. That's why I say I doubt her very existence.

SIGNORA SIRELLI. Heavens, he *is* trying to drive us mad!

LAUDISI. Well, we'll see, we'll see.

ALL [*confused voices*]. But other people have seen her, haven't they? She comes out in the courtyard, doesn't she? She writes messages to her mother. He's doing this just to make fun of us!

Scene 3

The same, CENTURI

CENTURI [*entering amid the general hubbub, excited, and announcing*]. The Governor is here! The Governor is here!

AGAZZI. The Governor here? What have you been up to?

CENTURI. I met him on his way over—with Signor Ponza—

SIRELLI. With Signor Ponza!

AGAZZI. Heavens, no! If he's with Ponza, they're probably going to visit the old lady next door. Please, Centuri, will you wait outside and ask the Governor to step in here for a moment as he promised me?

CENTURI. Certainly, sir. [*He leaves in haste through the door on the left.*]

AGAZZI. My friends, I must ask you to retire to the music room for a while.

SIGNORA SIRELLI. You'll put it to him properly, won't you? It's the only way, the only way!

AMALIA. This way, ladies, please!

AGAZZI. You'll stay, won't you, Sirelli? You too, Lamberto. [*The others all go into the music room. To* LAUDISI] But let me do the talking, won't you?

LAUDISI. I'll be glad to. In fact if you'd prefer me to leave too . . .

AGAZZI. Oh no, it's better if you stay. [*He closes the folding doors.*] Ah, here he comes.

Scene 4

LAUDISI, AGAZZI, SIRELLI, the GOVERNOR, CENTURI

GOVERNOR [*about sixty, tall, fat, an air of complaisant good nature. Entering by door on left*]. My dear Agazzi! Oh, you're here, are you, Sirelli? My dear Laudisi! [*He shakes hands all round.*]

LAUDISI. How are you, Governor?

AGAZZI. Come right in, Centuri, sit here, will you? Sirelli, you sit there. Will you sit here, Governor? I hope you don't mind my asking you to come here first?

GOVERNOR. I was intending to come, just as I promised. I'd have come afterward anyway. Well, Sirelli, I've been hearing about you. They tell me you're all inflamed and agitated over this matter of the new secretary—more agitated than anyone else!

SIRELLI. *That's* not quite true, Governor. I don't think you can find anyone in town who's not just as agitated as I am.

AGAZZI. That is so. Everybody's terribly agitated.

GOVERNOR. Well, I can't for the life of me understand why.

AGAZZI. Because it hasn't been your lot to see certain goings on. Now *we* have the old lady right next door, his mother-in-law, you know—

SIRELLI. Forgive me, Governor, but you haven't heard what she has to say, have you?

GOVERNOR. I was just going to see her. [*To* AGAZZI] I'd promised you I'd listen to her here as you wished. But her son-in-law came to beg me to go to her place. He was desperate about it—it's all the gossip that bothers him. Now the point is, do you think he'd send me to her if he weren't quite sure the visit would confirm his own version of the story?

AGAZZI. Certainly he would. When *he's* present, the old lady—.

SIRELLI [*cutting in*]. Would say whatever he wants her to say, Governor! And that's the proof that it's not she that's mad!

AGAZZI. We put it to the test, right here, only yesterday!

GOVERNOR. Well, yes, but he deliberately makes her believe it's he that's mad. He forewarned me of that. How otherwise could the poor old thing keep her illusion? But think what torture it is for poor Ponza!

SIRELLI. That is, if it's not *she* who permits *him* the illusion of believing her daughter dead—so he won't live in constant fear of her being taken away again! In that case, you must realize, Governor, it's the old lady who's being tortured now, not Ponza.

AGAZZI. Well, that's the point at issue. I'm sure *you*—[*to the* GOVERNOR] must be wondering—

SIRELLI. We're *all* wondering—

GOVERNOR. But are you? Not very seriously, I think. None of you seem to have any doubts about the matter. I'm on the other side, and I have no doubts either. What about you, Laudisi?

LAUDISI. Pardon me, Governor; I've promised my brother-in-law to hold my tongue.

AGAZZI [*with a start*]. Now really, what are you saying? If you're asked a question, reply for heaven's sake! You know why I asked him to be quiet, don't you? Because for the past two days he's been amusing himself making the mystery more mysterious.

LAUDISI. Don't believe him, Governor. It's just the other way round: I've been doing my best to clear the mystery up.

SIRELLI. Oh yes, and d'you know how? By maintaining it's impossible to discover the truth. By creating the suspicion that there's no woman in Ponza's house at all—but a ghost!

GOVERNOR [*enjoying it all*]. What, really? Not so bad!

AGAZZI. Oh, please! You know *him;* it's no use taking any notice of *him*.

LAUDISI. Though it was through me you were invited over, Governor.

GOVERNOR. Because you also think I'd do well to talk with the old lady next door?

LAUDISI. Nothing of the kind. You do best to stick by Signor Ponza's version of the story.

GOVERNOR. Oh, I see. So you agree that Signor Ponza—

LAUDISI [*quickly*]. No! I want all the others to stick by Signora Frola's version and make an end of the matter.

AGAZZI. You see how it is? Would you call that logic?

GOVERNOR. One moment. [*To* LAUDISI] In your opinion, then, what the old lady says is also trustworthy?

LAUDISI. Absolutely. From beginning to end. Like what *he* says.

GOVERNOR. What are we to make of it then—

SIRELLI. If what they say is contradictory?

AGAZZI [*irritated, with decision*]. Would you listen to me for a moment? I haven't committed myself. I lean to neither one version nor the other—and I don't intend to till later. *He* may be right, *she* may be right. The point is we must find out. And there's but one way to do so.

SIRELLI. And—[*pointing at* LAUDISI] he has suggested what it is.

GOVERNOR. He has? Well, let's hear it.

AGAZZI. Since none of the other evidence amounts to proof, the only thing is for you to use your authority and extract a confession from the wife!

GOVERNOR. Signora Ponza?

SIRELLI. Not in the presence of her husband, naturally.

AGAZZI. In private. So she'll tell the truth.

SIRELLI. So she'll explain whether she's the old lady's daughter as we think she must be—

AGAZZI. Or whether she's a second wife who's agreed to play the part of the old lady's daughter as Signor Ponza would have us believe—

GOVERNOR. And as I certainly believe myself! Well, by all means. This seems the only way to me too. Poor Ponza himself desires nothing better than to convince everyone he is right. He's been utterly accommodating. He'll be happier than anybody about this. And it will certainly ease *your* minds, my friends. Will you do something for me, Centuri? [CENTURI rises.] Go and bring Signor Ponza from next door. Tell him I'd like to see him a moment.

CENTURI. Certainly. [*Bows and leaves*]

AGAZZI. If only he consents!

GOVERNOR. He'll consent at once, just watch! We'll make an end of the whole matter in the space of a few minutes. Right here before your eyes.

AGAZZI. What? In *my* place?

SIRELLI. You think he'll want to bring his wife *here?*

GOVERNOR. Leave me alone. I said: right here. Because otherwise you'll all be thinking *I*—

AGAZZI. No, no, no! What are you saying?

SIRELLI. That? Never!

GOVERNOR. Come off it. Since you know I felt sure all along that *he* was in the right, you'd think I was just hushing the matter up, protecting a public servant. No, I say! I want you all to hear. [*Then to* AGAZZI] Is your wife at home?

AGAZZI. Yes, she's in the next room, with some other ladies . . .

GOVERNOR. Aha! Subversive activities[13] in the back room! You can hardly object if I make the place serve a more useful purpose. Let's set the stage. We'll put Ponza here. Will you and Sirelli sit opposite with me, Agazzi? That's it!

Scene 5

The same, CENTURI, PONZA

CENTURI. Signor Ponza!

GOVERNOR. Thank you, Centuri. Please bring him in.

[PONZA *appears in the doorway.*]

CENTURI. Come in, come right in, Signor Ponza.

[PONZA *bows.*]

GOVERNOR. Please be seated, my dear Ponza.

[PONZA *bows again and sits down.*]

GOVERNOR. You know these gentlemen . . . Sirelli . . .

[PONZA *rises and bows.*]

AGAZZI. Yes, I already introduced them. That is Laudisi, my brother-in-law.

[PONZA *bows.*]

GOVERNOR. I sent for you, my dear Ponza, to tell you that here, with my friends . . . [*No sooner has he started speaking than* PONZA *is visibly very disturbed, deeply agitated. The* GOVERNOR, *aware of this, stops.*] You wish to say something?

PONZA. Yes. I ask to be transferred to another town. As of today.

GOVERNOR. But why? You spoke so reasonably with me not long ago, so . . .

PONZA. Yes, but now I'm the target of insufferable persecution.

GOVERNOR. Now, come: let's not exaggerate!

AGAZZI [*to* PONZA]. Persecution, did you say? Do you mean by me?

PONZA. Persecution by everybody. And that's why I'm going. I'm going, Governor. A relentless, ferocious investigation[14] of my private life— that's what it is—and I won't stand for it. It will end in ruining the . . . labor of love that I'm devoting my life to—not counting the cost. I love and respect that poor old lady more than if she were my own mother; yet, yesterday, I was compelled to attack her with the most cruel violence. And now, in her apartment, I find her in such a state of degradation and over-excitement—

AGAZZI [*interrupting, calm*]. It's strange—because, to us, the old lady always spoke with the utmost calm. The over-excitement was all yours, Signor Ponza. And is so now!

PONZA. Because none of you know what you are making me go through!

GOVERNOR. Come, come, calm yourself, my dear Ponza! What is the matter? I am here. And you know with how much trust and sympathy I've always listened to you, isn't that true?

PONZA. It's true—as far as you're concerned. And I'm grateful, Governor.

GOVERNOR. Well then! Look, you love and respect your wife's mother as if she were your own. I'd like you to realize that my friends here are curious to find out the truth precisely because *they* are fond of the old lady too.

PONZA. But they are killing her, Governor. I warned them repeatedly.

GOVERNOR. Really, my dear Ponza, once this thing is cleared up, you'll not be troubled by them again. And we'll clear it up right away, there's no problem. You yourself can remove the last doubt from the minds of these friends—not from mine, I'm already convinced—in the simplest, surest way.

PONZA. How so, if they don't believe a word I speak?

AGAZZI. That is not true. When you came here, after your mother-in-law's first visit, to tell us she was mad, we all believed you. We were amazed but we believed you. [*to the* GOVERNOR] But immediately afterward, you understand, the old lady returned—

GOVERNOR. Yes, yes, I know, you told me . . . [*Continues, turning toward*

PONZA] She returned to give the version of the story which you your-self wish her to accept. It's surely not so hard to see that a painful doubt might arise in the mind of anyone who heard *her* after hearing *you*. What it boils down to is that our friends have had difficulty in completely believing you, my dear Ponza, since they heard what your mother-in-law had to say. There's only one thing to do. You and your mother-in-law must retire for a moment. *You* feel sure you are telling the truth, *I* feel sure you are too. So you can't have anything against having it *re*-told by the only person—besides the two of you—that's in a position to re-tell it.

PONZA. Who is that?

GOVERNOR. Why—your wife?

PONZA. My wife? [*With force and indignation*] Oh, no! Never!

GOVERNOR. And why not, may I ask?

PONZA. I'm to bring my wife here for the satisfaction of people who won't believe me?

GOVERNOR [*promptly*]. I beg your pardon, it's for *my* satisfaction. Is it really so hard to arrange?

PONZA. But, Governor! Not my wife! Don't ask that! Leave my wife out of this! Just believe *me!*

GOVERNOR. Now, really, if you talk this way, I too will start thinking you don't *want* us to believe you.

AGAZZI. He tried in every possible way to stop his mother-in-law coming here in the first place. Even at the cost of being rude to my wife and daughter.

PONZA [*bursting out in sheer exasperation*]. What do you all want of me, in God's name? You've had the old lady, wasn't that enough? Must you get your hands on my wife too? I cannot put up with this violence, Governor. My wife is not leaving our apartment! I won't hand her over. It's enough that *you* believe me. I'm filling out the blanks for my transfer. Then I go. [*He rises.*]

GOVERNOR [*bringing down his fist on the desk*]. Wait! In the first place you will not speak in that tone before Councillor Agazzi and me. I won't stand for it. *I* have shown *you* courtesy and deference. In the second place you are refusing to supply a proof which I—and not the oth-ers—am asking for. I am asking for it in *your* interest, I can't see how it can possibly harm you. I repeat: your obstinacy makes *me* begin to doubt you too. My colleague and I can perfectly well receive a lady—or even, if you prefer, come to your home . . .

PONZA. You make it a matter of duty?

GOVERNOR. I repeat: I am *asking* this for your own good. My position entitles me to *demand* it.

PONZA. Very well, very well. If that's how it is. I will bring my wife here, and have done with it. But who can guarantee that the old lady won't see her?

GOVERNOR. Yes . . . it's true she's just next door . . .

AGAZZI [*quickly*]. *We* could go to the Signora's apartment.

PONZA. No, no, it was you I was thinking of. I meant I don't want you to prepare any more of these catastrophic surprises.

AGAZZI. You needn't worry, as far as we're concerned.

GOVERNOR. Or, look, if it suits you better, you could take the lady to the Government Building.

PONZA. No, no, I'll bring her here at once. Then I'll go next door and keep an eye on Signora Frola. I'm going, Governor. Then it will be over, over! [*He leaves angrily.*]

Scene 6

The same, minus PONZA

GOVERNOR. I didn't expect this opposition on his part, I must confess.

AGAZZI. Now he'll go and make his wife say what *he* wants said, just watch.

GOVERNOR. No, no. Don't worry about that. I shall question the lady myself.

SIRELLI. Really, the way he's always so worked up!

GOVERNOR. No, no, it's the first time—the very first—that I've seen him this way. Perhaps it's the idea of bringing his wife—

SIRELLI. The idea of setting her free, you mean!

GOVERNOR. Oh, his keeping her locked up—after all, that can be explained without assuming he's mad!

SIRELLI. Excuse me, Governor, you still haven't heard the old lady, poor creature!

AGAZZI. He says himself he keeps his wife locked up because of her mother.

GOVERNOR. Even if that isn't the case, he might still keep her locked up. He might be jealous. He might simply be a jealous husband.

SIRELLI. To the extent of not having a maid or a cleaning woman? He compels his wife to do all the housework herself.

AGAZZI. And *he* does the shopping. Every morning.

CENTURI. That's true, sir. I've seen him. He carries his parcels home with a little boy to help him—

SIRELLI. —and the little boy stays outside!

GOVERNOR. But good heavens, he told me about that and sincerely deplored it!

LAUDISI [*playfully*]. Reliable sources of information report . . .

GOVERNOR. He does it to economize, Laudisi. Having to maintain two households . . .

SIRELLI. Well, we wouldn't criticize him from that viewpoint. But really, Governor, do you believe a second wife would take on the—

AGAZZI [*getting heated*]. The lowest household chores!—

SIRELLI [*continuing*]. For someone who was once her husband's mother-in-law and—to her—is a total stranger?

AGAZZI. Yes, yes, doesn't it seem a bit much?

GOVERNOR. It does, rather . . .

CENTURI. It certainly does . . .

LAUDISI [*interrupting*]. Too much for "a second wife"—if that's all she is.

GOVERNOR [*quickly*]. Let's admit—it *is* too much. Even this, however, can be explained—not, it's true, as generosity on her part—but definitely as jealousy on his. And, mad or not mad, he is jealous. That at least is established, it seems to me.

[*At this point the confused noise of many voices is heard from the music room.*]

AGAZZI. Heavens, what's going on in there?

Scene 7

The same, AMALIA

AMALIA [*rushes in through the folding doors in the utmost consternation, announcing*]. Signora Frola! Signora Frola is here!

AGAZZI. No, by God! Who sent for her!

AMALIA. No one. She came of her own accord.

GOVERNOR. No, for heaven's sake! Not now!! Have her sent away, Signora!

AGAZZI. Yes, at once! Don't let her in! Stop her at all costs! If he found her here, he'd think it was an ambush!

Scene 8

The same, SIGNORA FROLA, *and all the others*

SIGNORA FROLA *enters trembling, weeping, imploring, a handkerchief in her hand, in the midst of an excited crowd.*

SIGNORA FROLA. For pity's sake, good people, for pity's sake! You tell them, tell them all, Councillor!

AGAZZI [*coming forward, highly annoyed*]. I tell *you,* Signora, go away at once! You simply cannot stay here!

SIGNORA FROLA [*lost*]. But why? Why? [*To* AMALIA] I turn to you, you are kind . . .

AMALIA. But look, look, the Governor is here—

SIGNORA FROLA. You, Governor. For pity's sake! I wanted to come to you.

GOVERNOR. Please don't be impatient, Signora. At the moment I cannot take care of you. You really must leave at once.

SIGNORA FROLA. Yes, I *am* leaving. I'm leaving today. I'm going away, Governor, going away for good!

AGAZZI. No, no, Signora. Please be kind enough to withdraw to your apartment next door for just one moment. Do me this favor. You can talk with the Governor afterward.

SIGNORA FROLA. But why? What's the matter? What's the matter?

AGAZZI [*losing his patience*]. Your son-in-law is about to return. He will be here at any moment. You understand?

SIGNORA FROLA. Will he? In that case, yes . . . I'll be going . . . I'll be going at once. I only wanted to say this to you all: for pity's sake, stop! You believe you're doing good to me but you're doing me unspeakable harm! I shall be compelled to leave if you keep on acting like this. To be gone this very day and leave him in peace! What in the world do you want of him—here—now? What should he come here and do? Oh, Governor!

GOVERNOR. We want nothing of him, Signora, just don't worry. Be calm and leave us, I beg you.

AMALIA. Please leave, Signora, please oblige us!

SIGNORA FROLA. Oh dear, Signora, you people are depriving me of the only comfort I had left: to see my daughter, at least from a distance. [*She starts crying.*]

GOVERNOR. Who says so? You have no need to go away. We are asking you to leave the room for one moment. Don't worry!

SIGNORA FROLA. But I'm thinking of *him,* Governor! I came here to intercede with you all for him, not for myself!

GOVERNOR. Very well. You needn't worry on his account either, I give you my word. Everything will be taken care of, just see.

SIGNORA FROLA. How? With all these people persecuting him?

GOVERNOR. No, Signora, that's not true. I am here, and I'm on his side. Don't worry!

SIGNORA FROLA. Thank you. You mean, you've understood . . . ?

GOVERNOR. Yes, Signora, yes. I have understood.

SIGNORA FROLA. We are satisfied to live in this way. My daughter is satisfied. So . . . Well, you attend to it . . . because if you don't, there's nothing for it but for me to go away. Just that: go away and never see her again, even from a distance as at present . . . I *beg* you to leave him in peace!

[*At this point there is a movement in the crowd. All start making signs. Some look back into the music room. Suppressed exclamations*]

VOICES. Oh dear . . . here she is, here she is!

SIGNORA FROLA [*noting the dismay and disorder, groans in perplexity and trembles*]. What's the matter? What's the matter?

Scene 9

The same, SIGNORA PONZA, *then* PONZA

The crowd divides up on either hand to let SIGNORA PONZA *pass. She comes forward, erect, in mourning, her face hidden under a thick veil, black, impenetrable.*[15]

SIGNORA FROLA [*letting out a harrowing cry of frantic joy*]. Ah!!! Lina! Lina! Lina!

[*She rushes forward and embraces the veiled lady with all the thirst of a mother who hasn't embraced her daughter for years. At the same time* PONZA *is heard shouting outside. Immediately afterward he rushes in.*]

PONZA. Julia! Julia! Julia!

[*Hearing his cries,* SIGNORA PONZA, *though still in the arms of* SIGNORA FROLA, *grows rigid.* PONZA, *coming in, at once sees his mother-in-law thus desperately embracing his wife. He is furious and shrieks*].

Ah!!! Just as I said! Is this how you repay my good faith? Cowards!

SIGNORA PONZA [*Turning her veiled head, with almost austere solemnity*]. Don't be afraid, don't be afraid.[16] Go!

PONZA [*quietly, lovingly, to* SIGNORA FROLA]. Yes, let's be going, let's be going.

SIGNORA FROLA [*who has withdrawn from the embrace, trembling all over, humble, echoes his words at once, urgent*]. Yes, let's be going, let's be going . . .

[PONZA *and* SIGNORA FROLA *embrace and exchange caresses. Their weeping makes a plaintive duet. Whispering affectionate words to each other, they withdraw. Silence. The company watches them until they have quite disappeared. Then everybody turns round, dismayed and moved, to look at the veiled lady.*]

SIGNORA PONZA [*after having looked at them through her veil, says with dark solemnity*]. After this, what more can you want of me, ladies and gentlemen? There has been a misfortune here, as you see, which should remain hidden. Only in this way can the remedy work—the remedy our compassion has provided.

GOVERNOR [*moved*]. We should like to respect such compassion, Signora. We should wish you to tell us, however—

SIGNORA PONZA [*with slow, staccato speech*]. What? The truth? It is simply this. I am Signora Frola's daughter—

ALL [*with a gasp of pleasure*]. Ah!

SIGNORA PONZA [*without pausing, as above*]. And I am Signor Ponza's second wife—

ALL [*astonished, disappointed, in low voices*]. Oh! But . . . ?

SIGNORA PONZA [*without pausing, as above*]. And to myself I am no one. No one.

GOVERNOR. No, no, Signora, at least to yourself you must be either one or the other!

SIGNORA PONZA. No! To myself—I am the one that each of you thinks I am. [*She looks at them all through her veil just for an instant; and then withdraws. Silence*]

LAUDISI. That, my dear friends, was the voice of truth! [*He looks round at them with derisive defiance.*] Are you satisfied? [*He bursts out laughing.*[17]]

Translator's Notes from the 1954 Edition

The world premiere of this play took place at the Teatro Olimpia in Milan on June 18, 1917. By 1924 it had reached Dullin's Atelier in Paris; by 1925 the Lyric, Hammersmith, London; by 1927, the Theatre Guild, New York. In the French, English, and American productions, respectively, the part of Laudisi was played by Charles Dullin, Nigel Playfair, and Reginald Mason; that of Ponza by Corney, Claude Rains, and Edward G. Robinson; that of Signora Frola by Marcelle Dullin, Nancy Price, and Beryl Mercer.

The play was first published in the periodical *La nuova antologia* in 1918. The present English version is based on the definitive text in the collected works, viz., *Maschere nude*, Vol. II (Milan, Arnoldo Mondadori Editore, 1948). The Italian text has also been published in America, though with one short piece of bowdlerization, by D. C. Heath and Company in 1930, with introduction, notes, and vocabulary by Joseph Louis Russo; the only English version previously published is that of Arthur Livingston in *Three Plays* by Luigi Pirandello (E. P. Dutton and Company, 1922), reprinted with some slight changes in Luigi Pirandello, *Naked Masks: Five Plays*, edited by Eric Bentley (Everyman's Library [E. P. Dutton and Company, 1952]).

The new stage version was commissioned by Roger L. Stevens for performance at the Brattle Theatre, Cambridge, Massachusetts, in 1952 under the direction of the present editor. It was used, again under his direction, at the Westport Country Playhouse in Connecticut in the same year. In these two productions the part of Laudisi was played, respectively, by Philip Bourneuf and Alfred Drake; that of Ponza by Martin Gabel and Martin Kosleck; that of Signora Frola on both occasions by Mildred Dunnock. The play has also been televised in this version by Kraft Television.

The present editor first provided suggestions for a production of the play in *The Rocky Mountain Review* (Winter, 1946), in an essay entitled "Pirandello and Modern Comedy" which was subsequently incorporated in his book *The Playwright as Thinker*. His introduction to *Naked Masks*, reprinted in the book *In Search of Theater*, also includes a passage on *Right You Are*. For further literature about the play, the reader is referred to the general Pirandello bibliography in Appendix III of *Naked Masks*. To this might be added the article "Una tragedia italiana," by Giorgio Prosperi, in the magazine *Sipario*, November-December, 1946. The editor has read many reviews of English and American performances; has cited W. J. Turner's (below, page 60), which appeared in *The New Statesman and Nation*, October 3, 1925; but would wish to cite only one more, Stark Young's, which originally appeared in *The New Republic*, March 23, 1927, and is now more easily accessible in Mr. Young's volume *Immortal Shadows*.

RIGHT YOU ARE. This title has been used simply because so many people know the play by it. Also because no one has ever found an apt translation of the Italian *Così è (se vi pare)*. The first American edition is called *Right You Are (If You Think So!)*. At the first English performance, the title was *And That's the Truth!* Ludwig Lewisohn suggested *As You Like It*, and Arthur Livingston *And Thinking Makes It So*. Other attempts are *Right You Are (If You Think You Are)* and *Have It Your Own Way*. Literally, the Italian means "Thus it is if it seems thus to you," but this is impossible English; the nearest one can come to it is *It Is So (If You Think So)*, a title imposed upon the Livingston translation by the present editor in the Everyman's Library Pirandello. What no English version has rendered is the comical contrast between the pontifical main clause *(Così è)* and the colloquial parenthesis *(se vi pare)*.

CHARACTERS. "The administration of an Italian province is entrusted to a *prefetto*, appointed by the premier, assisted by a varying number of *consiglieri*" (Russo). *Prefetto* is here translated as governor, as the word *prefect* is not, in this meaning, in the Anglo-American vocabulary; *consigliere* is left as councillor, this being less misleading than any other word. The Italian for executive secretary reads simply *segretario*, but it is essential to understand that he would have workers under him and is not merely a clerk.

THE PLACE. THE TIME. In the short story which is the source of the play the town is called Valdana, a made-up name. But we are told on page 21 where Ponza and Frola come from, namely, a village in Marsica. Marsica is "a district in the Abruzzi bordering on Lazio. It was ravaged by one of the most terrific earthquakes of modern times on January 13, 1915. Avezzano, the most important town in the district, lost about 90 percent of its population of 11,500, Pescina had 4,500 victims, while some of the villages in the vicinity were literally wiped out. The total loss of life amounted to more than 30,000" (Russo). It is these facts (which deeply influenced another Italian writer: Ignazio Silone; see *The God That Failed*, ed. Crossman, pp. 92ff.) that give plausibility to the Ponza-Frola family's total loss of identification papers.

ACTS AND SCENES. The scene divisions of the Italian edition have been kept. In general (though Pirandello is not absolutely consistent), a new scene starts with the entrance or exit of an actor or actors. These scene divisions are very useful in rehearsing the play, especially since a list of the characters appearing in each scene is given at the head of it.

I. THE CURTAIN RISES. In Italy it is quite usual to wait half an hour for latecomers, after which the playwright can plunge in medias res, as Pirandello does here, and as we in England and America, who start pretty much on time, simply dare not do. The opening scene in the Anglo-American theater has the function of keeping the punctual part of the audience happy while the unpunctual part gets seated. Now the punctual people are the earnest and analytic people, the people likely to think that, in *Right You Are*, the social and historical background should be clearer. For their sake, in the Brattle Theatre production, a series of slides was projected on a curtain, which thereby became a screen. Lester Polakov had been to the New York Public Library and had found actual photographs of the 1915 earthquake. The pictures were preceded, accompanied, or followed by headlines, making a sequence as follows:

Slide One: JANUARY 15, 1910—REGION OF MARSICA RAVAGED BY EARTHQUAKE
Slide Two: photo with legend: AVEZZANO BEFORE
Slide Three: photo with legend: AVEZZANO AFTER
Slide Four: 11,500 DEAD IN AVEZZANO ALONE
Slide Five: photo of more ruins
Slide Six: FIRST SERVANT OF OUR STRICKEN PEOPLE HAS BEEN OUR KING
Slide Seven: photo of Victor Emmanuel III inspecting ruins
Slide Eight: THE FAMILY, THE FAMILY, FOREVER THE FAMILY!—VICTOR EMMAN-
    UEL III
Slide Nine: photo of Victor Emmanuel in the bosom of his family
Slide Ten: HIS SUFFERING PEOPLE—SURVIVORS OF THE EARTHQUAKE
Slide Eleven: photo of survivors amid ruins
Slide Twelve: photo of survivors living in tents
Slide Thirteen: MARCH 5, 1910—GOVERNOR OF OUR PROVINCE DECORATED BY
    KING FOR MASTERLY HANDLING OF DISPLACED PERSONS
Slide Fourteen: photo of Governor (i.e., of the actor cast for the role)
Slide Fifteen: IN OUR TOWN, COUNCILLOR AGAZZI PROVIDES GOVERNMENT JOBS
    FOR HOMELESS
Slide Sixteen: photo of Councillor Agazzi (also an actor)
Slide Seventeen: MAY 10, 1910. COUNCILLOR AGAZZI DECORATED BY GOVERNOR
    FOR SAVING SITUATION
Slide Eighteen: photo of Agazzi being decorated
Slide Nineteen: IN OUR TOWN THERE ARE NO DISPLACED PERSONS, THERE ARE
    ONLY BROTHERS AND SISTERS—AGAZZI
    The date was shifted from 1915 to 1910 because our Anglo-American audience
associates the former date too readily with the First World War and knows nothing
of the earthquake anyway. It would be desirable to show the Governor being
decorated by Victor Emmanuel in the above sequence if photographers could
solve the problem of getting the historic king together in one picture with a mem-
ber of the current cast. Some directors might like to use such slides before Acts
Two and Three, in which case the following sequence is suggested.
    Act Two:
Slide One: JULY 3, 1910—POLICE COMMISSIONER CENTURI TAKES UP PONZA
    CASE
Slide Two: photo of Centuri in uniform
Slide Three: WHEN IN DOUBT ASK A POLICEMAN—TWENTIETH-CENTURY PROV-
    ERB
Slide Four: JULY 4, 1910—CENTURI OPENS UP ARCHIVES. STAFF OF FIFTY TO
    STUDY RECORDS OF ALL BIRTHS, DEATHS, AND MARRIAGES
Slide Five: THE SPIRIT KILLETH BUT THE LETTER GIVETH LIFE—CENTURI
    Act Three:
Slide One: JULY 25, 1910—CENTURI TO ANNOUNCE FINDINGS TODAY
Slide Two: COUNCILLOR AGAZZI TO APPEAL TO GOVERNOR IF NOT SATISFIED
Slide Three: photo of Governor in Mussolini-like pose
Slide Four: THE GOVERNOR IS ALWAYS RIGHT—OLD ITALIAN SAYING
    2. LET'S SET THE STAGE. MOVE YOUR CHAIRS BACK A LITTLE. And later the
chairs are moved in again in several stages as the gossips get more and more inter-

ested in their visitors' narratives. These two lines are interpolations necessitated by
the stage business. "Let's set the stage," it is true, is not absolutely necessary. It is
a gag suggested by the nature of the particular action, the character speaking, and
the whole play: the "chorus" is always setting the stage for the drama of the Ponza-
Frolas. "Let's set the stage," a line never used by Pirandello, is repeated a number
of times in this version and, in production, culminated in a big laugh on the very
last repetition (the Governor's use of it in Act Three).

    3. ACT TWO, SCENE ONE. Pirandello situated the second and third acts in the
study adjoining the drawing room of the first act. Where a revolving stage is
available, the easiest solution is to place both rooms on it, with each room almost
as wide as the proscenium arch; so that in Act One, we can see just a little of the
study, and in the following acts, we can see a little of the drawing room. But what
to do if there is no revolving stage? Pirandello himself envisaged two sets with a
complete change of scene between the first two acts. Then, in the second act, when
he wants to introduce sounds from the drawing room, he has them spoken in the
wings—and "wings" is the word, as it is clear that he thinks throughout in terms
of the baroque tradition with entrances left, right, and center.

    Against following the playwright's lead there are two arguments of quite dif-
ferent kinds. The first is purely practical and perhaps purely American: the cost of
building two sets is too high. The second is that "voices off" from the wings now
seem very old-fashioned or simply ineffective. (Signora Frola plays the piano in
one room, Signor Ponza overhears her from the next. Would it not be better if we
could see *both* parties?) It was with these two arguments in mind that I asked Lester
Polakov to devise a scheme whereby the two rooms could be presented to the
audience simultaneously. In the Polakov arrangement, the main action all takes
place in the drawing room, but there is another room behind it (upstage), called
the music room because the piano is in it, yet also functioning as a corridor or
entrance hall to the drawing room by virtue of its oblong shape. It is in fact one of
the two entrances to this set; the butler brings Ponza and Frola through it in Act
One. The other entrance, leading directly to the drawing room, is used whenever
there is no time for the more ceremonious and, as it were, processional entrance.
The music room can be completely open to the drawing room, as it should be in
Act One. It can be curtained off—as for the music scene in Act Two. Or it can be
shut off by folding doors—to shut out the crowd in Act Three. In the handling of
this crowd, incidentally, the dual set has many advantages, most notably, that dialogue can be audibly spoken in the drawing room while a rather noisy crowd is on
stage but in the music room. In Act Two, the sudden unveiling of Frola at the
piano is much more theatrical than her entrance from the wings could be. And
there is one respect in which the dual arrangement assists the drama throughout. If
the drawing room is rather garish and in bad taste, the music room can be macabre
and dark. Such a contrast is to be found in many an Italian palazzo, where you
arrive at the plush, modern living room through ancient and unlit galleries. Polakov's drawing room was a bureaucrat's showpiece (over the folding doors was Victor Emmanuel in stained glass; on the walls, trophies from Tripoli; chairs in gilt
and gold on the floor; and above the doorway the motto *Veritas*), while the music
room, at the bidding of the lighting man, could veer from Robert Adam to Charles
Addams, and seemed to bring in Ponza, Frola, and, above all, the Veiled Lady from
another world.

In Acts Two and Three, the stage directions, and very occasionally the dialogue, have had to be adapted to this staging. Producers who wish to revert to the original arrangement should have little difficulty in doing the necessary rewriting for themselves. In any event, the earlier English version, which follows Pirandello in this respect, is at their disposal.

4. THE LARGE MIRROR. Lester Polakov had the ingenuity so to set the angle of the mirror that a good portion of the audience could see Laudisi in it: the little vaudeville act is greatly improved if what we see is only an image while what we hear comes from a face we cannot see. The speech itself proved the hardest bit in the play to English. As far as the sense goes, the trouble mainly stems from our not having a word for *fantasma*. The homonym *phantasm*, in spoken dialogue, means precisely nothing. The Italian word being both abstract, like *fantasy*, and concrete, like *ghost*, the former word has been used earlier in Act Two where an abstraction was called for, the latter in Act Three, where the joke is that the crowd thinks Laudisi refers to an actual spirit. The mirror speech is the bridge between these two passages, and for that reason both words, *fantasy* and *ghost*, have been worked in. Such an exigency forces the translator, of course, into a heavier style than the original. Even so, the solution is not complete. Pirandello talks of carrying your *fantasma* inside you, and a *ghost* has never been considered so portable. There is also a problem in communicating Pirandello's brand of relativism in *any* English words, since Anglo-Saxon readers tend to assume he is saying that everything is unreal and truth is nowhere to be found, whereas what he is trying to say is that everything is real and truth is everywhere to be found. The mirror itself arouses expectations Pirandello does not gratify. What we are prepared to get is the simple contrast (as in E. E. Cummings's *him*) between the *me* I know and that part of *me* which other people know. Pirandello is out for bigger game!

Here are three alternative versions of the speech, beginning with the most literal one. The second, the clearest and most explanatory version, is the worst as English speech and therefore as theater; and here is the problem in a nutshell: we have to carry over Pirandello's meaning, yet it is even more urgent to give the actor something (literally and figuratively) to play with.

1. Ah, so there you are! Well, old fellow, which of us two is the madman? Yes, I know, I say *you* and you point at *me*. Come now, between you and me, we understand each other pretty well, the two of us. The only trouble is, the others don't see you as I do! So what becomes of you, my dear chap? The "you" that is seen by other people—what must it be for me? Why, a creature of fantasy, a figment, an idea, an image. Well, you see *these* madmen? They ignore the image they carry in themselves—in their own souls—and, driven by curiosity, go running after images of other people—thinking those are quite a different matter.

2. Ah, so there you are! Well, old boy, which of us two is the madman? Oh yes, I know, I say *you* and you point your finger at *me*. So far, so good: between the two of us, well, we understand each other, don't we? The only trouble is, the others don't see you the same way I do. They simply have an idea, a conception, of you. That is, you only exist in their imagination, you're a figment, a creature of fantasy. Now what can *I* make of their idea of *you*? Well, I can have an *idea* of it—and so you become, for me, an idea of an idea, a conception of a conception. So—even for me—you're a figment, a creature of fantasy—a ghost. Every man jack of us carries such a ghost in his breast. But do we act accordingly? By no means. Most of

us prefer to ignore what we carry within ourselves—our idea of other people's idea of ourselves—and to go running after something more external—our idea of other people, which we believe to be no idea at all, no ghost, no fantasy, but sheer reality, sheer truth. This is what our friends here are doing, driven by the demon of curiosity.

3. (Laudisi is shaking his own hand and echoing Sirelli) Goodbye, Lamberto, goodbye, Lamberto! Lamberto? Who's that? Where is he? Where? (Seeing his image in the mirror and drawing a long breath) Ahh! So there you are! Signor Lamberto, good morning! And, by the way, old boy, which of us two is the madman? Yes, I know, I say *you* and you point your finger at *me*. But I know you pretty well, don't I? Or do I? I know you at pretty close quarters anyway. I know you a little better than I know the others. You're not me of course, I don't know me, you're— an image in the glass. But *other* people! They're an image in a less reliable glass than this, a much less literal-minded glass. I see other people only in the distorting mirror of my own mind. In fact what I take for other people—why, they're just creatures of my own fantasy, phantoms, ghosts, and what other people take for me, *that's* not me, it's *you*, Signor Lamberto. And, what's more, it's you as they see you and not you as I see you! You know *these* madmen? "Let's set the stage, Signor Ponza will be sitting here, I'll put Signora Frola there . . ." They don't waste much time looking at their *own* image, do they? They concentrate on hunting down other people. And they don't realize they're only hunting their own fantasies, the Ponza *they* take him for, the Frola they take *her* for . . .

5. SIGNORA NENNI. It is hard to understand why Pirandello left Signora Nenni silent for so long. On the assumption that she is a great listener, it is possible to have her silently repeating with her lips what Laudisi says. Certain key words that have been on her mind might even become audible, in which case Laudisi will have to hear her and respond. For example, *Laudisi:* A forged document, understand? *Signora Nenni* (grasping at the fascinating and appalling word): Forged?! *Laudisi:* Forged. And then again a few seconds later, *Laudisi:* Signor Ponza comes along and says they're forged. *Signora Nenni* (indignant this time, as at the discovery of treason): Forged! *Laudisi* (mimicking her horror): Forged. No longer embarrassed at Signora Nenni's being left out of the scene, the director will now have to take care she doesn't monopolize it; the device amuses the audience so much that the actress playing Signora Nenni will repeat every word Laudisi utters unless she is forcibly restrained from doing so.

6. WITH THAT MAN. Some audiences are more quickwitted than others. A director who decides that his audience is slow-witted should assume that they have not, at this point, grasped what Agazzi's "great idea" is and that it must be restated. A restatement can be interpolated here in Dina's speech by deleting "with the man. If he found them closed . . ." and substituting the following: "with Signor Ponza. The doors must be left open so we can be heard talking in the music room. Father will use this as an excuse to bring us all in here. With Signora Frola. If he found the doors closed and couldn't hear a sound from the music room . . . Well, you know Father." At the end of Laudisi's next speech, after "convinced," the following can be added: "already that it's Ponza who's mad?"

7. "NINA MAD THROUGH LOVE." Pirandello names this eighteenth-century opera (by Paisiello) but does not give a name to the melody he describes. The only tune in the opera which the description seems to fit is a soprano aria, "Il mio ben,

quando verrà?" And what makes one fairly certain that this is what Pirandello referred to is that the aria has appeared in modern song collections, whereas a score of the opera is practically impossible to come by. The American producer will find the item in *Italian Songs of the Seventeenth and Eighteenth Centuries,* published by Schirmer. Only an actress who can play the piano fairly well will be able to manage the performance herself, for the piece, being a song and not a piano solo, is printed in three clefs. It also entails technical difficulties such as playing three against two.

8. BURSTS OUT LAUGHING. Since Act Two would send the audience into the lobby in much the same frame of mind as Act One, it might be shrewder to have no intermission at all at this point. If the stagehands need a couple of minutes to rearrange the furniture, the music from the preceding scene can be played again. It could even be sung this time by a soprano appearing before the curtain except that the modern audience is far too well educated and will ask what such a little entr'acte "symbolizes."

9. ACT THREE, SCENE TWO. It is not worth presenting a crowd unless it can be both large and well trained: ideally, we should see a cross section of an Italian town from the postman to the priest, from the schoolmaster with his books to the farmer's daughter carrying chickens home in a basket. Since at Westport the crowd that was provided two days before the opening looked like *La Traviata* at a girls' college, it was eliminated altogether; it may be useful to prospective producers to know that the play works quite well without a crowd—or rather that the cast without extras can itself seem quite a crowd. With or without extras, this scene is the most dangerous one of the play in that there is a strong chance of its dragging, and the moment is the one above all others—half an hour before the end—when a play must not drag. The problem is to give Laudisi's intellectual fooling all the physicality of farce. This can be done by building the earlier part of the scene as a chase, a rushing from one side of the stage to the other and back again in pursuit of the elusive harlequin. In the latter part of the scene (beginning with "Columbus's egg"), Laudisi is no longer pursued; he is the pursuer. He can force the "crowd" into a clump and buzz annoyingly around them like a wasp. He can even resume his teasing of Signora Nenni whenever he comes near her. She will naturally be fascinated by the word "ghost" and the repetition-gag can be brought to an hysterico-farcical climax with the phrase "to doubt it" if Laudisi refuses to let her have the last word and repeats her repetitions in a mad to-and-fro until the others clasp their heads and scream. The first turning point ("Columbus's egg") where Laudisi puts in Sirelli's head the idea of bringing Signora Ponza over is followed by a second ("you're all sure she exists") where Laudisi plants the notion that she is a ghost. At each turning point the action must, as it were, shift into a higher gear, so that top speed is reached at the announcement of the Governor's arrival.

10. THE GOVERNOR'S OPINION. *Right You Are* is the story of a contest between Ponza and Frola, a contest for *credence,* and everyone in the theatre is betting on the issue. First, Signora Frola is the favorite, then Ponza comes out in front, then Frola leads again, and so forth. Pirandello is at pains to keep the race a close one: whoever had the last word has always got ahead but has always been followed by a last word from the other. Yet, although the two have been evenly balanced in actual power, there has been no balance in the sympathy that has been aroused: it has all gone to Frola. And a danger in any production of the play is that the audience's sympathy for Frola may place them conclusively on her side. It is to deal with this

danger that Pirandello brings the Governor in. He is Ponza's only real supporter, but being Governor his authority is assumed (in the Italian context) fully to counterbalance that of all the Agazzis and hoi polloi combined. In a way, it is but the pattern of the second act all over again. Frola gains steadily in sympathy, but her position is then assailed by sheer *force majeur*. Ponza's change of mood is so abrupt we *have* to believe him: how could he have calmed down so quickly if the outburst had not been deliberate? In the third act, against Frola's charm and sincerity are marshalled the authority and worldly wisdom of a governor. By the time Signora Ponza makes her concluding announcement, the betting out front should be even. Whether it is so or not will depend principally on the actor playing the Governor. The part needs a Sydney Greenstreet.

11. COLUMBUS'S EGG. When once the way has been shown, nothing is easier than to follow it. Columbus applied this principle to his voyages by asking on a famous occasion if any present could make an egg stand on its end. When the others had tried in vain, he struck the egg gently on one end, then stood it on the broken part. Producers of *Right You Are* who think their audience will not understand Laudisi's exclamation can change it to "Eureka!" (though perhaps it is better to risk mystifying half the audience if there is some assurance that the other half gets the point; the mystification, in any event, is slight; and few people, when they are mystified, know it).

12. THE GHOST OF A SECOND WIFE IF SIGNORA FROLA IS RIGHT. THE GHOST OF HER DAUGHTER IF SIGNOR PONZA IS RIGHT. Actors will ask, "Shouldn't it be the other way round? After all, it's Ponza who believes it's a second wife and Frola who thinks it's her daughter." Exactly: if Ponza is right, Frola's daughter is not there, Frola only imagines this, creates the fantasy or ghost of it, and vice versa. But by this time you could probably say the opposite and few spectators would know the difference.

13. SUBVERSIVE ACTIVITIES. If the phrase seems not to belong to 1910 it can be dropped. Literally, the Italian means "the headquarters of a conspiracy" (the word "conspiracy" is also still to be seen in our newspapers). In any case, the actor should not try for a laugh on the line or it will kill what often proved the biggest laugh in the play, which comes immediately afterward on "Let's set the stage."

14. FEROCIOUS INVESTIGATION. This passage, it may be noted in passing, is translated literally.

15. THICK VEIL, BLACK, IMPENETRABLE. In the American premiere of 1927 Armina Marshall's veil was not impenetrable or even thick, and two years earlier, on the occasion of the London premiere, the poet and critic W. J. Turner had suggested that Signora Ponza should wear no veil at all. It is true that, on the literal plane, nothing would be given away by her not wearing a veil. Seeing the lady's face, we still receive no shock of recognition; we do not know her. But, it might be retorted, that is why the revelation can only be an anticlimax—aside from its being contrary to Pirandello's instructions and, more important, to the meaning of his play.

16. DON'T BE AFRAID. How should the lines of Signora Ponza be spoken? The formal, almost hieratic, style of the lines encourages the actress to attempt some formalized style of utterance. The present editor can only say that in his experience the role has been more effective when played as a real woman with natural emo-

tions. The tone of her first line can be firm, helpful, loving: the only kind of for-malization the line needs is, perhaps, that the first "don't be afraid" be spoken to Ponza, the second to Frola, the "Go!" to both. The tone of the lines Signora Ponza speaks to the crowd should be ironic, gently bitter. She despairs of having them really understand, so she (deliberately?) provokes them with a riddle; and whether she knows it or not, there is one present who will understand: Laudisi, whose laugh will grow out of the silence following his very quiet "Are you satisfied?" and carry the meaning of the riddle to that outer world, the audience. After "I am Signora Frola's daughter," there is a long intake of breath from the crowd; at last the secret seems to be out. A little more deliberately, perhaps mockingly, Signora Ponza adds: "And I am Signor Ponza's second wife." General and utter confusion. Then her tone sinks to a lost sadness for: "And to myself I am no one. No one." By this time even the imperturbable Governor is perturbed. "No, no, Signora," he stammers, "at least to yourself you must be either one or the other!" There is exas-peration in his "must be" as if to say: "you really can't upset a governor's equanim-ity this way, how unreasonable can life get?" Signora Ponza delivers her parting shot with an absolute calm and simplicity, "Sono colei che mi si crede," which means "I am that one who I am believed to be." Like the title of the play, this key line defies pithy, idiomatic translation. "I am whoever you choose to have me" is wrong in two respects. *Colei* does not mean "whoever" but "that particular woman," a difference with broad philosophical implications. Nor can the imper-sonal *si crede* be translated "you choose" in this context, for the "you" will seem to refer to the governor, who has just spoken. In both his productions, the present translator used the line "I am she who each of you thinks I am," the "each of you" justifying itself by reference to Pirandello's philosophy: the veiled lady is not merely she who the governor thinks she is, or she who people collectively think she is, but she who each man separately and differently thinks she is. Yet the phrase "she who," though it can be put over in the theatre by a pause between the two words, seems rather queer, and actresses are tempted to say "she who*m*" which makes matters worse. So for this book another version has been hazarded: "I am the one that each of you thinks I am." Even this demands a slight pause (after "the one").

17. BURSTS OUT LAUGHING. One of the nicest problems of the performance is: what to do with Laudisi's laughs at the end of each act? The editor's memory of a great production at the Comédie Française in 1938 is that, each time, the whole stage was dimmed out except for a spot on Laudisi's face and that the laugh which came from the pinpoint of light (and from the throat of Jean Debucourt) was quiet, sardonic, regular—an even, Mephistophelean ripple. At Westport, this lighting and this type of laughter were used only at the end of the play. In the other acts it was thought best not to cut Laudisi off from the others—he had been off in his corner quite enough—but to play up his relationship to them. In the first act, Alfred Drake changed "You're looking each other over?" to "You're looking for something?" and then, as they blankly returned his amused gaze, was overcome by a great gust of good-humored laughter. In the second act, the couch, upon which the action of the whole had been centered, was exploited by Laudisi. He stood behind it and feigned surprise at not finding Ponza and Frola seated there. Ringing laughter was again used, but this time harshly, sarcastically.

Six Characters in Search
of an Author

CHARACTERS OF THE PLAY-IN-THE-MAKING

The Father
The Mother
The Son, aged 22
The Stepdaughter, 18

The Boy, 14
The Little Girl, 4
    (these two last do not speak)
Then, called into being: Madam
    Pace

ACTORS IN THE COMPANY

The Director (Direttore-
    Capocomico)
Leading Lady
Leading Man
Second Actress
Ingenue
Juvenile Lead
Other actors and actresses

Stage Manager
Prompter
Property Man
Technician
Director's Secretary
Stage Door Man
Stage Crew

THE PLACE: *The stage of a playhouse.*

The play has neither acts nor scenes. The performance should be interrupted twice: first—without any lowering of the curtain—when the Director and the chief among the Characters retire to put the scenario together and the Actors leave the stage; second when the Technician lets the curtain down by mistake.

When the audience arrives in the theater, the curtain is raised; and the stage, as normally in the daytime, is without wings or scenery and almost completely dark and empty. From the beginning we are to receive the impression of an un-rehearsed performance.

Two stairways, left and right respectively, connect the stage with the auditorium.

On stage the dome of the prompter's box has been placed on one side of the box itself. On the other side, at the front of the stage, a small table and an armchair with its back to the audience, for the DIRETTORE-CAPOCOMICO [DI-RECTOR].

Two other small tables of different sizes with several chairs around them have also been placed at the front of the stage, ready as needed for the rehearsal. Other chairs here and there, left and right, for the actors, and at the back, a piano, on one side and almost hidden.

As soon as the houselights dim, the TECHNICIAN *is seen entering at the door on stage. He is wearing a blue shirt, and a tool bag hangs from his belt. From a corner at the back he takes several stagebraces, then arranges them on the floor downstage, and kneels down to hammer some nails in. At the sound of the hammering, the* STAGE MANAGER *comes running from the door that leads to the dressing rooms.*

STAGE MANAGER. Oh! What are you doing?

TECHNICIAN. What am I doing? Hammering.

STAGE MANAGER. At this hour? [*He looks at the clock*] It's ten-thirty already. The Director will be here any moment. For the rehearsal.

TECHNICIAN. I gotta have time to work, too, see.

STAGE MANAGER. You will have. But not now.

TECHNICIAN. When?

STAGE MANAGER. Not during rehearsal hours. Now move along, take all this stuff away, and let me set the stage for the second act of, um, *The Game of Role Playing.*

[*Muttering, grumbling, the* TECHNICIAN *picks up the stage-braces and goes away. Meanwhile, from the door on stage, the* ACTORS OF THE COMPANY *start coming in, both men and women, one at a time at first, then in twos, at random, nine or ten of them, the number one would expect as the cast in rehearsals of Pirandello's play, "The Game of Role Playing,"[1] which is the order of the day. They enter, greet the* STAGE MANAGER *and each other, all saying good-morning to all. Several go to their dressing rooms. Others, among them the* PROMPTER, *who has a copy of the script rolled up under his arm, stay on stage, waiting for*

the DIRECTOR *to begin the rehearsal. Meanwhile, either seated in conversa-*
tional groups, or standing, they exchange a few words among themselves. One
lights a cigarette, one complains about the part he has been assigned, one reads
aloud to his companions items of news from a theater journal. It would be well if
both the Actresses and the Actors wore rather gay and brightly colored clothes
and if this first improvised scene [scena a soggetto] *combined vivacity with*
naturalness. At a certain point, one of the actors can sit down at the piano and
strike up a dance tune. The younger actors and actresses start dancing.]

STAGE MANAGER [*clapping his hands to call them to order*]. All right, that's
   enough of that. The Director's here.

[*The noise and the dancing stop at once. The Actors turn and look toward the*
auditorium from the door of which the DIRECTOR *is now seen coming. A bowler*
hat on his head, a walking stick under his arm, and a big cigar in his mouth,
he walks down the aisle and, greeted by the Actors, goes on stage by one of the
two stairways. The SECRETARY *hands him his mail: several newspapers and a*
script in a wrapper.]

DIRECTOR. Letters?
SECRETARY. None. That's all the mail there is.
DIRECTOR [*handing him the script*]. Take this to my room. [*Then, looking*
   around and addressing himself to the STAGE MANAGER] We can't see
   each other in here. Want to give us a little light?
STAGE MANAGER. OK.

[*He goes to give the order, and shortly afterward, the whole left side of the stage*
where the Actors are is lit by a vivid white light. Meanwhile, the PROMPTER *has*
taken up his position in his box. He uses a small lamp and has the script open in
front of him.]

DIRECTOR [*clapping his hands*]. Very well, let's start. [*To the* STAGE MAN-
   AGER] Someone missing?
STAGE MANAGER. The Leading Lady.
DIRECTOR. As usual! [*He looks at the clock*] We're ten minutes late already.
   Fine her for that, would you, please? Then she'll learn to be on time.

[*He has not completed his rebuke when the voice of the* LEADING LADY *is heard*
from the back of the auditorium.]

LEADING LADY. No, no, for Heaven's sake! I'm here! I'm here! [*She is*
   dressed all in white with a big, impudent hat on her head and a cute little
   dog in her arms. She runs down the aisle and climbs one of the sets of stairs
   in great haste.]

DIRECTOR. You've sworn an oath always to keep people waiting.

LEADING LADY. You must excuse me. Just couldn't find a taxi. But you haven't even begun, I see. And I'm not on right away. [*Then, calling the* STAGE MANAGER *by name, and handing the little dog over to him*] *Would you please shut him in my dressing room?*

DIRECTOR [*grumbling*]. And the little dog to boot! As if there weren't enough dogs around here. [*He claps his hands again and turns to the* PROMPTER.] Now then, the second act of *The Game of Role Playing*. [*As he sits down in his armchair*] Quiet, gentlemen. Who's on stage?

[*The Actresses and Actors clear the front of the stage and go and sit on one side, except for the three who will start the rehearsal and the* LEADING LADY *who, disregarding the* DIRECTOR's *request, sits herself down at one of the two small tables.*]

DIRECTOR [*to the* LEADING LADY]. You're in this scene, are you?

LEADING LADY. Me? No, no.

DIRECTOR [*irritated*]. Then how about getting up, for Heaven's sake?

[*The* LEADING LADY *rises and goes and sits beside the other Actors who have already gone to one side.*]

DIRECTOR [*to the* PROMPTER]. Start, start.

PROMPTER [*reading from the script*]. "In the house of Leone Gala. A strange room, combined study and dining room."

DIRECTOR [*turning to the* STAGE MANAGER]. We'll use the red room.

STAGE MANAGER [*making a note on a piece of paper*]. Red room. Very good.

PROMPTER [*continuing to read from the script*]. "The table is set and the desk has books and papers on it. Shelves with books on them, and cupboards with lavish tableware. Door in the rear through which one goes to Leone's bedroom. Side door on the left through which one goes to the kitchen. The main entrance is on the right."

DIRECTOR [*rising and pointing*]. All right, now listen carefully. That's the main door. This is the way to the kitchen. [*Addressing himself to the Actor playing the part of Socrates*] You will come on and go out on this side. [*To the* STAGE MANAGER] The compass at the back. And curtains. [*He sits down again.*]

STAGE MANAGER [*making a note*]. Very good.

PROMPTER [*reading as before*]. "Scene One. Leone Gala, Guido Venanzi, Filippo called Socrates." [*To the* DIRECTOR] Am I supposed to read the stage directions, too?

DIRECTOR. Yes, yes, yes! I've told you that a hundred times!

PROMPTER [*reading as before*]. "At the rise of the curtain, Leone Gala, wearing a chef's hat and apron, is intent on beating an egg in a saucepan with a wooden spoon. Filippo, also dressed as a cook, is beating another egg. Guido Venanzi, seated, is listening."

LEADING ACTOR [*to the* DIRECTOR]. Excuse me, but do I really have to wear a chef's hat?

DIRECTOR [*annoyed by this observation*]. I should say so! It's in the script. [*And he points at it.*]

LEADING ACTOR. But it's ridiculous, if I may say so.

DIRECTOR [*leaping to his feet, furious*]. "Ridiculous, ridiculous!" What do you want me to do? We never get a good play from France any more, so we're reduced to producing plays by Pirandello, a fine man and all that, but neither the actors, the critics, nor the audience are ever happy with his plays, and if you ask me, he does it all on purpose. [*The Actors laugh. And now he rises and coming over to the* LEADING ACTOR *shouts:*] A cook's hat, yes, my dear man! And you beat eggs. And you think you have nothing more on your hands than the beating of eggs? Guess again. You symbolize the shell of those eggs. [*The Actors resume their laughing, and start making ironical comments among themselves.*] Silence! And pay attention while I explain. [*Again addressing himself to the* LEADING ACTOR] Yes, the shell: that is to say, the empty *form* of reason without the *content* of instinct, which is blind. You are reason, and your wife is instinct in the game of role playing. You play the part assigned you, and you're your own puppet—of your own free will. Understand?

LEADING ACTOR [*extending his arms, palms upward*]. Me? No.

DIRECTOR [*returning to his place*]. Nor do I. Let's go on. Wait and see what I do with the ending. [*In a confidential tone*] I suggest you face three-quarters front. Otherwise, what with the abstruseness of the dialogue, and an audience that can't hear you, good-bye play! [*Again clapping*] Now, again, order! Let's go.

PROMPTER. Excuse me, sir, may I put the top back on the prompter's box? There's rather a draft.

DIRECTOR. Yes, yes, do that.

[*The* STAGE DOOR MAN *has entered the auditorium in the meanwhile, his braided cap on his head. Proceeding down the aisle, he goes up on stage to announce to the* DIRECTOR *the arrival of the Six Characters, who have also entered the auditorium, and have started following him at a certain distance, a little lost and perplexed, looking around them.*

Whoever is going to try and translate this play into scenic terms must take all possible measures not to let these Six Characters get confused with the Actors of the Company. Placing both groups correctly, in accordance with the stage directions, once the Six are on stage, will certainly help, as will lighting the two groups in contrasting colors. But the most suitable and effective means to be suggested here is the use of special masks for the Characters: masks specially made of material which doesn't go limp when sweaty and yet masks which are not too heavy for the Actors wearing them, cut out and worked over so they leave eyes, nostrils, and mouth free. This will also bring out the inner significance of the play. The Characters in fact should not be presented as ghosts but as created realities, unchanging constructs of the imagination, and therefore more solidly real than the Actors with their fluid naturalness. The masks will help to give the impression of figures constructed by art, each one unchangeably fixed in the expression of its own fundamental sentiment, thus:

remorse *in the case of the* FATHER; revenge *in the case of the* STEP-DAUGHTER; disdain *in the case of the* SON; grief *in the case of the* MOTHER, *who should have wax tears fixed in the rings under her eyes and on her cheeks, as with the sculpted and painted images of the* mater dolorosa *in church. Their clothes should be of special material and design, without extravagance, with rigid, full folds like a statue, in short not suggesting a material you might buy at any store in town, cut out and tailored at any dressmaker's.*

The FATHER *is a man of about fifty, hair thin at the temples, but not bald, thick mustache coiled round a still youthful mouth that is often open in an uncertain, pointless smile. Pale, most notably on his broad forehead: blue eyes, oval, very clear and piercing; dark jacket and light trousers: at times gentle and smooth, at times he has hard, harsh outbursts.*

The MOTHER *seems scared and crushed by an intolerable weight of shame and self-abasement. Wearing a thick black crepe widow's veil, she is modestly dressed in black, and when she lifts the veil, the face does not show signs of suffering, and yet seems made of wax. Her eyes are always on the ground.*

The STEPDAUGHTER, *eighteen, is impudent, almost insolent. Very beautiful, and also in mourning, but mourning of a showy elegance. She shows contempt for the timid, afflicted, almost humiliated manner of her little brother, rather a mess of a* BOY, *fourteen, also dressed in black, but a lively tenderness for her little sister, a* LITTLE GIRL *of around four, dressed in white with black silk sash round her waist.*

The SON, *twenty-two, tall, almost rigid with contained disdain for the* FATHER *and supercilious indifference toward the* MOTHER, *wears a mauve topcoat and a long green scarf wound round his neck.]*

STAGE DOOR MAN [*beret in hand*]. Excuse me, your honor.

DIRECTOR [*rudely jumping on him*]. What is it now?

STAGE DOOR MAN [*timidly*]. There are some people here asking for you.

[*The* DIRECTOR *and the Actors turn in astonishment to look down into the auditorium.*]

DIRECTOR [*furious again*]. But I'm rehearsing here! And you know perfectly well no one can come in during rehearsal! [*Turning again toward the house*] Who are these people? What do they want?

THE FATHER [*stepping forward, followed by the others, to one of the two little stairways to the stage*]. We're here in search of an author.

DIRECTOR [*half angry, half astounded*]. An author? What author?

FATHER. Any author, sir.

DIRECTOR. There's no author here at all. It's not a new play we're rehearsing.

STEPDAUGHTER [*very vivaciously as she rushes up the stairs*]. Then so much the better, sir! *We* can be your new play!

ONE OF THE ACTORS [*among the racy comments and laughs of the others*]. Did you hear that?

FATHER [*following the* STEPDAUGHTER *onstage*]. Certainly, but if the author's not here . . . [*to the* DIRECTOR] Unless *you'd* like to be the author?

[*The* MOTHER, *holding the* LITTLE GIRL *by the hand, and the* BOY *climb the first steps of the stairway and remain there waiting. The* SON *stays morosely below.*]

DIRECTOR. Is this your idea of a joke?

FATHER. Heavens, no! Oh, sir, on the contrary: we bring you a painful drama.

STEPDAUGHTER. We can make your fortune for you.

DIRECTOR. Do me a favor, and leave. We have no time to waste on madmen.

FATHER [*wounded, smoothly*]. Oh, sir, you surely know that life is full of infinite absurdities which, brazenly enough, do not need to appear probable, because they're true.

DIRECTOR. What in God's name are you saying?

FATHER. I'm saying it can actually be considered madness, sir, to force oneself to do the opposite: that is, to give probability to things so they will seem true. But permit me to observe that, if this is madness, it is also the *raison d'être* of your profession.

[*The Actors become agitated and indignant.*]

DIRECTOR [*rising and looking him over*]. It is, is it? It seems to you an affair
for madmen, our profession?

FATHER. Well, to make something seem true which is not true . . . without
any need, sir: just for fun . . . Isn't it your job to give life on stage to
creatures of fantasy?

DIRECTOR [*immediately, making himself spokesman for the growing indignation of his Actors*]. Let me tell you something, my good sir. The actor's
profession is a very noble one. If, as things go nowadays, our new
playwrights give us nothing but stupid plays, with puppets in them
instead of men, it is our boast, I'd have you know, to have given life—
on these very boards—to immortal works of art.

[*Satisfied, the Actors approve and applaud their* DIRECTOR.]

FATHER [*interrupting and bearing down hard*]. Exactly! That's just it. You
have created living beings—*more* alive than those that breathe and
wear clothes! Less real, perhaps; but more true! We agree completely!

[*The Actors look at each other, astounded.*]

DIRECTOR. What? You were saying just now . . .

FATHER. No, no, don't misunderstand me. You shouted that you hadn't
time to waste on madmen. So I wanted to tell you that no one knows
better than you that Nature employs the human imagination to carry
her work of creation on to a higher plane!

DIRECTOR. All right, all right. But what are you getting at, exactly?

FATHER. Nothing, sir. I only wanted to show that one may be born to this
life in many modes, in many forms: as tree, as rock, water or butterfly
. . . or woman. And that . . . characters are born too.

DIRECTOR [*his amazement ironically feigned*]. And you—with these companions of yours—were born a character?

FATHER. Right, sir. And alive, as you see.

[*The* DIRECTOR *and the Actors burst out laughing as at a joke.*]

FATHER [*wounded*]. I'm sorry to hear you laugh, because, I repeat, we
carry a painful drama within us, as you all might deduce from the
sight of that lady there, veiled in black.

[*As he says this, he gives his hand to the* MOTHER *to help her up the last steps
and, still holding her by the hand, he leads her with a certain tragic solemnity*

to the other side of the stage, which is suddenly bathed in fantastic light. The LITTLE GIRL *and the* BOY *follow the* MOTHER; *then the* SON, *who stands on one side at the back; then the* STEPDAUGHTER *who also detaches herself from the others—downstage and leaning against the proscenium arch. At first astonished at this development, then overcome with admiration, the Actors now burst into applause as at a show performed for their benefit.*]

DIRECTOR [*bowled over at first, then indignant*]. Oh, stop this! Silence please! [*Then, turning to the Characters*] And you, leave! Get out of here! [*To the* STAGE MANAGER] *For God's sake, get them out!*

STAGE MANAGER [*stepping forward but then stopping, as if held back by a strange dismay*]. Go! Go!

FATHER [*to the* DIRECTOR]. No, look, we, um—

DIRECTOR [*shouting*]. I tell you we've got to work!

LEADING MAN. It's not right to fool around like this . . .

FATHER [*resolute, stepping forward*]. I'm amazed at your incredulity! You're accustomed to seeing the created characters of an author spring to life, aren't you, right here on this stage, the one confronting the other? Perhaps the trouble is there's no script *there* [*pointing to the* PROMPTER's *box*] with us in it?

STEPDAUGHTER [*going right up to the* DIRECTOR, *smiling, coquettish*]. Believe me, we really are six characters, sir. Very interesting ones at that. But lost. Adrift.

FATHER [*brushing her aside*]. Very well: lost, adrift. [*Going right on*] In the sense, that is, that the author who created us, made us live, did not wish, or simply and materially was not able, to place us in the world of art. And that was a real crime, sir, because whoever has the luck to be born a living character can also laugh at death. He will never die! The man will die, the writer, the instrument of creation; the creature will never die! And to have eternal life it doesn't even take extraordinary gifts, nor the performance of miracles. Who was Sancho Panza? Who was Don Abbondio?[2] But they live forever because, as live germs, they have the luck to find a fertile matrix, an imagination which knew how to raise and nourish them, make them live through all eternity!

DIRECTOR. That's all well and good. But what do you people want here?

FATHER. We want to live, sir.

DIRECTOR [*ironically*]. Through all eternity?

FATHER. No, sir. But for a moment at least. In you.

AN ACTOR. Well, well, well!

LEADING LADY. They want to live in us.

JUVENILE LEAD [*pointing to the* STEPDAUGHTER]. Well, I've no objection, so long as I get that one.

FATHER. Now look, look. The play is still in the making. [*To the* DIRECTOR] But if you wish, and your actors wish, we can make it right away. Acting in concert.

LEADING MAN [*annoyed*]. Concert? We don't put on concerts! We do plays, dramas, comedies!

FATHER. Very good. That's why we came.

DIRECTOR. Well, where's the script?

FATHER. Inside us, sir. [*The Actors laugh.*] The drama is inside us. It *is* us. And we're impatient to perform it. According to the dictates of the passion within us.

STEPDAUGHTER [*scornful, with treacherous grace, deliberate impudence*]. My passion—if you only knew, sir! My passion—for him! [*She points to the* FATHER *and makes as if to embrace him but then breaks into a strident laugh.*]

FATHER [*an angry interjection*]. You keep out of this now. And please don't laugh that way!

STEPDAUGHTER. No? Then, ladies and gentlemen, permit me. A two months' orphan, I shall dance and sing for you all. Watch how! [*She mischievously starts to sing "Beware of Chu Chin Chow" by Dave Stamper, reduced to fox trot or slow one-step by Francis Salabert: the first verse, accompanied by a step or two of dancing.[3] While she sings and dances, the Actors, especially the young ones, as if drawn by some strange fascination, move toward her and half raise their hands as if to take hold of her. She runs away and when the Actors burst into applause she just stands there, remote, abstracted, while the DIRECTOR protests.*]

ACTORS AND ACTRESSES [*laughing and clapping*]. Brava! Fine! Splendid!

DIRECTOR [*annoyed*]. Silence! What do you think this is, a night spot? [*Taking the* FATHER *a step or two to one side, with a certain amount of consternation*] Tell me something. Is she crazy?

FATHER. Crazy? Of course not. It's much worse than that.

STEPDAUGHTER [*running over at once to the* DIRECTOR]. Worse! Worse! Not crazy but worse! Just listen: I'll play it for you right now, this drama, and at a certain point you'll see me—when this dear little thing—[*She takes the* LITTLE GIRL *who is beside the* MOTHER *by the hand and leads her to the* DIRECTOR.]—isn't she darling? [*Takes her in her arms and kisses her.*] Sweetie! Sweetie! [*Puts her down again and adds with almost involuntary emotion.*] Well, when God suddenly takes this little sweetheart away from her poor mother, and that idiot there—[*thrusting the* BOY *forward, rudely seizing him by a sleeve*] does the stupidest of things, like the nitwit that he is, [*with a shove she drives him back toward the* MOTHER] then you will see me take to my heels. Yes, ladies and gentlemen, take to my heels! I can hardly wait for that moment. For after what happened between him and me—[*She points to the* FATHER *with a horrible wink.*] something very intimate, you understand—I can't stay in such company any longer, witnessing the anguish of our mother on account of that fool there—[*She points to the* SON.] Just look at him, look at him!—how indifferent, how frozen, because he is the legitimate son, that's what he is, full of contempt for me, for him [*the* BOY], and for that little creature [*the* LITTLE GIRL], because we three are bastards, d'you see? bastards. [*Goes to the* MOTHER *and embraces her.*] And this poor mother, the common mother of us all, he—well, he doesn't want to acknowledge her as *his* mother too, and he looks down on her, that's what he does, looks on her as only the mother of us three bastards, the wretch! [*She says this rapidly in a state of extreme excitement. Her voice swells to the word: "bastards!" and descends again to the final "wretch," almost spitting it out.*]

MOTHER [*to the* DIRECTOR, *with infinite anguish*]. In the name of these two small children, sir, I implore you . . . [*She grows faint and sways.*] Oh, heavens . . .

FATHER [*rushing over to support her with almost all the Actors who are astonished and scared*]. Please! Please, a chair, a chair for this poor widow!

ACTORS [*rushing over*].—Is it true then?—She's *really* fainting?

DIRECTOR. A chair!

[*One of the Actors proffers a chair. The others stand around, ready to help. The* MOTHER, *seated, tries to stop the* FATHER *from lifting the veil that hides her face.*]

FATHER [*to the* DIRECTOR]. Look at her, look at her . . .

MOTHER. Heavens, no, stop it!

FATHER. Let them see you. [*He lifts her veil.*]

MOTHER [*rising and covering her face with her hands, desperate*]. Oh, sir, please stop this man from carrying out his plan. It's horrible for me!

DIRECTOR [*surprised, stunned*]. I don't know where we're at! What's this all about? [*To the* FATHER] Is this your wife?

FATHER [*at once*]. Yes, sir, my wife.

DIRECTOR. Then how is she a widow, if you're alive?

[*The Actors relieve their astonishment in a loud burst of laughter.*]

FATHER [*wounded, with bitter resentment*]. Don't laugh! Don't laugh like that! Please! Just that is her drama, sir. She had another man. Another man who should be here!

MOTHER [*with a shout*]. No! No!

STEPDAUGHTER. He had the good luck to die. Two months ago, as I told you. We're still in mourning, as you see.

FATHER. But he's absent, you see, not just because he's dead. He's absent— take a look at her, sir, and you will understand at once!—Her drama wasn't in the love of two men for whom she was incapable of feeling anything—except maybe a little gratitude [not to me, but to him]— She is not a woman, she is a mother!—And her drama—a powerful one, very powerful—is in fact all in those four children which she bore to her two men.

MOTHER. *My* men? Have you the gall to say I wanted two men? It was him, sir. He forced the other man on me. Compelled—yes, compelled— me to go off with him!

STEPDAUGHTER [*cutting in, roused*]. It's not true!

MOTHER [*astounded*]. How d'you mean, not true?

STEPDAUGHTER. It's not true! It's not true!

MOTHER. And what can you know about it?

STEPDAUGHTER. It's not true. [*To the* DIRECTOR] Don't believe it. Know why she says it? For his sake. [*Pointing to the* SON] His indifference tortures her, destroys her. She wants him to believe that, if she abandoned him when he was two, it was because he [*the* FATHER] compelled her to.

MOTHER [*with violence*]. He did compel me, he did compel me, as God is my witness! [*To the* DIRECTOR] Ask him if that isn't true. [*Her husband*] Make him tell him. [*The* SON] She couldn't know anything about it.

STEPDAUGHTER. With my father, while he lived, I know you were always happy and content. Deny it if you can.

MOTHER. I don't deny it, I don't . . .

STEPDAUGHTER. He loved you, he cared for you! [*To the* BOY, *with rage*] Isn't that so? Say it! Why don't you speak, you dope?

MOTHER. Leave the poor boy alone. Why d'you want to make me out ungrateful, daughter? I have no wish to offend your father! I told him [*the* FATHER] I didn't abandon my son and my home for my own pleasure. It wasn't my fault.

FATHER. That's true, sir. It was mine.

[*Pause*]

LEADING MAN [*to his companions*]. What a show!

LEADING LADY. And *they* put it on—for us.

JUVENILE LEAD. Quite a change!

DIRECTOR [*who is now beginning to get very interested*]. Let's listen to this, let's listen! [*And saying this, he goes down one of the stairways into the auditorium, and stands in front of the stage, as if to receive a spectator's impression of the show.*]

SON [*without moving from his position, cold, quiet, ironic*]. Oh yes, you can now listen to the philosophy lecture. He will tell you about the Demon of Experiment.

FATHER. You are a cynical idiot, as I've told you a hundred times. [*To the* DIRECTOR, *now in the auditorium*] He mocks me, sir, on account of that phrase I found to excuse myself with.

SON [*contemptuously*]. Phrases!

FATHER. Phrases! Phrases! As if they were not a comfort to everyone: in the face of some unexplained fact, in the face of an evil that eats into us, to find a word that says nothing but at least quiets us down!

STEPDAUGHTER. Quiets our guilt feelings too. That above all.

FATHER. Our guilt feelings? Not so. I have never quieted my guilt feelings with words alone.

STEPDAUGHTER. It took a little money as well, didn't it, it took a little dough! The hundred lire he was going to pay me, ladies and gentlemen!

[*Movement of horror among the Actors.*]

SON [*with contempt toward the* STEPDAUGHTER]. That's filthy.

STEPDAUGHTER. Filthy? The dough was there. In a small pale blue envelope on the mahogany table in the room behind the shop. Madam Pace's [*she pronounces it "Pah-chay"*] shop. One of those Madams who lure us poor girls from good families into their *ateliers* under the pretext of selling *Robes et Manteaux*.

SON. And with those hundred lire he was going to pay she has bought the right to tyrannize over us all. Only it so happens—I'd have you know—that he never actually incurred the debt.

STEPDAUGHTER. Oh, oh, but we were really going to it, I assure you! [*She bursts out laughing.*]

MOTHER [*rising in protest*]. Shame, daughter! Shame!

STEPDAUGHTER [*quickly*]. Shame? It's my revenge! I am frantic, sir, frantic to live it, live that scene! The room . . . here's the shopwindow with the coats in it; there's the bed-sofa; the mirror; a screen; and in front of the window the little mahogany table with the hundred lire in the pale blue envelope. I can see it. I could take it. But you men should turn away now: I'm almost naked. I don't blush any more. It's he that blushes now. [*Points to the* FATHER.] But I assure you he was very pale, very pale, at that moment. [*To the* DIRECTOR] You must believe me, sir.

DIRECTOR. You lost me some time ago.

FATHER. Of course! Getting it thrown at you like that! Restore a little order, sir, and let *me* speak. And never mind this ferocious girl. She's trying to heap opprobrium on me by withholding the relevant explanations!

STEPDAUGHTER. This is no place for longwinded narratives!

FATHER. I said—explanations.

STEPDAUGHTER. Oh, certainly. Those that suit your turn.

[*At this point, the* DIRECTOR *returns to the stage to restore order.*]

FATHER. But that's the whole root of the evil. Words. Each of us has, inside him, a world of things—to everyone, his world of things. And how can we understand each other, sir, if, in the words I speak, I put the sense and value of things as they are inside me, whereas the man who hears them inevitably receives them in the sense and with the value they have for him, the sense and value of the world inside him? We think we understand each other but we never do. Consider: the compassion, all the compassion I feel for this woman [*the* MOTHER] has been received by her as the most ferocious of cruelties!

MOTHER. You ran me out of the house.

FATHER. Hear that? Ran her out. It *seemed to her* that I ran her out.

MOTHER. You can talk; I can't . . . But, look, sir, after he married me . . . and who knows why he did? I was poor, of humble birth . . .

FATHER. And that's why. I married you for your . . . humility. I loved you for it, believing . . . [*He breaks off, seeing her gestured denials; seeing the impossibility of making himself understood by her, he opens his arms wide in a gesture of despair, and turns to the* DIRECTOR] See that? She says No. It's scarifying, isn't it, sir, scarifying, this deafness of hers, this mental deafness! She has a heart, oh yes, where her children are concerned! But she's deaf, deaf in the brain, deaf, sir, to the point of desperation!

STEPDAUGHTER [*to the* DIRECTOR]. All right, but now make him tell you what his intelligence has ever done for us.

FATHER. If we could only foresee all the evil that can result from the good we believe we're doing!

[*At this point, the* LEADING LADY, *who has been on hot coals seeing the* LEAD-ING MAN *flirt with the* STEPDAUGHTER, *steps forward and asks of the* DIREC-TOR:]

LEADING LADY. Excuse me, is the rehearsal continuing?

DIRECTOR. Yes, of course! But let me listen a moment.

JUVENILE LEAD. This is something quite new.

INGENUE. Very interesting!

LEADING LADY. If that sort of thing interests you. [*And she darts a look at the* LEADING MAN.]

DIRECTOR [*to the* FATHER]. But you must give us *clear* explanations. [*He goes and sits down.*]

FATHER. Right. Yes. Listen. There was a man working for me. A poor man. As my secretary. Very devoted to me. Understood *her* [*the* MOTHER] very well. There was mutual understanding between them. Nothing wrong in it. They thought no harm at all. Nothing off-color about it. No, no, he knew his place, as she did. They didn't do anything wrong. Didn't even think it.

STEPDAUGHTER. So he thought it *for* them. And did it.

FATHER. It's not true! I wanted to do them some good. And myself too, oh yes, I admit. I'd got to this point, sir: I couldn't say a word to either of them but they would exchange a significant look. The one would consult the eyes of the other, asking how what I had said should be taken, if they didn't want to put me in a rage. That sufficed, you will understand, to keep me continually in a rage, in a state of unbearable exasperation.

DIRECTOR. Excuse me, why didn't you fire him, this secretary?

FATHER. Good question! That's what I did do, sir. But then I had to see that poor woman remain in my house, a lost soul. Like an animal without a master that one takes pity on and carries home.

MOTHER. No, no, it's—

FATHER [*at once, turning to her to get it in first*]. Your son? Right?

MOTHER. He'd already snatched my son from me.

FATHER. But not from cruelty. Just so he'd grow up strong and healthy. In touch with the soil.

STEPDAUGHTER [*pointing at the latter, ironic*]. And just look at him!

FATHER [*at once*]. Uh? Is it also my fault if he then grew up this way? I sent him to a wet nurse, sir, in the country, a peasant woman. I didn't find her [*the* MOTHER] strong enough, despite her humble origin. I'd married her for similar reasons, as I said. All nonsense maybe, but there we are. I always had these confounded aspirations toward a certain solidity, toward what is morally sound. [*Here the* STEPDAUGHTER *bursts out laughing.*] Make her stop that! It's unbearable!

DIRECTOR. Stop it. I can't hear, for Heaven's sake!

[*Suddenly, again, as the* DIRECTOR *rebukes her, she is withdrawn and remote, her laughter cut off in the middle. The* DIRECTOR *goes down again from the stage to get an impression of the scene.*]

FATHER. I couldn't bear to be with that woman any more. [*Points to the* MOTHER] Not so much, believe me, because she irritated me, and even made me feel physically ill, as because of the pain—a veritable anguish—that I felt on her account.

MOTHER. And he sent me away!

FATHER. Well provided for. And to that man. Yes, sir. So she could be free of me.

MOTHER. And so *he* could be free.

FATHER. That, too. I admit it. And much evil resulted. But I intended good. And more for her than for me, I swear it! [*He folds his arms across his chest. Then, suddenly, turning to the* MOTHER] I never lost sight of you, never lost sight of you till, from one day to the next, unbeknown to me, he carried you off to another town. He noticed I was interested in her, you see, but that was silly, because my interest was absolutely pure, absolutely without ulterior motive. The interest I took in her new family, as it grew up, had an unbelievable tenderness to it. Even she should bear witness to that! [*He points to the* STEPDAUGHTER.]

STEPDAUGHTER. Oh, very much so! I was a little sweetie. Pigtails over my shoulders. Panties coming down a little bit below my skirt. A little sweetie. He would see me coming out of school, at the gate. He would come and see me as I grew up . . .

FATHER. This is outrageous. You're betraying me!

STEPDAUGHTER. I'm not! What do you mean?

FATHER. Outrageous. Outrageous. [*Immediately, still excited, he continues in a tone of explanation, to the* DIRECTOR.] My house, sir, when she had left it, at once seemed empty. [*Points to the* MOTHER] She was an incubus. But she filled my house for me. Left alone, I wandered through these rooms like a fly without a head. This fellow here [*the* SON] was raised away from home. Somehow, when he got back, he didn't seem mine any more. Without a mother between me and him, he grew up on his own, apart, without any relationship to me, emotional or intellectual. And then—strange, sir, but true—first I grew curious, then I was gradually attracted toward *her* family, which I had brought into being. The thought of *this* family began to fill the void around me. I had to—really had to—believe she was at peace, absorbed in the simplest cares of life, lucky to be away and far removed from the complicated torments of my spirit. And to have proof of this, I would go and see that little girl at the school gate.

STEPDAUGHTER. Correct! He followed me home, smiled at me and, when I was home, waved to me, like this! I would open my eyes wide and look at him suspiciously. I didn't know who it was. I told mother. And she guessed right away it was him. [*The* MOTHER *nods.*] At first she didn't want to send me back to school for several days. When I did go, I saw him again at the gate—the clown!—with a brown paper bag in his hand. He came up to me, caressed me, and took from the bag a lovely big Florentine straw hat with a ring of little May roses round it—for me!

DIRECTOR. You're making too long a story of this.

SON [*contemptuously*]. Story is right! Fiction! Literature!

FATHER. Literature? This is life, sir. Passion!

DIRECTOR. Maybe! But not actable!

FATHER. I agree. This is all preliminary. I wouldn't *want* you to act it. As you see, in fact, she [*the* STEPDAUGHTER] is no longer that little girl with pigtails—

STEPDAUGHTER. —and the panties showing below her skirt!

FATHER. The drama comes now, sir. Novel, complex—

STEPDAUGHTER [*gloomy, fierce, steps forward*].—What my father's death meant for us was—

FATHER [*Not giving her time to continue*].—poverty, sir. They returned, unbeknownst to me. She's so thickheaded. [*Pointing to the* MOTHER] It's true she can hardly write herself, but she could have had her daughter write, or her son, telling me they were in need!

MOTHER. But, sir, how could I have guessed he felt the way he did?

FATHER. Which is just where you always went wrong. You could never guess how I felt about anything!

MOTHER. After so many years of separation, with all that had happened . . .

FATHER. And is it my fault if that fellow carried you off as he did? [*Turning to the* DIRECTOR] From one day to the next, as I say. He'd found some job someplace. I couldn't even trace them. Necessarily, then, my interest dwindled, with the years. The drama breaks out, sir, unforeseen and violent, at their return. When I, alas, was impelled by the misery of my still living flesh . . . Oh, and what misery that is for a man who is alone, who has not wanted to form debasing relationships, not yet old enough to do without a woman, and no longer young enough to go and look for one without shame! Misery? It's horror, horror, because no woman can give him love any more.—Knowing this, one should go without! Well, sir, on the outside, when other people are watching, each man is clothed in dignity: but, on the inside, he knows what unconfessable things are going on within him. One gives way, gives way to temptation, to rise again, right afterward, of course, in a great hurry to put our dignity together again, complete, solid, a stone on a grave that hides and buries from our eyes every sign of our shame and even the very memory of it! It's like that with everybody. Only the courage to say it is lacking—to say certain things.

STEPDAUGHTER. The courage to do them, though—everybody's got that.

FATHER. Everybody. But in secret. That's why it takes more courage to say them. A man only has to say them and it's all over: he's labeled a cynic. But, sir, he isn't! He's just like everybody else. Better! He's better because he's not afraid to reveal, by the light of intelligence, the red stain of shame, there, in the human beast, which closes its eyes to it. Woman—yes, woman—what is she like, actually? She looks at us, inviting, tantalizing. You take hold of her. She's no sooner in your arms than she shuts her eyes. It is the sign of her submission. The sign with which she tells the man: Blind yourself for I am blind.

STEPDAUGHTER. How about when she no longer keeps them shut? When she no longer feels the need to hide the red stain of shame from herself by closing her eyes, and instead, her eyes dry now and impassive, sees the shame of the man, who has blinded himself even without love? They make me vomit, all those intellectual elaborations, this philosophy that begins by revealing the beast and then goes on to excuse it and save its soul . . . I can't bear to hear about it! Because when a man feels obliged to *reduce* life this way, reduce it all to "the beast," throwing overboard every vestige of the truly human, every aspiration after chastity, all feelings of purity, of the ideal, of duties, of modesty, of shame, then nothing is more contemptible, more nauseating than his wretched guilt feelings! Crocodile tears!

DIRECTOR. Let's get to the facts, to the facts! This is just discussion.

FATHER. Very well. But a fact is like a sack. When it's empty, it won't stand up. To make it stand up you must first pour into it the reasons and feelings by which it exists. I couldn't know that—when that man died and they returned here in poverty—she went out to work as a dressmaker to support the children, nor that the person she went to work for was that . . . that Madam Pace!

STEPDAUGHTER. A highclass dressmaker, if you'd all like to know! To all appearances, she serves fine ladies, but then she arranges things so that the fine ladies serve *her* . . . without prejudice to ladies not so fine!

MOTHER. Believe me, sir, I never had the slightest suspicion that that old witch hired me because she had her eye on my daughter . . .

STEPDAUGHTER. Poor mama! Do you know, sir, what the woman did when I brought her my mother's work? She would point out to me the material she'd ruined by giving it to my mother to sew. And she deducted for that, she deducted. And so, you understand, *I* paid, while that poor creature thought she was making sacrifices for me and those two by sewing, even at night, Madam Pace's material!

[*Indignant movements and exclamations from the Actors.*]

DIRECTOR[*without pause*]. And there, one day, you met—

STEPDAUGHTER [*pointing to the* FATHER].—him, him, yes sir! An old client! Now there's a scene for you to put on! Superb!

FATHER. Interrupted by her—the mother—

STEPDAUGHTER [*without pause, treacherously*].—almost in time!—

FATHER [*shouting*]. No, no, *in* time! Because, luckily, I recognized the girl in time. And I took them all back, sir, into my home. Now try to visualize my situation and hers, the one confronting the other—she as you see her now, myself unable to look her in the face any more.

STEPDAUGHTER. It's too absurd! But—afterward—was it possible for me to be a modest little miss, virtuous and well-bred, in accordance with those confounded aspirations toward a certain solidity, toward what is morally sound?

FATHER. And therein lies the drama, sir, as far as I'm concerned: in my awareness that each of us thinks of himself as *one* but that, well, it's not true, each of us is many, oh so many, sir, according to the possibilities of being that are in us. We are one thing for this person, another for that! Already *two* utterly different things! And with it all, the illusion of being always one thing for all men, and always this one thing in every single action. It's not true! Not true! We realize as much when, by some unfortunate chance, in one or another of our acts, we find ourselves suspended, hooked. We see, I mean, that we are not wholly in that act, and that therefore it would be abominably unjust to judge us by that act alone, to hold us suspended, hooked, in the pillory, our whole life long, as if our life were summed up in that act!

Now do you understand this girl's treachery? She surprised me in a place, in an act, in which she should never have had to know me—I couldn't be that way for her. And she wants to give me a reality such as I could never had expected I would have to assume for her, the reality of a fleeting moment, a shameful one, in my life! This, sir, this is what I feel most strongly. And you will see that the drama will derive tremendous value from this. But now add the situation of the others! His . . . [*He points to the* SON.]

SON [*shrugging contemptuously*]. Leave me out of this! It's none of my business.

FATHER. What? None of your business?

SON. None. And I *want* to be left out. I wasn't made to be one of you, and you know it.

STEPDAUGHTER. We're common, aren't we?—And he's so refined.—But from time to time I give him a hard, contemptuous look, and he looks down at the ground. You may have noticed that, sir. He looks down at the ground. For he knows the wrong he's done me.

SON [*hardly looking at her*]. Me?

STEPDAUGHTER. You! You! I'm on the streets because of you! [*A movement of horror from the Actors*] Did you or did you not, by your attitude, deny us—I won't say the intimacy of home but even the hospitality which puts guests at their ease? We were the intruders, coming to invade the kingdom of your legitimacy! I'd like to have you see, sir, certain little scenes between just him and me! He says I tyrannized over them all. But it was entirely because of his attitude that I started to exploit the situation he calls filthy, a situation which had brought me into his home with my mother, who is also *his* mother, *as its mistress!*

SON [*coming slowly forward*]. They can't lose, sir, three against one, an easy game. But figure to yourself a son, sitting quietly at home, who one fine day sees a young woman arrive, an impudent type with her nose in the air, asking for his father, with whom she has heaven knows what business; and then he sees her return, in the same style, accompanied by that little girl over there; and finally he sees her treat his father—who can say why?—in a very ambiguous and cool manner, demanding money, in a tone that takes for granted that he *has* to give it, has to, is obligated—

FATHER. —but I *am* obligated: it's for your mother!

SON. How would I know? When, sir, [*to the* DIRECTOR] have I ever seen her? When have I ever heard her spoken of. One day I see her arrive

with her, [*the* STEPDAUGHTER] with that boy, with that little girl.
They say to me: "It's your mother too, know that?" I manage to figure
out from her carryings-on [*pointing at the* STEPDAUGHTER] why they
arrived in our home from one day to the next . . . What I'm feeling
and experiencing I can't put into words, and wouldn't want to. I
wouldn't want to confess it, even to myself. It cannot therefore result
in any action on my part. You can see that. Believe me, sir, I'm a character that, dramatically speaking, remains unrealized. I'm out of place
in their company. So please leave me out of it all!

FATHER. What? But it's just because you're so—

SON [*in violent exasperation*].—I'm so what? How would *you* know? When
did you ever care about me?

FATHER. *Touché! Touché!* But isn't even that a dramatic situation? This
withdrawnness of yours, so cruel to me, and to your mother who, on
her return home is seeing you almost for the first time, a grown man
she doesn't recognize, though she knows you're her son . . . [*Pointing
out the* MOTHER *to the* DIRECTOR] Just look at her, she's crying.

STEPDAUGHTER [*angrily, stamping her foot*]. Like the fool she is!

FATHER [*pointing her out to the* DIRECTOR]. And she can't abide him, you
know. [*Again referring to the* SON]—He says it's none of his business.
The truth is he's almost the pivot of the action. Look at that little boy,
clinging to his mother all the time, scared, humiliated . . . It's all because of *him*. [*the* SON] Perhaps the most painful situation of all is that
little boy's: he feels alien, more than all the others, and the poor little
thing is so mortified, so anguished at being taken into our home—
out of charity, as it were . . . [*Confidentially*] He's just like his father:
humble, doesn't say anything . . .

DIRECTOR. He won't fit anyway. You've no idea what a nuisance children
are on stage.

FATHER. But he wouldn't be a nuisance for long. Nor would the little girl,
no, she's the first to go . . . [4]

DIRECTOR. Very good, yes! The whole thing interests me very much indeed. I have a hunch, a definite hunch, that there's material here for a
fine play!

STEPDAUGHTER [*trying to inject herself*]. With a character like me in it!

FATHER [*pushing her to one side in his anxiety to know what the* DIRECTOR
will decide]. You be quiet!

DIRECTOR [*going right on, ignoring the interruption*]. Yes, it's new stuff . . .

FATHER. Very new!

DIRECTOR. You had some gall, though, to come and throw it at me this way . . .

FATHER. Well, you see, sir, born as we are to the stage . . .

DIRECTOR. You're amateurs, are you?

FATHER. No. I say: "born to the stage" because . . .

DIRECTOR. Oh, come on, you must have done some acting!

FATHER. No, no, sir, only as every man acts the part assigned to him—by himself or others—in this life. In me you see passion itself, which—in almost all people, as it rises—invariably becomes a bit theatrical . . .

DIRECTOR. Well, never mind! Never mind about that!—You see, my dear sir, without the author . . . I could direct you to an author . . .

FATHER. No, no, look: you be the author!

DIRECTOR. Me? What are you talking about?

FATHER. Yes, you. You. Why not?

DIRECTOR. Because I've never been an author, that's why not!

FATHER. Couldn't you be one now, hm? There's nothing to it. Everyone's doing it. And your job is made all the easier by the fact that you have us—here—alive—right in front of your nose!

DIRECTOR. It wouldn't be enough.

FATHER. Not enough? Seeing us live our own drama . . .

DIRECTOR. I know, but you always need someone to write it!

FATHER. No. Just someone to take it down, maybe, since you have us here—in action—scene by scene. It'll be enough if we piece together a rough sketch for you, then you can rehearse it.

DIRECTOR [tempted, goes up on stage again]. Well, I'm almost, almost tempted . . . Just for kicks . . . We could actually rehearse . . .

FATHER. Of course you could! What scenes you'll see emerge! I can list them for you right away.

DIRECTOR. I'm tempted . . . I'm tempted . . . Let's give it a try . . . Come to my office. [Turns to the Actors] Take a break, will you? But don't go away. We'll be back in fifteen or twenty minutes. [To the FATHER] Let's see what we can do . . . Maybe we can get something very extraordinary out of all this . . .

FATHER. We certainly can. Wouldn't it be better to take them along? [He points to the Characters.]

DIRECTOR. Yes, let them all come. [Starts going off, then comes back to address the Actors] Now don't forget. Everyone on time. Fifteen minutes.

[DIRECTOR and Six Characters cross the stage and disappear. The Actors stay there and look at one another in amazement.]

LEADING MAN. Is he serious? What's he going to do?

JUVENILE. This is outright insanity.

A THIRD ACTOR. We have to improvise a drama right off the bat?

JUVENILE LEAD. That's right. Like Commedia dell'Arte.

LEADING LADY. Well, if he thinks *I'm* going to lend myself to that sort of
    thing . . .

INGENUE. Count me out.

A FOURTH ACTOR [*alluding to the Characters*]. I'd like to know who those
    people are.

THE THIRD ACTOR. Who would they be? Madmen or crooks!

JUVENILE LEAD. And he's going to pay attention to them?

INGENUE. Carried away by vanity! Wants to be an author now . . .

LEADING MAN. It's out of this world. If this is what the theater is coming
    to, my friends . . .

A FIFTH ACTOR. I think it's rather fun.

THE THIRD ACTOR. Well! We shall see. We shall see. [*And chatting thus
    among themselves, the Actors leave the stage, some using the little door at
    the back, others returning to their dressing rooms.*]

*The curtain remains raised. The performance is interrupted by a twenty-minute
intermission.*

Bells ring. The performance is resumed.[5]

   *From dressing rooms, from the door, and also from the house, the Actors,
the* STAGE MANAGER, *the* TECHNICIAN, *the* PROMPTER, *the* PROPERTY MAN
return to the stage; at the same time the DIRECTOR *and the Six Characters
emerge from the office.*

   As soon as the house lights are out, the stage lighting is as before.

DIRECTOR. Let's go, everybody! Is everyone here? Quiet! We're begin-
    ning. [*Calls the* TECHNICIAN *by name.*]

TECHNICIAN. Here!

DIRECTOR. Set the stage for the parlor scene. Two wings and a backdrop
    with a door in it will do, quickly please!

[*The* TECHNICIAN *at once runs to do the job, and does it while the* DIREC-
TOR *works things out with the* STAGE MANAGER, *the* PROPERTY MAN, *the*
PROMPTER, *and the Actors. This indication of a set consists of two wings, a drop
with a door in it, all in pink and gold stripes.*]

DIRECTOR [*to the* PROPERTY MAN]. See if we have some sort of bed-sofa in
    the prop room.

PROPERTY MAN. Yes, sir, there's the green one.

STEPDAUGHTER. No, no, not green! It was yellow, flowered, plush, and very big. Extremely comfortable.

PROPERTY MAN. Well, we have nothing like that.

DIRECTOR. But it doesn't matter. Bring the one you have.

STEPDAUGHTER. Doesn't matter? Madam Pace's famous chaise longue!

DIRECTOR. This is just for rehearsal. Please don't meddle! [*To the* STAGE MANAGER] See if we have a display case—long and rather narrow.

STEPDAUGHTER. The table, the little mahogany table for the pale blue envelope!

STAGE MANAGER [*to the* DIRECTOR]. There's the small one. Gilded.

DIRECTOR. All right. Get that one.

FATHER. A large mirror.

STEPDAUGHTER. And the screen. A screen, please, or what'll I do?

STAGE MANAGER. Yes, ma'am, we have lots of screens, don't worry.

DIRECTOR [*to the* STEPDAUGHTER]. A few coat hangers?

STEPDAUGHTER. A great many, yes.

DIRECTOR [*to the* STAGE MANAGER]. See how many we've got, and have them brought on.

STAGE MANAGER. Right, sir, I'll see to it.

[*The* STAGE MANAGER *also hurries to do his job and while the* DIRECTOR *goes on talking with the* PROMPTER *and then with the Characters and the Actors, has the furniture carried on by stagehands and arranges it as he thinks fit.*]

DIRECTOR [*to the* PROMPTER]. Meanwhile you can get into position. Look: this is the outline of the scenes, act by act. [*He gives him several sheets of paper.*] You'll have to be a bit of a virtuoso today.

PROMPTER. Shorthand?

DIRECTOR [*Pleasantly surprised*]. Oh, good! You know shorthand?

PROMPTER. I may not know prompting, but shorthand . . . [*Turning to a stagehand*] Get me some paper from my room—quite a lot—all you can find!

[*The stagehand runs off and returns a little later with a wad of paper which he gives to the* PROMPTER.]

DIRECTOR [*Going right on, to the* PROMPTER]. Follow the scenes line by line as we play them, and try to pin down the speeches, at least the most important ones. [*Then, turning to the Actors*] Clear the stage please, everyone! Yes, come over to this side and pay close attention. [*He indicates the left.*]

LEADING LADY. Excuse me but—

DIRECTOR [*forestalling*]. There'll be no improvising, don't fret.

LEADING MAN. Then what are we to do?

DIRECTOR. Nothing. For now, just stop, look, and listen. Afterward you'll be given written parts. Right now we'll rehearse. As best we can. With them doing the rehearsing for us. [*He points to the Characters.*]

FATHER [*amid all the confusion on stage, as if he'd fallen from the clouds*]. We're rehearsing? How d'you mean?

DIRECTOR. Yes, for them. You rehearse for them. [*Indicates the Actors.*]

FATHER. But if we are the characters . . .

DIRECTOR. All right, you're characters, but, my dear sir, characters don't perform here, actors perform here. The characters are there, in the script [*He points to the* PROMPTER's *box.*]—when there *is* a script!

FATHER. Exactly! Since there isn't, and you gentlemen have the luck to have them right here, alive in front of you, those characters . . .

DIRECTOR. Oh, great! Want to do it all yourselves? Appear before the public, do the acting yourselves?

FATHER. Of course. Just as we are.

DIRECTOR [*Ironically*]. I'll bet you'd put on a splendid show!

LEADING MAN. Then what's the use of staying?

DIRECTOR [*without irony, to the Characters*]. Don't run away with the idea that you can act! That's laughable . . . [*And in fact the Actors laugh.*] Hear that? They're laughing. [*Coming back to the point*] I was forgetting. I must cast the show. It's quite easy. It casts itself. [*To the* SECOND ACTRESS] You, ma'am, will play the Mother. [*To the* FATHER] You'll have to find her a name.

FATHER. Amalia, sir.

DIRECTOR. But that's this lady's real name. We wouldn't want to call her by her real name!

FATHER. Why not? If that is her name . . . But of course, if it's to be this lady . . . [*He indicates the* SECOND ACTRESS *with a vague gesture.*] To me *she* [*The* MOTHER] is Amalia. But suit yourself . . . [*He is getting more and more confused.*] I don't know what to tell you . . . I'm beginning to . . . oh, I don't know . . . to find my own words ringing false, they sound different somehow.

DIRECTOR. Don't bother about that, just don't bother about it. We can always find the right sound. As for the name, if you say Amalia, Amalia it shall be; or we'll find another. For now, we'll designate the characters thus: [*To the* JUVENILE LEAD] You're the Son. [*To the* LEADING LADY] You, ma'am, are of course the Stepdaughter.

STEPDAUGHTER [*excitedly*]. What, what? That one there is me? [*She bursts out laughing.*]

DIRECTOR [*mad*]. What is there to laugh at?

LEADING LADY [*aroused*]. No one has ever dared laugh at me! I insist on respect—or I quit!

STEPDAUGHTER. But, excuse me, I'm not laughing at you.

DIRECTOR [*to the* STEPDAUGHTER]. You should consider yourself honored to be played by . . .

LEADING LADY [*without pause, contemptuously*].—"That one there!"

STEPDAUGHTER. But I wasn't speaking of you, believe me. I was speaking of me. I don't see me in you, that's all. I don't know why . . . I guess you're just not like me!

FATHER. That's it, exactly, my dear sir! What is *expressed* in us . . .

DIRECTOR. Expression, expression! You think that's your business? Not at all!

FATHER. Well, but what *we* express . . .

DIRECTOR. But you don't. You don't express. You provide us with raw material. The actors give it body and face, voice and gesture. They've given expression to much loftier material, let me tell you. Yours is on such a small scale that, if it stands up on stage at all, the credit, believe me, should all go to my actors.

FATHER. I don't dare contradict you, sir, but it's terribly painful for us who are as you see us—with these bodies, these faces—

DIRECTOR [*cutting in, out of patience*].—that's where make-up comes in, my dear sir, for whatever concerns the face, the remedy is make-up!

FATHER. Yes. But the voice, gesture—

DIRECTOR. Oh, for Heaven's sake! You can't exist here! Here the actor acts you, and that's that!

FATHER. I understand, sir. But now perhaps I begin to guess also why our author who saw us, alive as we are, did not want to put us on stage. I don't want to offend your actors. God forbid! But I feel that seeing myself acted . . . I don't know by whom . . .

LEADING MAN [*rising with dignity and coming over, followed by the gay young Actresses who laugh*]. By me, if you've no objection.

FATHER [*humble, smooth*]. I'm very honored, sir. [*He bows.*] But however much art and willpower the gentleman puts into absorbing me into himself . . . [*He is bewildered now.*]

LEADING MAN. Finish. Finish.

[*The Actresses laugh.*]

FATHER. Well, the performance he will give, even forcing himself with make-up to resemble me, well, with that figure [*all the Actors laugh*] he can hardly play me as I am. I shall rather be—even apart from the face—what he interprets me to be, as he feels I am—if he feels I am anything—and not as I feel myself inside myself. And it seems to me that whoever is called upon to judge us should take this into account.

DIRECTOR. So now you're thinking of what the critics will say? And I was still listening! Let the critics say what they want. We will concentrate on putting on your play! [*He walks away a little, and looks around.*] Come on, come on. Is the set ready? [*To the Actors and the Characters*] Don't clutter up the stage, I want to be able to see! [*He goes down from the stage.*] Let's not lose any more time! [*To the* STEPDAUGHTER] Does the set seem pretty good to you?

STEPDAUGHTER. Oh! But I can't recognize it!

DIRECTOR. Oh my God, don't tell me we should reconstruct Madam Pace's back room for you! [*To the* FATHER] Didn't you say a parlor with flowered wallpaper?

FATHER. Yes, sir. White.

DIRECTOR. It's not white. Stripes. But it doesn't matter. As for furniture we're in pretty good shape. That little table—bring it forward a bit! [*Stagehands do this. To the* PROPERTY MAN] Meanwhile you get an envelope, possibly a light blue one, and give it to the gentleman. [*indicating the* FATHER]

PROPERTY MAN. A letter envelope?

DIRECTOR AND FATHER. Yes, a letter envelope.

PROPERTY MAN. I'll be right back. [*He exits.*]

DIRECTOR. Come on, come on. It's the young lady's scene first. [*The* LEADING LADY *comes forward.*] No, no, wait. I said the young lady. [*Indicating the* STEPDAUGHTER] You will just watch—

STEPDAUGHTER [*adding, without pause*].—watch me live it!

LEADING LADY [*resenting this*]. I'll know how to live it too, don't worry, once I put myself in the role!

DIRECTOR [*raising his hands to his head*]. Please! No more chatter! Now, scene one. The Young Lady with Madam Pace. Oh, and how about this Madam Pace? [*Bewildered, looking around him, he climbs back on stage.*]

FATHER. She isn't with us, sir.

DIRECTOR. Then what do we do?

FATHER. But she's alive. She's alive too.

DIRECTOR. Fine. But where?

FATHER. I'll tell you. [*Turning to the Actresses*] If you ladies will do me the
favor of giving me your hats for a moment.

THE ACTRESSES [*surprised a little, laughing a little, in chorus*].—What?—
Our hats?—What does he say?—Why?—Oh, dear!

DIRECTOR. What are you going to do with the ladies' hats?

[*The Actors laugh.*]

FATHER. Oh, nothing. Just put them on these coathooks for a minute. And
would some of you be so kind as to take your coats off too?

ACTORS [*as before*]. Their coats too?—And then?—He's nuts!

AN ACTRESS OR TWO [*as above*].—But why?—Just the coats?

FATHER. Just so they can be hung there for a moment. Do me this favor.
Will you?

ACTRESSES [*taking their hats off, and one or two of them their coats, too, continuing to laugh, and going to hang the hats here and there on the coathooks*].—Well, why not?—There!—This is getting to be really
funny!—Are we to put them on display?

FATHER. Exactly! That's just right, ma'am: on display!

DIRECTOR. May one inquire *why* you are doing this?

FATHER. Yes, sir. If we set the stage better, who knows but she may come
to us, drawn by the objects of her trade . . . [*Inviting them to look toward the entrance at the back*] Look! Look!

[*The entrance at the back opens, and* MADAM PACE *walks a few paces downstage, a hag of enormous fatness with a pompous wig of carrot-colored wool and
a fiery red rose on one side of it,* à l'espagnole, *heavily made up, dressed with
gauche elegance in garish red silk, a feathered fan in one hand and the other
hand raised to hold a lighted cigarette between two fingers. At the sight of this
apparition, the* DIRECTOR *and the Actors at once dash off the stage with a yell
of terror, rushing down the stairs and making as if to flee up the aisle. The*
STEPDAUGHTER, *on the other hand, runs to* MADAM PACE—*deferentially, as
to her boss.*]

STEPDAUGHTER [*running to her*]. Here she is, here she is!

FATHER [*beaming*]. It's she! What did I tell you? Here she is!

DIRECTOR [*overcoming his first astonishment, and incensed now*]. What tricks
are these?

[*The next four speeches are more or less simultaneous.*]

LEADING MAN. What goes on around here?

JUVENILE LEAD. Where on earth did she come from?

INGENUE. They must have been holding her in reserve.

LEADING LADY. Hocus pocus! Hocus pocus!

FATHER [*dominating these protests*]. Excuse me, though! Why, actually, would you want to destroy this prodigy in the name of vulgar truth, this miracle of a reality that is born of the stage itself—called into being by the stage, drawn here by the stage, and shaped by the stage— and which has more right to live on the stage than you have because it is much truer? Which of you actresses will later re-create Madam Pace? This lady *is* Madam Pace. You must admit that the actress who re-creates her will be less true than this lady—who is Madam Pace. Look: my daughter recognized her, and went right over to her. Stand and watch the scene!

[*Hesitantly, the* DIRECTOR *and the Actors climb back on stage. But the scene between the* STEPDAUGHTER *and* MADAM PACE *has begun during the protest of the Actors and the* FATHER*'s answer: sotto voce, very quietly, in short natu- rally—as would never be possible on a stage. When, called to order by the* FA- THER, *the Actors turn again to watch, they hear* MADAM PACE, *who has just placed her hand under the* STEPDAUGHTER*'s chin in order to raise her head, talk unintelligibly. After trying to hear for a moment, they just give up.*]

DIRECTOR. Well?

LEADING MAN. What's she saying?

LEADING LADY. One can't hear a thing.

JUVENILE LEAD. Louder!

STEPDAUGHTER [*leaving* MADAM PACE, *who smiles a priceless smile, and walking down toward the Actors*]. Louder, huh? How d'you mean: louder? These aren't things that can be said louder. *I* was able to say them loudly—to shame him [*indicating the* FATHER]—that was my revenge. For Madam, it's different, my friends: it would mean—jail.

DIRECTOR. Oh my God! It's like that, is it? But, my dear young lady, in the theater one must be heard. And even we couldn't hear you, right here on the stage. How about an audience out front? There's a scene to be done. And anyway you *can* speak loudly—it's just between yourselves, we won't be standing here listening like now. Pretend you're alone. In a room. The back room of the shop. No one can hear you. [*The* STEP- DAUGHTER *charmingly and with a mischievous smile tells him No with a repeated movement of the finger.*] Why not?

STEPDAUGHTER [*sotto voce, mysteriously*]. There's someone who'll hear if she [MADAM PACE] speaks loudly.

DIRECTOR [*in consternation*]. Is someone else going to pop up now?

[*The Actors make as if to quit the stage again.*]

FATHER. No, no, sir. She means me. I'm to be there—behind the door—waiting. And Madam knows. So if you'll excuse me. I must be ready for my entrance. [*He starts to move.*]

DIRECTOR [*stopping him*]. No, wait. We must respect the exigencies of the theater. Before you get ready—

STEPDAUGHTER [*interrupting him*]. Let's get on with it! I tell you I'm dying with desire to live it, to live that scene! If he's ready, I'm more than ready!

DIRECTOR [*shouting*]. But first we have to get that scene out of you and her! [*Indicating* MADAM PACE] Do you follow me?

STEPDAUGHTER. Oh dear, oh dear, she was telling me things you already know—that my mother's work had been badly done once again, the material is ruined, and I'm going to have to bear with her if I want her to go on helping us in our misery.

MADAM PACE [*coming forward with a great air of importance*]. Si, si, senor, porque yo no want profit. No advantage, no.

DIRECTOR [*almost scared*]. What, what? She talks like *that?!*

[*All the Actors loudly burst out laughing.*]

STEPDAUGHTER [*also laughing*]. Yes, sir, she talks like that—halfway between Spanish and English—very funny, isn't it?

MADAM PACE. Now that is not good manners, no, that you laugh at me! Yo hablo the English aś good I can, senor!

DIRECTOR. And it *is* good! Yes! Do talk that way, ma'am! It's a sure-fire effect! There couldn't be anything better to, um, soften the crudity of the situation! Do talk that way! It's fine!

STEPDAUGHTER. Fine! Of course! To have certain propositions put to you in a lingo like that. Sure fire, isn't it? Because, sir, it seems almost a joke. When I hear there's "an old senor" who wants to "have good time conmigo," I start to laugh—don't I, Madam Pace?

MADAM PACE. Old, viejo, no. Viejito—leetle beet old, si, darling? Better like that: if he no give you fun, he bring you prudencia.

MOTHER [*jumping up, to the stupefaction and consternation of all the Actors, who had been taking no notice of her, and who now respond to her shouts with a start and, smiling, try to restrain her, because she has grabbed* MADAM PACE's *wig and thrown it on the floor*]. Witch! Witch! Murderess! My daughter!

STEPDAUGHTER [*running over to restrain her* MOTHER]. No, no, mama, no, please!

FATHER [*running over too at the same time*]. Calm down, calm down! Sit here.

MOTHER. Then send that woman away!

STEPDAUGHTER [*to the* DIRECTOR, *who also has run over*]. It's not possible, not possible that my mother should be here!

FATHER [*also to the* DIRECTOR.] They can't be together. That's why, you see, the woman wasn't with us when we came. Their being together would spoil it, you understand.

DIRECTOR. It doesn't matter, doesn't matter at all. This is just a preliminary sketch. Everything helps. However confusing the elements, I'll piece them together somehow. [*Turning to the* MOTHER *and sitting her down again in her place*] Come along, come along, ma'am, calm down: sit down again.

STEPDAUGHTER [*who meanwhile has moved center stage again. Turning to* MADAM PACE]. All right, let's go!

MADAM PACE. Ah, no! No thank you! Yo aqui no do nada with your mother present.

STEPDAUGHTER. Oh, come on! Bring in that old senor who wants to have good time conmigo! [*Turning imperiously to all the others*] Yes, we've got to have it, this scene!—Come on, let's go! [*To* MADAM PACE] You may leave.

MADAM PACE. Ah si, I go, I go, go seguramente . . . [*She makes her exit furiously, putting her wig back on, and looking haughtily at the Actors who applaud mockingly.*]

STEPDAUGHTER [*to the* FATHER]. And you can make your entrance. No need to go out and come in again. Come here. Pretend, you're already in. Right. Now I'm here with bowed head, modest, huh? Let's go! Speak up! With a different voice, the voice of someone just in off the street: "Hello, miss."

DIRECTOR [*by this time out front again*]. Now look: are you directing this, or am I? [*To the* FATHER *who looks undecided and perplexed.*] Do it, yes. Go to the back. Don't leave the stage, though. And then come forward.

[*The* FATHER *does it, almost dismayed. Very pale; but already clothed in the reality of his created life, he smiles as he approaches from the back, as if still alien to the drama which will break upon him. The Actors now pay attention to the scene which is beginning.*]

DIRECTOR [*softly, in haste, to the* PROMPTER *in the box*]. And you, be ready now, ready to write!

The Scene

FATHER [*coming forward, with a different voice*]. Hello, miss.

STEPDAUGHTER [*with bowed head and contained disgust*]. Hello.

FATHER [*scrutinizing her under her hat which almost hides her face and noting that she is very young, exclaims, almost to himself, a little out of complaisance and a little out of fear of compromising himself in a risky adventure*]. Oh . . . —Well, I was thinking, it wouldn't be the first time, hm? The first time you came here.

STEPDAUGHTER [*as above*]. No, sir.

FATHER. You've been here other times? [*And when the* STEPDAUGHTER *nods*] More than one? [*He waits a moment for her to answer, then again scrutinizes her under her hat; smiles; then says*] Well then, hm . . . it shouldn't any longer be so . . . May I take this hat off for you?

STEPDAUGHTER [*without pause, to forestall him, not now containing her disgust*]. No, sir, *I* will take it off! [*And she does so in haste, convulsed.*]

[*The* MOTHER, *watching the scene with the* SON *and with the two others, smaller and more her own, who are close to her all the time, forming a group at the opposite side of the stage from the Actors, is on tenterhooks as she follows the words and actions of* FATHER *and* STEPDAUGHTER *with varied expression: grief, disdain, anxiety, horror, now hiding her face, now emitting a moan.*]

MOTHER. Oh God! My God!

FATHER [*is momentarily turned to stone by the moaning; then he reassumes the previous tone*]. Now give it to me: I'll hang it up for you. [*He takes the hat from her hands.*] But I could wish for a little hat worthier of such a dear, lovely little head! Would you like to help me choose one? From the many Madam has?—You wouldn't?

INGENUE [*interrupting*]. Oh now, come on, those are *our* hats!

DIRECTOR [*without pause, very angry*]. Silence, for Heaven's sake, don't try to be funny!—This is the stage. [*Turning back to the* STEPDAUGHTER] Would you begin again, please?

STEPDAUGHTER [*beginning again*]. No, thank you, sir.

FATHER. Oh, come on now, don't say no. Accept one from me. To please me . . . There are some lovely ones you know. And we would make Madam happy. Why else does she put them on display?

STEPDAUGHTER. No, no, sir, look: I wouldn't even be able to wear it.

FATHER. You mean because of what the family would think when they saw you come home with a new hat on? Think nothing of it. Know how to handle that? What to tell them at home?

STEPDAUGHTER [*breaking out, at the end of her rope*]. But that's not why, sir. I couldn't wear it because I'm . . . as you see me. You might surely have noticed! [*Points to her black attire.*]

FATHER. In mourning, yes. Excuse me. It's true: I do see it. I beg your pardon. I'm absolutely mortified, believe me.

STEPDAUGHTER [*forcing herself and plucking up courage to conquer her contempt and nausea*]. Enough! Enough! It's for me to thank you, it is not for you to be mortified or afflicted. Please pay no more attention to what I said. Even for me, you understand . . . [*She forces herself to smile and adds*] I need to forget I am dressed like this.

DIRECTOR [*interrupting, addressing himself to the* PROMPTER *in his box, and going up on stage again*]. Wait! Wait! Don't write. Leave that last sentence out, leave it out! [*Turning to the* FATHER *and* STEPDAUGHTER] It's going very well indeed. [*Then to the* FATHER *alone*] This is where you go into the part we prepared. [*To the Actors*] Enchanting, that little hat scene, don't you agree?

STEPDAUGHTER. Oh, but the best is just coming. Why aren't we continuing?

DIRECTOR. Patience one moment. [*Again addressing himself to the Actors*] Needs rather delicate handling, of course . . .

LEADING MAN. —With a certain *ease*—

LEADING LADY. Obviously. But there's nothing to it. [*To the* LEADING MAN] We can rehearse it at once, can't we?

LEADING MAN. As far as I'm . . . Very well, I'll go out and make my entrance. [*And he does go out by the back door, ready to re-enter.*]

DIRECTOR [*to the* LEADING LADY]. And so, look, your scene with that Madam Pace is over. I'll write it up later. You are standing . . . Hey, where are you going?

LEADING LADY. Wait. I'm putting my hat back on . . . [*She does so, taking the hat from the hook.*]

DIRECTOR. Oh yes, good.—Now, you're standing here with your head bowed.

STEPDAUGHTER [*amused*]. But she's not wearing black!

LEADING LADY. I *shall* wear black! And I'll carry it better than you!

DIRECTOR [*to the* STEPDAUGHTER]. Keep quiet, please! Just watch. You can learn something. [*Claps his hands*] Get going, get going! The entrance! [*And he goes back out front to get an impression of the stage.*]

[*The door at the back opens, and the* LEADING MAN *comes forward, with the relaxed, waggish manner of an elderly Don Juan. From the first speeches, the*

performance of the scene by the Actors is quite a different thing, without, how-
ever, having any element of parody in it—rather, it seems corrected, set to rights.
Naturally, the STEPDAUGHTER *and the* FATHER, *being quite unable to recog-*
nize themselves in this LEADING LADY *and* LEADING MAN *but hearing them*
speak their own words express in various ways, now with gestures, now with
smiles, now with open protests, their surprise, their wonderment, their suffering,
etc., as will be seen forthwith.

The PROMPTER'*s voice is clearly heard from the box.*[6]]

LEADING MAN. Hello, miss.

FATHER [*without pause, unable to contain himself*]. No, no!

[*The* STEPDAUGHTER, *seeing how the* LEADING MAN *makes his entrance, has
burst out laughing.*]

DIRECTOR [*coming from the proscenium, furious*]. Silence here! And stop
   that laughing at once! We can't go ahead till it stops.

STEPDAUGHTER [*coming from the proscenium*]. How can I help it? This lady
   [*the* LEADING LADY] just stands there. If she's supposed to be me, let
   me tell you that if anyone said hello to me in that manner and that
   tone of voice, I'd burst out laughing just as I actually did!

FATHER [*coming forward a little too*]. That's right . . . the manner, the tone
   . . .

DIRECTOR. Manner! Tone! Stand to one side now, and let me see the rehearsal.

LEADING MAN [*coming forward*]. If I'm to play an old man entering a house
   of ill—

DIRECTOR. Oh, pay no attention, please. Just begin again. It was going
   fine. [*Waiting for the Actor to resume*] Now then . . .

LEADING MAN. Hello, miss.

LEADING LADY. Hello.

LEADING MAN [*recreating the* FATHER'*s gesture of scrutinizing her under her
   hat, but then expressing very distinctly first the complaisance and then the
   fear*]. Oh . . . Well . . . I was thinking it wouldn't be the first time, I
   hope . . .

FATHER [*unable to help correcting him*]. Not "I hope." "Would it?" "Would
   it?"

DIRECTOR. He says: "would it?" A question.

LEADING MAN [*pointing to the* PROMPTER]. I heard: "I hope."

DIRECTOR. Same thing! "Would it." Or: "I hope." Continue, continue.—
   Now, maybe a bit less affected . . . Look, I'll do it for you. Watch me

. . . [*Returns to the stage, then repeats the bit since the entrance*]—Hello,
miss.

LEADING LADY. Hello.

DIRECTOR. Oh, well . . . I was thinking . . . [*Turning to the* LEADING MAN
to have him note how he has looked at the LEADING LADY *under her hat*]
Surprise . . . fear and complaisance. [*Then, going on, and turning to the*
LEADING LADY] It wouldn't be the first time, would it? The first time
you came here. [*Again turning to the* LEADING MAN *with an inquiring
look*] Clear? [*To the* LEADING LADY] Then you say: No, sir. [*Back to the*
LEADING MAN] How shall I put it? Plasticity! [*Goes back out front.*]

LEADING LADY. No, sir.

LEADING MAN. You came here other times? More than one?

DIRECTOR. No, no, wait. [*Indicating the* LEADING LADY] First let her nod.
"You came here other times?"

[*The* LEADING LADY *raises her head a little, closes her eyes painfully as if in
disgust, then nods twice at the word "Down" from the* DIRECTOR.]

STEPDAUGHTER [*involuntarily*]. Oh, my God! [*And she at once puts her
hand on her mouth to keep the laughter in.*]

DIRECTOR [*turning round*]. What is it?

STEPDAUGHTER [*without pause*]. Nothing, nothing.

DIRECTOR [*to the* LEADING MAN]. That's your cue. Go straight on.

LEADING MAN. More than one? Well then, hm . . . it shouldn't any longer
be so . . . May I take this little hat off for you?

[*The* LEADING MAN *says this last speech in such a tone and accompanies it with
such a gesture that the* STEPDAUGHTER, *her hands on her mouth, much as she
wants to hold herself in, cannot contain her laughter, which comes bursting out
through her fingers irresistibly and very loud.*]

LEADING LADY [*returning to her place, enraged*]. Now look, I'm not going
to be made a clown of by that person!

LEADING MAN. Nor am I. Let's stop.

DIRECTOR [*to the* STEPDAUGHTER, *roaring*]. Stop it! Stop it!

STEPDAUGHTER. Yes, yes. Forgive me, forgive me . . .

DIRECTOR. You have no manners! You're presumptuous! So there!

FATHER [*seeking to intervene*]. That's true, yes, that's true, sir, but forgive
. . .

DIRECTOR [*on stage again*]. Forgive nothing! It's disgusting!

FATHER. Yes, sir. But believe me, it has such a strange effect—

DIRECTOR. Strange? Strange? What's strange about it?

FATHER. I admire your actors, sir, I really admire them, this gentleman [LEADING MAN] and that lady [LEADING LADY] but assuredly . . . well, they're not us . . .

DIRECTOR. So what? How *could* they be you, if they're the actors?

FATHER. Exactly, the actors! And they play our parts well, both of them. But of course, to us, they seem something else—that tries to be the same but simply isn't!

DIRECTOR. How d'you mean: isn't? What is it then?

FATHER. Something that . . . becomes theirs. And stops being ours.

DIRECTOR. Necessarily! I explained that to you!

FATHER. Yes. I understand, I do under—

DIRECTOR. Then that will be enough! [*Turning to the Actors.*] We'll be rehearsing by ourselves as we usually do. Rehearsing with authors present has always been hell, in my experience. There's no satisfying them. [*Turning to the* FATHER *and the* STEPDAUGHTER] Come along then. Let's resume. And let's hope you find it possible not to laugh this time.

STEPDAUGHTER. Oh, no, I won't be laughing this time around. My big moment comes up now. Don't worry!

DIRECTOR. Very well, when she says: "Please pay no more attention to what I said . . . Even for me—you understand . . ." [*Turning to the* FATHER] You'll have to cut right in with: "I understand, oh yes, I understand . . ." and ask her right away—

STEPDAUGHTER [*interrupting*]. Oh? Ask me what?

DIRECTOR. —why she is in mourning.

STEPDAUGHTER. No, no, look: when I told him I needed to forget I was dressed like this, do you know what his answer was? "Oh, good! Then let's take that little dress right off, shall we?"

DIRECTOR. Great! Terrific! It'll knock 'em right out of their seats!

STEPDAUGHTER. But it's the truth.

DIRECTOR. Truth, is it? Well, well, well. This is the theater! Our motto is: truth up to a certain point!

STEPDAUGHTER. Then what would you propose?

DIRECTOR. You'll see. You'll see it. Just leave me alone.

STEPDAUGHTER. Certainly not. From my nausea—from all the reasons one more cruel than another why I am what I am, why I am "that one there"—you'd like to cook up some romantic, sentimental concoction, wouldn't you? He asks me why I'm in mourning, and I tell him, through my tears, that Papa died two months ago! No, my dear sir! He has to say what he did say: "Then let's take that little dress right off, shall we?" And I, with my two-months mourning in my heart, went back there—you see? behind that screen—and—my fingers quivering with shame, with loathing—I took off my dress, took off my corset . . .

DIRECTOR [*running his hands through his hair*]. Good God, what are you saying?

STEPDAUGHTER [*shouting frantically*]. The truth, sir, the truth!

DIRECTOR. Well, yes, of course, that must be the truth . . . and I quite understand your horror, young lady. Would you try to understand that all that is impossible *on the stage?*

STEPDAUGHTER. Impossible? Then, thanks very much, I'm leaving.

DIRECTOR. No, no, look . . .

STEPDAUGHTER. I'm leaving, I'm leaving! You went in that room, you two, didn't you, and figured out "what is possible on the stage"? Thanks very much. I see it all. He wants to skip to the point where he can act out his [*exaggerating*] spiritual travail! But I want to play *my* drama. Mine!

DIRECTOR [*annoyed, and shrugging haughtily*]. Oh well, *your* drama. This is not just your drama, if I may say so. How about the drama of the others? His drama [*the* FATHER], hers [*the* MOTHER]? We can't let one character hog the limelight, just taking the whole stage over, and overshadowing all the others! Everything must be placed within the frame of one harmonious picture! We must perform only what is performable! I know as well as you do that each of us has a whole life of his own inside him and would like to bring it all out. But the difficult thing is this: to bring out only as much as is needed—in relation to the others—and in this to *imply* all the rest, *suggest* what remains inside! Oh, it would be nice if every character could come down to the footlights and tell the audience just what is brewing inside him—in a fine monologue or, if you will, a lecture! [*Good-natured, conciliatory*] Miss, you will have to *contain yourself*. And it will be in your interest. It could make a bad impression—let me warn you—this tearing fury, this desperate disgust—since, if I may say so, you confessed having been with others at Madam Pace's—before him—more than once!

STEPDAUGHTER [*lowering her head, pausing to recollect, a deeper note in her voice*]. It's true. But to me the others are also *him*, all of them equally!

DIRECTOR [*not getting it*]. The others? How d'you mean?

STEPDAUGHTER. People "go wrong." And wrong follows on the heels of wrong. Who is responsible, if not whoever it was who first brought them down? Isn't that always the case? And for me that is him. Even before I was born. Look at him, and see if it isn't so.

DIRECTOR. Very good. And if he has so much to feel guilty about, can't you appreciate how it must weigh him down? So let's at least permit him to act it out.

STEPDAUGHTER. And how, may I ask, how could he act out all that "noble" guilt, all those so "moral" torments, if you propose to spare him the horror of one day finding in his arms—after having bade her take off the black clothes that marked her recent loss—a woman now, and already gone wrong—that little girl, sir, that little girl whom he used to go watch coming out of school?

[*She says these last words in a voice trembling with emotion. The* MOTHER, *hearing her say this, overcome with uncontrollable anguish, which comes out first in suffocated moans and subsequently bursts out in bitter weeping. The emotion takes hold of everyone. Long pause.*]

STEPDAUGHTER [*as soon as the* MOTHER *gives signs of calming down, somber, determined*]. We're just among ourselves now. Still unknown to the public. Tomorrow you will make of us the show you have in mind. You will put it together in your way. But would you like to really see— our drama? Have it explode—the real thing?

DIRECTOR. Of course. Nothing I'd like better. And I'll use as much of it as I possibly can!

STEPDAUGHTER. Very well. Have this Mother here go out.

MOTHER [*ceasing to weep, with a loud cry*]. No, no! Don't allow this, don't allow it!

DIRECTOR. I only want to take a look, ma'am.

MOTHER. I can't, I just can't!

DIRECTOR. But if it's already happened? Excuse me but I just don't get it.

MOTHER. No, no, it's happening now. It's always happening. My torment is not a pretense! I am alive and present—always, in every moment of my torment—it keeps renewing itself, it too is alive and always present. But those two little ones over there—have you heard them speak? They cannot speak, sir, not any more! They still keep clinging to me—to keep my torment alive and present. For themselves they don't exist, don't exist any longer. And she [*the* STEPDAUGHTER], she just fled, ran away from me, she's lost, lost . . . If I see her before me now, it's for the same reason: to renew the torment, keep it always alive and present forever—the torment I've suffered on her account too—forever!

FATHER [*solemn*]. The eternal moment, sir, as I told you. She [*the* STEP-
DAUGHTER] is here to catch me, fix me, hold me there in the pillory,
hanging there forever, hooked, in that single fleeting shameful moment of my life! She cannot give it up. And, actually, sir, *you* cannot
spare me.

DIRECTOR. But I didn't say I wouldn't use that. On the contrary, it will be
the nucleus of the whole first act. To the point where she [*the*
MOTHER] surprises you.

FATHER. Yes, exactly. Because that is the sentence passed upon me: all our
passion which has to culminate in her [*the* MOTHER'*s*] final cry!

STEPDAUGHTER. It still rings in my ears. It's driven me out of my mind,
that cry!—You can present me as you wish, sir, it doesn't matter. Even
dressed. As long as at least my arms—just my arms—are bare. Because it was like this. [*She goes to the* FATHER *and rests her head on his
chest.*] I was standing like this with my head on his chest and my arms
round his neck like this. Then I saw something throbbing right here
on my arm. A vein. Then, as if it was just this living vein that dis-
gusted me, I jammed my eyes shut, like this, d'you see? and buried my
head on his chest. [*Turning to the* MOTHER] Scream, scream, mama!
[*Buries her head on the* FATHER'*s chest and with her shoulders raised as if
to avoid hearing the scream she adds in a voice stifled with torment.*]
Scream as you screamed then!

MOTHER [*rushing forward to part them*]. No! My daughter! My daughter!
[*Having pulled her from him*] Brute! Brute! It's my daughter, don't you
see—my daughter!

DIRECTOR [*the outburst having sent him reeling to the footlights, while the
Actors show dismay*]. Fine! Splendid! And now: curtain, curtain!

FATHER [*running to him, convulsed*]. Right! Yes! Because that, sir, is how
it actually was!

DIRECTOR [*in admiration and conviction*]. Yes, yes, of course! Curtain! Curtain!

[*Hearing this repeated cry of the* DIRECTOR, *the* TECHNICIAN *lets down the
curtain, trapping the* DIRECTOR *and the* FATHER *between curtain and footlights.*]

DIRECTOR [*looking up, with raised arms*]. What an idiot! I say Curtain,
meaning that's how the act should end, and they let down the actual
curtain! [*He lifts a corner of the curtain so he can get back on stage. To the*
FATHER] Yes, yes, fine, splendid! Absolutely sure fire! Has to end that

way. I can vouch for the first act. [*Goes behind the curtain with the* FA-THER.]

[*When the curtain rises we see that the stagehands have struck that first "indication of a set," and have put on stage in its stead a small garden fountain. On one side of the stage, the Actors are sitting in a row, and on the other are the Characters. The* DIRECTOR *is standing in the middle of the stage, in the act of meditating with one hand, fist clenched, on his mouth.*]

DIRECTOR [*shrugging after a short pause*]. Yes, well then, let's get to the second act. Just leave it to me as we agreed beforehand and everything will be all right.

STEPDAUGHTER. Our entrance into his house [*the* FATHER] in spite of him. [*the* SON]

DIRECTOR [*losing patience*]. Very well. But leave it all to me, I say.

STEPDAUGHTER. In spite of him. Just let that be clear.

MOTHER [*shaking her head from her corner*]. For all the good that's come out of it . . .

STEPDAUGHTER [*turning quickly on her*]. It doesn't matter. The more damage to us, the more guilt feelings for him.

DIRECTOR [*still out of patience*]. I understand, I understand. All this will be taken into account, especially at the beginning. Rest assured.

MOTHER [*supplicatingly*]. Do make them understand, I beg you, sir, for my conscience sake, for I tried in every possible way—

STEPDAUGHTER [*continuing her* MOTHER's *speech, contemptuously*]. To placate me, to advise me not to give him trouble. [*To the* DIRECTOR] Do what she wants, do it because it's true. I enjoy the whole thing very much because, look: the more she plays the suppliant and tries to gain entrance into his heart, the more he holds himself aloof: he's an absentee! How I relish this!

DIRECTOR. We want to get going—on the second act, don't we?

STEPDAUGHTER. I won't say another word. But to play it all in the garden, as you want to, won't be possible.

DIRECTOR. Why won't it be possible?

STEPDAUGHTER. Because he [*the* SON] stays shut up in his room, on his own. Then again we need the house for the part about this poor bewildered little boy, as I told you.

DIRECTOR. Quite right. But on the other hand, we can't change the scenery in view of the audience three or four times in one act, nor can we stick up signs—

LEADING MAN. They used to at one time . . .

DIRECTOR. Yes, when the audiences were about as mature as that little girl.

LEADING LADY. They got the illusion more easily.

FATHER [*suddenly, rising*]. The illusion, please don't say illusion! Don't use that word! It's especially cruel to us.

DIRECTOR [*astonished*]. And why, if I may ask?

FATHER. Oh yes, cruel, cruel! You should understand that.

DIRECTOR. What word would you have us use anyway? The illusion of creating here for our spectators—

LEADING MAN. —By our performance—

DIRECTOR. —the illusion of a reality.

FATHER. I understand, sir, but perhaps you do not understand us. Because, you see, for you and for your actors all this—quite rightly—is a game—

LEADING LADY [*indignantly interrupting*]. Game! We are not children, sir. We act in earnest.

FATHER. I don't deny it. I just mean the game of your art which, as this gentleman rightly says, must provide a perfect illusion of reality.

DIRECTOR. Yes, exactly.

FATHER. But consider this. We [*he quickly indicates himself and the other five Characters*], we have no reality outside this illusion.

DIRECTOR [*astonished, looking at his Actors who remain bewildered and lost*]. And that means?

FATHER [*after observing them briefly, with a pale smile*]. Just that, ladies and gentlemen. How should we have any other reality? What for you is an illusion, to be created, is for us our unique reality. [*Short pause. He takes several short steps toward the* DIRECTOR, *and adds*] But not for us alone, of course. Think a moment. [*He looks into his eyes.*] Can you tell me who you are? [*And he stands there pointing his first finger at him.*]

DIRECTOR [*Upset, with a half-smile*]. How do you mean, who I am? I am I.

FATHER. And if I told you that wasn't true because you are me?

DIRECTOR. I would reply that you are out of your mind. [*The Actors laugh.*]

FATHER. You are right to laugh: because this is a game. [*To the* DIRECTOR] And you can object that it's only in a game that that gentleman there [LEADING MAN], who is himself, must be me, who am *myself*. I've caught you in a trap, do you see that?

[*Actors start laughing again.*]

DIRECTOR [*Annoyed*]. You said all this before. Why repeat it?

FATHER. I won't—I didn't intend to say that. I'm inviting you to emerge from this game. [*He looks at the* LEADING LADY *as if to forestall what she might say.*] This game of art which you are accustomed to play here with your actors. Let me again ask quite seriously: Who are you?

DIRECTOR [*turning to the Actors, amazed and at the same time irritated*]. The gall of this fellow! Calls himself a character and comes here to ask me who I am!

FATHER [*dignified, but not haughty*]. A character, sir, can always ask a man who he is. Because a character really has his own life, marked with his own characteristics, by virtue of which he is always someone. Whereas, a man—I'm not speaking of you now—*a man* can be no one.

DIRECTOR. Oh sure. But you are asking me! And I am the manager, understand?

FATHER [*quite softly with mellifluous modesty*]. Only in order to know, sir, if you as you now are see yourself . . . for example, at a distance in time. Do you see the man you once were, with all the illusions you had then, with everything, inside you and outside, as it seemed then—as it was then for you!—Well sir, thinking back to those illusions which you don't have any more, to all those things which no longer seem to be what at one time they were for you, don't you feel, not just the boards of this stage, but the very earth beneath slipping away from you? For will not all that you feel yourself to be now, your whole reality of today, as it is now, inevitably seem an illusion tomorrow?

DIRECTOR [*who has not followed exactly, but has been staggered by the plausibilities of the argument*]. Well, well, what do you want to prove?

FATHER. Oh nothing sir. I just wanted to make you see that if *we* [*pointing again at himself and the other Characters*] have no reality outside of illusion, it would be well if you should distrust your reality because, though you breathe it and touch it today, it is destined like that of yesterday to stand revealed to you tomorrow as illusion.

DIRECTOR [*deciding to mock him*]. Oh splendid! And you'll be telling me next that you and this play that you have come to perform for me are truer and more real than I am.

FATHER [*quite seriously*]. There can be no doubt of that, sir.

DIRECTOR. Really?

FATHER. I thought you had understood that from the start.

DIRECTOR. More real than me?

FATHER. If your reality can change overnight . . .

DIRECTOR. Of course it can, it changes all the time, like everyone else's.

FATHER [*with a cry*]. But ours does not, sir. You see, that is the difference. It does not change, it cannot ever change or be otherwise because it is already fixed, it is what is, just that, forever—a terrible thing, sir!—an immutable reality. You should shudder to come near us.[7]

DIRECTOR [*suddenly struck by a new idea, he steps in front of the* FATHER]. I should like to know, however, when anyone ever saw a character get out of his part and set about expounding and explicating it, delivering lectures on it. Can you tell me? I have never seen anything like that.

FATHER. You have never seen it, sir, because authors generally hide the travail of their creations. When characters are alive and turn up, living, before their author, all that author does is follow the words and gestures which they propose to him. He has to want them to be as they themselves want to be. Woe betide him if he doesn't! When a character is born, he at once acquires such an independence, even of his own author, that the whole world can imagine him in innumerable situations other than those the author thought to place him in. At times he acquires a meaning that the author never dreamt of giving him.

DIRECTOR. Certainly, I know that.

FATHER. Then why all this astonishment at us? Imagine what a misfortune it is for a character such as I described to you—given life in the imagination of an author who then wished to deny him life—and tell me frankly: isn't such a character, given life and left without life, isn't he right to set about doing just what we are doing now as we stand here before you, after having done just the same—for a very long time, believe me—before *him,* trying to persuade him, trying to push him . . . I would appear before him sometimes, sometimes she [*looks at* STEPDAUGHTER] would go to him, sometimes that poor mother . . .

STEPDAUGHTER [*coming forward as if in a trance*]. It's true. I too went there, sir, to tempt him, many times, in the melancholy of that study of his, at the twilight hour, when he would sit stretched out in his armchair, unable to make up his mind to switch the light on, and letting the evening shadows invade the room, knowing that these shadows were alive with us and that we were coming to tempt him . . . [*As if she saw herself still in that study and felt only annoyance at the presence of all of these Actors*] Oh, if only you would all go away! Leave us alone! My mother there with her son—I with this little girl—the boy there always alone—then I with him [*the* FATHER]—then I by myself, I by myself . . . in those shadows. [*Suddenly she jumps up as if she wished to take hold of herself in the vision she has of herself lighting up the shadows and alive.*] Ah my life! What scenes, what scenes we went there to propose to him: I, I tempted him more than the others.

FATHER. Right, but perhaps that was the trouble: you insisted too much. You thought you could seduce him.

STEPDAUGHTER. Nonsense. He wanted me that way. [*She comes up to the* DIRECTOR *to tell him as in confidence.*] If you ask me, sir, it was because he was so depressed, or because he despised the theater the public knows and wants . . .

DIRECTOR. Let's continue. Let's continue, for Heaven's sake. Enough theories, I'd like some facts. Give me some facts.

STEPDAUGHTER. It seems to me that we have already given you more facts than you can handle—with our entry into his [*the* FATHER'S] house! You said you couldn't change the scene every five minutes or start hanging signs.

DIRECTOR. Nor can we, of course not, we have to combine the scenes and group them in one simultaneous close-knit action. Not your idea at all. You'd like to see your brother come home from school and wander through the house like a ghost, hiding behind the doors, and brooding on a plan which—how did you put it—?

STEPDAUGHTER. —shrivels him up, sir, completely shrivels him up, sir.

DIRECTOR. "Shrivels!" What a word! All right then: his growth was stunted except for his eyes. Is that what you said?

STEPDAUGHTER. Yes, sir. Just look at him. [*She points him out next to the* MOTHER.]

DIRECTOR. Good girl. And then at the same time you want this little girl to be playing in the garden, dead to the world. Now, the boy in the house, the girl in the garden, is that possible?

STEPDAUGHTER. Happy in the sunshine! Yes, that is my only reward, her pleasure, her joy in that garden! After the misery, the squalor of a horrible room where we slept, all four of us, she with me: just think, of the horror of my contaminated body next to hers! She held me tight, oh so tight with her loving innocent little arms! In the garden she would run and take my hand as soon as she saw me. She did not see the big flowers, she ran around looking for the teeny ones and wanted to show them to me, oh the joy of it!

[*Saying this and tortured by the memory she breaks into prolonged desperate sobbing, dropping her head onto her arms which are spread out on the work table. Everyone is overcome by her emotion. The* DIRECTOR *goes to her almost paternally and says to comfort her*]

DIRECTOR. We'll do the garden. We'll do the garden, don't worry, and you'll be very happy about it. We'll bring all the scenes together in the garden. [*Calling a stagehand by name*] Hey, drop me a couple of trees, will you, two small cypress trees, here in front of the fountain.

[*Two small cypress trees are seen descending from the flies. A* STAGEHAND *runs on to secure them with nails and a couple of braces.*]

DIRECTOR [*to the* STEPDAUGHTER]. Something to go on with anyway. Gives us an idea. [*Again calling the* STAGEHAND *by name*] Hey, give me a bit of sky.

STAGEHAND [*From above*]. What?

DIRECTOR. Bit of sky, a backcloth, to go behind that fountain. [*A white backdrop is seen descending from the flies.*] Not white, I said sky. It doesn't matter, leave it, I'll take care of it. [*Shouting*] Hey, Electrician, put these lights out. Let's have a bit of atmosphere, lunar atmosphere, blue background, and give me a blue spot on that backcloth. That's right. That's enough. [*At his command a mysterious lunar scene is created which induces the Actors to talk and move as they would on an evening in the garden beneath the moon.*] [*To* STEPDAUGHTER] You see? And now instead of hiding behind doors in the house the boy could move around here in the garden and hide behind trees. But it will be difficult, you know, to find a little girl to play the scene where she shows you the flowers. [*Turning to the* BOY] Come down this way a bit. Let's see how this can be worked out. [*And when the* BOY *doesn't move*] Come on, come on. [*Then dragging him forward he tries to make him hold his head up but it falls down again every time.*] Oh dear, another problem, this boy . . . What *is* it? . . . My God, he'll have to say something . . . [*He goes up to him, puts a hand on his shoulder and leads him behind one of the tree drops.*] Come on. Come on. Let me see. You can hide a bit here . . . Like this . . . You can stick your head out a bit to look . . . [*He goes to one side to see the effect. The* BOY *has scarcely run through the actions when the Actors are deeply affected; and they remain quite overwhelmed.*] Ah! Fine! Splendid! [*He turns again to the* STEPDAUGHTER.] If the little girl surprises him looking out and runs over to him, don't you think she might drag a few words out of him too?

STEPDAUGHTER [*jumping to her feet*]. Don't expect him to speak while *he's* here. [*She points to the* SON.] You have to send *him* away first.

SON [*going resolutely toward one of the two stairways*]. Suits me. Glad to go. Nothing I want more.

DIRECTOR [*immediately calling him*]. No. Where are you going? Wait.

[*The* MOTHER *rises, deeply moved, in anguish at the thought that he is really going. She instinctively raises her arms as if to halt him, yet without moving away from her position.*]

SON [*arriving at the footlights, where the* DIRECTOR *stops him*]. I have absolutely nothing to do here. So let me go please. Just let me go.

DIRECTOR. How do you mean, you have nothing to do?

STEPDAUGHTER [*placidly, with irony*]. Don't hold him! He won't go.

FATHER. He has to play the terrible scene in the garden with his mother.

SON [*unhesitating, resolute, proud*]. I play nothing. I said so from the start. [*To the* DIRECTOR] Let me go.

STEPDAUGHTER [*running to the* DIRECTOR *to get him to lower his arms so that he is no longer holding the* SON *back*]. Let him go. [*Then turning to the* SON *as soon as the* DIRECTOR *has let him go*] Very well, go. [*The* SON *is all set to move toward the stairs but, as if held by some occult power, he cannot go down the steps. While the Actors are both astounded and deeply troubled, he moves slowly across the footlights straight to the other stairway. But having arrived there he remains poised for the descent but unable to descend. The* STEPDAUGHTER, *who has followed him with her eyes in an attitude of defiance, bursts out laughing.*] He can't, you see. He can't. He has to stay here, has to. Bound by a chain, indissolubly. But if I who do take flight, sir, when that happens which has to happen, and precisely because of the hatred I feel for him, precisely so as not to see him again—very well, if *I* am still here and can bear the sight of him and his company—you can imagine whether *he* can go away. He who really must, must remain here with that fine father of his and that mother there who no longer has any other children. [*Turning again to the* MOTHER] Come on, Mother, come on. [*Turning again to the* DIRECTOR *and pointing to the* MOTHER] Look, she got up to hold him back. [*To the* MOTHER, *as if exerting a magical power over her*] Come. Come . . . [*Then to the* DIRECTOR] You can imagine how little she wants to display her love in front of your actors. But so great is her desire to get at him that—look, you see—she is even prepared to live her scene.

[*In fact the* MOTHER *has approached and no sooner has the* STEPDAUGHTER *spoken her last words than she spreads her arms to signify consent.*]

SON [*without pause*]. But *I* am not, *I* am not. If I can not go I will stay here, but I repeat: I will play nothing.

FATHER [*to the* DIRECTOR, *enraged*]. You can force him, sir.

SON. No one can force me.

FATHER. I will force you.

STEPDAUGHTER. Wait, wait. First the little girl must be at the fountain. [*She runs to take the* LITTLE GIRL, *drops on her knees in front of her, takes her little face in her hands.*] My poor little darling, you look bewildered with those lovely big eyes of yours. Who knows where you think you are? We are on a stage my dear. What is a stage? It is a place where you play at being serious, a place for play-acting, where we will now play-act. But seriously! For real! You too . . . [*She embraces her, presses her to her bosom and rocks her a little.*] Oh, little darling, little darling, what an ugly play you will enact! What a horrible thing has been planned for you, the garden, the fountain . . . All pretense, of course, that's the trouble, my sweet, everything is make-believe here, but perhaps for you, my child, a make-believe fountain is nicer than a real one for playing in, hmm? It will be a game for the others, but not for you, alas, because you are real, my darling, and are actually playing in a fountain that is real, beautiful, big, green with many bamboo plants reflected in it and giving it shade. Many, many ducklings can swim in it, breaking the shade to bits. You want to take hold of one of these ducklings . . . [*With a shout that fills everyone with dismay*] No! No, my Rosetta! Your mother is not looking after you because of that beast of a son. A thousand devils are loose in my head . . . and *he* . . . [*She leaves the* LITTLE GIRL *and turns with her usual hostility to the* BOY.] And what are you doing here, always looking like a beggar child? It will be your fault too if this little girl drowns—with all your standing around like that. As if I hadn't paid for everybody when I got you all into this house. [*Grabbing one of his arms to force him to take a hand out of his pocket*] What have you got there? What are you hiding? Let's see this hand. [*Tears his hand out of his pocket, and to the horror of everyone discovers that it holds a small revolver. She looks at it for a moment as if satisfied and then says*] Ah! Where did you get that and how? [*And as the* BOY *in his confusion, with his eyes staring and vacant all the time, does not answer her*] Idiot, if I were you I wouldn't have killed myself, I would have killed one of those two—or both of them—the father and the son! [*She hides him behind the small cypress tree from which he had been looking out, and she takes the* LITTLE GIRL *and hides her in the fountain, having her lie down in it in such a way as to be quite hidden. Finally, the* STEPDAUGHTER *goes down on her knees with her face in her hands, which are resting on the rim of the fountain.*]

DIRECTOR. Splendid! [*Turning to the* SON] And at the same time . . .

SON [*with contempt*]. And at the same time, nothing. It is not true, sir. There was never any scene between me and her. [*He points to the* MOTHER.] Let her tell you herself how it was.

[*Meanwhile the* SECOND ACTRESS *and the* JUVENILE LEAD *have detached themselves from the group of Actors. The former has started to observe the* MOTHER, *who is opposite her, very closely. And the other has started to observe the* SON. *Both are planning how they will recreate the roles.*]

MOTHER. Yes, it is true, sir. I had gone to his room.

SON. My room, did you hear that? Not the garden.

DIRECTOR. That is of no importance. We have to rearrange the action, I told you that.

SON [*noticing that the* JUVENILE LEAD *is observing him*]. What do *you* want?

JUVENILE LEAD. Nothing. I am observing you.

SON [*turning to the other side where the* SECOND ACTRESS *is*]. Ah, and here we have you to re-create the role, eh? [*He points to the* MOTHER.]

DIRECTOR. Exactly, exactly. You should be grateful, it seems to me, for the attention they are giving you.

SON. Oh yes, thank you. But you still haven't understood that you cannot do this drama. We are not inside you, not in the least, and your actors are looking at us from the outside. Do you think it's possible for us to live before a mirror which, not content to freeze us in the fixed image it provides of our expression, also throws back at us an unrecognizable grimace purporting to be ourselves?

FATHER. That is true. That is true. You must see that.

DIRECTOR [*to the* JUVENILE LEAD *and the* SECOND ACTRESS]. Very well, get away from here.

SON. No good. I won't cooperate.

DIRECTOR. Just be quiet a minute and let me hear your mother. [*To the* MOTHER] Well? You went into his room?

MOTHER. Yes sir, into his room. I was at the end of my tether. I wanted to pour out all of the anguish which was oppressing me. But as soon as he saw me come in—

SON. —There was no scene. I went away. I went away so there would be no scene. Because I have never made scenes, never, understand?

MOTHER. That's true. That's how it was. Yes.

DIRECTOR. But now there's got to be a scene between you and him. It is indispensable.

MOTHER. As for me, sir, I am ready. If only you could find some way to have me speak to him for one moment, to have me say what is in my heart.

FATHER [*going right up to the* SON, *very violent*]. You will do it! For your mother! For your mother!

SON [*more decisively than ever*]. I will do nothing!

FATHER [*grabbing him by the chest and shaking him*]. By God, you will obey! Can't you hear how she is talking to you? Aren't you her son?

SON [*grabbing his* FATHER]. No! No! Once and for all let's have done with it!

[*General agitation. The* MOTHER, *terrified, tries to get between them to separate them.*]

MOTHER [*as before*]. Please, please!

FATHER [*without letting go of the* SON]. You must obey, you must obey!

SON [*wrestling with his* FATHER *and in the end throwing him to the ground beside the little stairway, to the horror of everyone*]. What's this frenzy that's taken hold of you? To show your shame and ours to everyone? Have you no restraint? I won't cooperate, I won't cooperate! And that is how I interpret the wishes of the man who did not choose to put us on stage.

DIRECTOR. But you came here.

SON [*pointing to his* FATHER]. He came here—not me!

DIRECTOR. But aren't you here too?

SON. It was he who wanted to come, dragging the rest of us with him, and then getting together with you to plot not only what really happened, but also—as if that did not suffice—*what did not happen*.

DIRECTOR. Then tell me. Tell me what did happen. Just tell me. You came out of your room without saying a thing?

SON [*after a moment of hesitation*]. Without saying a thing. In order not to make a scene.

DIRECTOR [*driving him on*]. Very well, and then, what did you do then?

SON [*while everyone looks on in anguished attention, he moves a few steps on the front part of the stage*]. Nothing . . . crossing the garden . . . [*He stops, gloomy, withdrawn.*]

DIRECTOR [*always driving him on to speak, impressed by his reticence*]. Very well, crossing the garden?

SON [*desperate, hiding his face with one arm*]. Why do you want to make me say it, sir? It is horrible.

[*The* MOTHER *trembles all over, and stifles groans, looking toward the fountain.*]

DIRECTOR [*softly, noticing this look of hers, turning to the* SON, *with growing apprehension*]. The little girl?

SON [*looking out into the auditorium*]. Over there—in the fountain . . .

FATHER [*on the ground, pointing compassionately toward the* MOTHER]. And she followed him, sir.

DIRECTOR [*to the* SON, *anxiously*]. And then you . . .

SON [*slowly, looking straight ahead all the time*]. I ran out. I started to fish her out . . . but all of a sudden I stopped. Behind those trees I saw something that froze me: the boy, the boy was standing there, quite still. There was madness in the eyes. He was looking at his drowned sister in the fountain. [*The* STEPDAUGHTER, *who has been bent over the fountain, hiding the* LITTLE GIRL, *is sobbing desperately, like an echo from the bottom. Pause*] I started to approach and then . . .

[*From behind the trees where the* BOY *has been hiding, a revolver shot rings out.*]

MOTHER [*running up with a tormented shout, accompanied by the* SON *and all the Actors in a general tumult*]. Son! My son! [*And then amid the hub-bub and the disconnected shouts of the others*] Help! Help!

DIRECTOR [*amid the shouting, trying to clear a space while the* BOY *is lifted by his head and feet and carried away behind the backcloth*]. Is he wounded, is he wounded, really?

[*Everyone except the* DIRECTOR *and the* FATHER, *who has remained on the ground beside the steps, has disappeared behind the backcloth which has served for a sky, where they can still be heard for a while whispering anxiously. Then from one side and the other of this curtain, the Actors come back on stage.*]

LEADING LADY [*re-entering from the right, very much upset*]. He's dead! Poor boy! He's dead! What a terrible thing!

LEADING MAN [*re-entering from the left, laughing*]. How do you mean, dead? Fiction, fiction, one doesn't believe such things.

OTHER ACTORS [*on the right*]. Fiction? Reality! Reality! He is dead!

OTHER ACTORS [*on the left*]. No! Fiction! Fiction!

FATHER [*rising, and crying out to them*]. Fiction indeed! Reality, reality, gentlemen, reality! [*Desperate, he too disappears at the back.*]

DIRECTOR [*at the end of his rope*]. Fiction! Reality! To hell with all of you! Lights, lights, lights! [*At a single stroke the whole stage and auditorium is flooded with very bright light. The* DIRECTOR *breathes again, as if freed from an incubus, and they all look each other in the eyes, bewildered and lost.*] Things like this don't happen to me, they've made me lose a whole day. [*He looks at his watch.*] Go, you can all go. What could we do now anyway? It is too late to pick up the rehearsal where we left off. See you this evening. [*As soon as the Actors have gone he talks to the* ELECTRICIAN *by name.*] Hey, Electrician, lights out. [*He has hardly said the words when the theater is plunged for a moment into complete darkness.*] Hey, for God's sake, leave me at least one light! I like to see where I am going!

[*Immediately, from behind the backcloth, as if the wrong switch had been pulled, a green light comes on which projects the silhouettes, clear-cut and large, of the Characters, minus the* BOY *and the* LITTLE GIRL. *Seeing the silhouettes, the* DIRECTOR, *terrified, rushes from the stage. At the same time the light behind the backcloth goes out and the stage is again lit in nocturnal blue as before.*

Slowly, from the right side of the curtain, the SON *comes forward first, followed by the* MOTHER *with her arms stretched out toward him; then from the left side, the* FATHER. *They stop in the middle of the stage and stay there as if in a trance. Last of all from the right, the* STEPDAUGHTER *comes out and runs toward the two stairways. She stops on the first step, to look for a moment at the other three, and then breaks into a harsh laugh before throwing herself down the steps; she runs down the aisle between the rows of seats; she stops one more time and again laughs, looking at the three who are still on stage; she disappears from the auditorium, and from the lobby her laughter is still heard. Shortly thereafter the curtain falls.*]

Translator's Notes

The theater envisaged is of the type most usual where and when the play was written—Italy, 1921. Attempts to substitute a non-Italian type of theater of a later date break down because unless very drastic changes are made in the script, you are still left with items that don't properly fit. You cannot, for example, pretend this is an Off-Broadway theater in 1970 if you then proceed to call a character "Sècond Actress"—Actor's Equity Association hasn't a single member who would accept the title. With such things in mind, the translator decided simply to translate. And so the reader has the job of imagining a theater he is probably not familiar with—a theater in which, for example, there is a prompter in a prompter's box, center stage.

The second most important personage in the play is called, in the original, Direttore-Capocomico. A Direttore is a managing director or manager. Capocomico one would first be inclined to translate as Actor Manager, and the Actor Managers of the Victorian age did direct the plays. The only trouble here is that Pirandello's Capocomico obviously does not act. He is a Director-Manager, and I think there is, in American English, no alternative to calling him the Director, even though the present-day Italian word for that is Regista. It is a matter of the evolution of this particular profession. The Direttore-Capocomico is an intermediate figure between the old Actor Managers and the new Directors. Pirandello gets to the latter in a later play, *Tonight We Improvise*.

One note on the stage directions. In this play, there are few personal names, so that characters are generally referred to as just *him* or *her*. This forces the author to insert very many parentheses on the pattern of "Pointing to the Father." When possible, the translator has taken the liberty of shortening these to just (to stick to the example) "the Father" in parentheses.

The Italian text followed is that of the *Maschere Nude* as reprinted by Mondadori in 1948. This represents Pirandello's final revision of the play. The translation published in America by the E. P. Dutton Company was based on an earlier Italian text, namely, on the first edition of 1921. The three substantial passages in the first edition which Pirandello cut from his later revisions are included here in footnotes, so that the American reader gets a chance to see what Pirandello's changes amounted to. (No detailed study of *all* the changes has as yet been made, it would seem. The present translator is aware of three different stages of revision: the final version, the second edition [1923], and the first edition [1921].) The Dutton text, by Edward Storer, is literal but often erroneous. There is an accurate, and therefore helpful, translation of the first edition into French by Benjamin Crémieux.

1. *Il giuoco delle parti*, published in English as *The Rules of the Game*.

2. A humble priest in Manzoni's *The Betrothed*.

3. Pirandello gives four lines of the song in French, and hitherto the English translators have followed him. However, the song is an American one, music by Dave Stamper, lyrics by Gene Buck, from the Ziegfeld Follies, 1917. Here are the words:

In a fairy book a Chinese crook
Has won such wondrous fame
But nowadays he appears in plays
And Chu Chin Chow's his name.
With his forty thieves he now achieves
A great success each night.
Just lend an ear and listen here
And I will put you right:
    Beware of Chu Chin Chow!
    Take care, he's coming now!
    He's a robber from the Orient
    And he's filled with Chinese sentiment.
    At night when lights are low
    He wanders to and fro.
    He's the master of his art.
    He can steal a girlie's heart.
    Love he'll plunder, he's a wonder:
    Chu Chin Chow!
Mister Chu Chin Chow you must allow
Has a manner all his own
For he does not woo as others do
He's never quite alone.
With his forty jugs he carries hugs
And kisses to bestow.
'Tis in the sand he'll win your hand,
This Chinese Romeo.
    Beware of Chu Chin Chow, etc.

(Copyright 1917 by T. B. Harms and Francis, Day and Hunter.)

4. The first edition had the Father continue as follows:—"Because, finally, the drama is all in this: when the mother reenters my home, the family she had elsewhere, which was being, as it were, superimposed on the first one, comes to an end, it's alien, it can't grow in this soil. The little girl dies, the little boy comes to a tragic end, the older girl flees. And so, after all the torment, there remain—we three—myself, the mother, the son. And when the alien family is gone, we too find ourselves alien—the one to the other. We find ourselves utterly desolated. As he (pointing to the Son) scornfully said, it's the revenge of the Demon of Experiment which, alas, I carry inside me, a demon that makes me seek an impossible good, which is what happens when absolute faith is lacking—the faith that enables us humbly to accept life as it is—instead, in our pride, we try to take it over, creating for other persons a reality we consider to be in their line; but sir, it isn't; each of us has his own reality within him, to be respected before God, even when it harms us."

5. In the first edition, a passage follows most of which is found at a later point of the revised text. But this interesting speech of the Son was dropped: "Perform this! . . . As if there were any reason! But he (the Father) has found the meaning. As if everyone couldn't find the meaning of anything that happens in this life, *his* meaning, corresponding to *his* presuppositions! (Pause) He complains, this man, of having been discovered *where* he shouldn't have been and doing *what* he shouldn't have been doing—caught in an act which should have remained hidden, outside that reality which he should have sustained for other people. And I? Hasn't he acted in such a way as to force me to discover what no son should ever discover? That father and mother are alive and are man and woman, for each other, outside that reality of father and mother which we give them. For, as soon as this reality is uncovered, our life is no longer tied to that man and that woman except at a single point—one which will only shame them, should we see it!"

6. In Italian rehearsals, traditionally, the prompter reads all the lines a few seconds ahead of the actors until the latter have completely memorized their roles, if indeed they ever do.

7. In the first edition, the following passage occurs here:

FATHER. If you are truly conscious that your reality, on the other hand, your reality in time is an ephemeral and extremely fleeting illusion which you unconsciously invent, today in this day and tomorrow in some other way according to cases, according to conditions and will and feelings which you invent with the intellect which shows them to you today in one way and tomorrow . . . who knows how: illusions of reality as acted out in that fatuous comedy of life which does not end, which can not ever end because, if tomorrow it should end, then good bye, all is finished.

DIRECTOR. In the name of God, I wish you at least would stop your philosophizing and let's see if we might end this play which you people have brought me! Too much reasoning, too much reasoning, my dear sir.—You know you almost seem to me a . . . [*He interrupts and looks him over from top to toe*] . . . exactly, yes: You introduced yourself here as a—let's put it this way—as a character created by an author who decided not to make a play out of you. Correct?

FATHER. That's the simple truth, sir.

DIRECTOR. Cut it out. None of us believes you. Such things can't be seriously believed, you must know that. You know what I rather think is going on? I think that you are adopting the manner of a certain author whom I particularly detest—let me admit that—although, unfortunately, I've had to put on some of his works. I happen to have been rehearsing one of them when you all came. [*Turning to the Actors*] Think what we gained by the exchange! From the frying pan into the fire!

FATHER. I don't know, sir, what author you may be alluding to, but believe me, I feel, I feel what I think. And only those who do not think about what they feel would say I am just reasoning: they are blind to their own feelings. I know, I know that many consider such self-blinding much more human, but the opposite is true, sir, for man never reasons so much—on or off the point—as when he suffers. He wants to see the cause of his sufferings, he wants to know who is giving them to him, if this is just or unjust. When, on the other hand, he is enjoying himself, he just accepts the enjoyment and stops reasoning—as if to enjoy oneself were a right. Only the animals suffer without reasoning, sir. Yet put on stage a man who reasons in the midst of his suffering, and everyone will object. But let him suffer like an animal and everyone will say: "Oh, yes, he is human."

DIRECTOR. And in the meanwhile you go on reasoning, huh?

FATHER. Because I suffer, sir. I am not reasoning, I am crying aloud the why and wherefore of my suffering.

Emperor Henry

CHARACTERS

First Valet
Second Valet
Harald [*whose real name is Franco*] ⎫
Landolf [*whose real name is Lolo*] ⎪
Ordulf [*whose real name is Momo*] ⎬ *supposed Privy Councillors*
Bertold [*whose real name is Fino*] ⎭
Giovanni, *the butler*
Marquis Carlo Di Nolli
Baron Tito Belcredi
Dr. Dionisio Genoni, *a psychiatrist*
Countess Matilda Spina, *the Baron's mistress*
Frida, *her daughter, engaged to the Marquis*
"Henry the Fourth, Emperor of Germany" [*the Marquis's uncle*]

THE PLACE: *A solitary villa in the*
Umbrian countryside.

THE TIME: *"The present"—the play was*
first performed in 1922.

ACT I

A hall in the villa got up in every way to pass for the throne room of the German Emperor Henry the Fourth in his imperial residence at Goslar, Hanover. But in the middle of the ancient furnishings two large modern oil paintings—life-size portraits—stand out from the back wall. They are supported, not far above the ground, on a sort of pedestal or ledge of carved wood which runs the whole length of the wall. [It is broad and protrudes so you can sit on it as on a long bench.] Between the two portraits is the throne itself—the imperial chair and its low baldachin—which is, as it were, inserted in the pedestal dividing it into two parts. The two portraits represent a lady and a gentleman, both young, rigged up in carnival costumes, one as the Emperor Henry the Fourth and the other as Countess Matilda of Tuscany. Doors to left and right.

Two valets, in eleventh-century costume, are lying on the ledge. Suddenly they jump down, in surprise, apparently, running to place themselves, stiff as statues, at the foot of the throne, one on each side, with their halberds. Soon afterward, by the second door on the right, HARALD, LANDOLF, ORDULF, *and* BERTOLD *come in. These young men are paid by the* MARQUIS CARLO DI NOLLI *to pretend to be privy councillors—regal vassals, belonging to the lower aristocracy, at the court of the* EMPEROR. *They are therefore dressed as German knights of the eleventh century. The last of them,* BERTOLD [*his real name is Fino*], *is doing the job for the first time. His three companions are amusing themselves telling him everything. The whole scene should be played with extreme vivacity.*

LANDOLF [*to* BERTOLD, *as if following up an explanation*]. And this is the throne room!

HARALD. At Goslar!

ORDULF. Or, if you'd prefer that, in his castle in the Harz Mountains!

HARALD. Or at Worms.

LANDOLF. It jumps around a bit. According to the scene we're acting out. Now here, now there—

ORDULF. Now in Saxony—

HARALD. Now in Lombardy—

LANDOLF. Now on the Rhine.

FIRST VALET [*holding his position, hardly moving his lips*]. Sss, Sss!

HARALD [*hearing and turning*].What's the matter?

FIRST VALET [*still like a statue, in an undertone*]. Well, is he coming or isn't he? [*The allusion is to the* EMPEROR.]

ORDULF. He isn't. He's sleeping. Take it easy.

SECOND VALET [*dropping the pose as his partner does so, taking a long breath, and going to lie down again on the ledge*]. Well, for Christ's sake, why didn't you say so before?

BERTOLD [*who has been observing everything in mixed amazement and perplexity, walking around the room and looking at it, then looking at his clothes and his companions' clothes*]. But look . . . this room . . . these clothes. . . . *What* Henry the Fourth? . . . I don't quite get it—is it Henry the Fourth of France or Henry the Fourth of England?

[*At this demand,* LANDOLF, HARALD, *and* ORDULF *burst into loud laughter.*]

LANDOLF [*laughing all the time and pointing at* BERTOLD *as if inviting the others—who also go on laughing—to continue making fun of him*]. Is it Henry the Fourth of France?

ORDULF. Or Henry the Fourth of England?

HARALD. Why, my dear child, it's Henry the Fourth of *Germany!*

ORDULF. The great and tragic emperor—

LANDOLF. —who repented and knelt in the snow before the Pope at Canossa! And day by day in this room we keep the war going—the terrible war between Church and State—

ORDULF. —between Pope and emperor!

BERTOLD [*covering his head with his hands to protect himself against this avalanche of information*]. I see, I see! I just didn't get it. Clothes like this. A room like this. I was right: these are *not* sixteenth-century clothes!

HARALD. Sixteenth century, indeed!

ORDULF. We're between the year 1000 and the year 1100.

LANDOLF. Count it up yourself: if we're in the snow at Canossa on January 25, 1077 . . .

BERTOLD [*more distressed than ever*]. My God, this is a disaster!

ORDULF. It certainly is, if you thought it was the *French* court.

BERTOLD. The *English* court, I studied up on *English* history, I was reading Shakespeare and everything . . .

LANDOLF. My dear man, *where* were you educated? Still, you're only a couple of centuries out.

BERTOLD [*getting angry*]. But why in God's name couldn't they have told me it was Henry the Fourth of Germany! I had two weeks to study the thing up—I can't tell you the number of books I've had my nose in!

HARALD. Look, dear boy. Didn't you know that poor Tony was called Adalbert, Bishop of Bremen, in this house?

BERTOLD. Adalbert, Bishop of . . . ? How'd I know that?

LANDOLF. Well, you see how it was: when Tony died, the Marquis . . .

BERTOLD. Ah, so it *was* the Marquis. Then why on earth didn't he tell me that . . . ?

HARALD. Maybe he thought you knew, dear boy.

LANDOLF. He wasn't going to take anyone else on. There were three of us left, and he thought we'd be enough. But then *he* took to shouting, "Adalbert driven out, Adalbert driven out!" Poor Tony, you see, it didn't seem to *him* Tony had died, it seemed to *him* the bishops of Mainz and Cologne had driven Adalbert out!

BERTOLD [*taking his head in his two hands and keeping it there*]. But I never heard a word of all this!

ORDULF. So here you are, my dear fellow.

HARALD. And the trouble is that we don't know who *you* are either, dear boy!

BERTOLD. Even you don't know? You don't know what part I'm to play?

ORDULF. Well, um—Bertold.

BERTOLD. Bertold? Who's he? *Why* Bertold?

LANDOLF. "They've driven Adalbert away from me? Then I want Bertold, I want Bertold!"—He took to shouting *that*.

HARALD. The three of us just stared at each other. Who the devil could this Bertold be?

ORDULF. So here you are, my dear fellow—Bertold.

LANDOLF. And what a wonderful job you'll make of it.

BERTOLD [*rebelling and starting to go*]. Oh, no! Not for me, thank you! I'm going, I'm going.

HARALD [*while he and* ORDULF *hold him back, amid laughter*]. Calm down, dear boy, calm down!

ORDULF. You won't be the Bertold of the story.

LANDOLF. Comfort yourself with the thought that even we don't really know who we are. He's Harald, he's Ordulf, I'm Landolf. . . . That's what we're *called*, and by now we've got used to it, but who *are* we? Names. Names of the period. And that's what you'll be—a name—of the period: Bertold. Only one of us, the late lamented Tony, ever had a good part, a part out of the story—the Bishop of Bremen. He looked like a real bishop, he was marvelous, poor Tony!

HARALD. God, how the dear boy would study: read, read, read!

LANDOLF. And he gave orders. Even to his Majesty. Oh, yes, he knew how to put himself over. Guided him. Was a tutor. An adviser, in effect. *We're* privy councillors, for that matter. But with us it's just for appearances: because the history books say the Emperor was hated by the *higher* aristocracy for surrounding himself at court with young men of the *lower* aristocracy.

ORDULF. That's us, my dear fellow.

LANDOLF. It really is a shame, because, well, with these clothes we could make a sensational appearance on the stage. In a costume play. They go over big these days. The Life and Loves of Henry the Fourth— what a story! Material not for one but for half a dozen tragedies! And now look at us! Just look at the four of us—and those two unfortunates standing by the throne like stuck pigs. [*He points at the two valets.*]—No one—no one puts us on stage, no one gives us scenes to act. We've got the—what do you call it?—we've got the *form*—but we don't have the *content!* We're worse off than the Emperor's real privy councillors because, well, it's true no one had given *them* a part to play either, but they didn't know they *had* to play one, they played it because they played it, it wasn't a part, it was their life, see what I mean? They acted in their own interests, they fought their rivals, they sold investitures, and so forth, while we . . . here are we in this beautiful court, dressed up as you see, and for what? To do what? To do nothing. . . . Six puppets hanging on the green room wall.

HARALD. No, no, dear boy, pardon me, but our replies do have to be in character.

LANDOLF. Yes, as far as that goes—

BERTOLD. And you said we do nothing! How'm I going to reply in character? I've got myself all prepared for Henry of England, and now someone calling himself Henry of Germany comes . . . comes butting in!

[LANDOLF, ORDULF, HARALD *start laughing again.*]

HARALD. You'd better attend to it, dear boy—

ORDULF. —and we'll help you, my dear fellow—

HARALD. —we've lots of books in there, my dear man—but first we'll just run through the main points—

ORDULF. —so you'll have a general idea—

HARALD. Look at this! [*Turns him around and shows him the* COUNTESS MATILDA's *portrait on the back wall.*] Who's that, for example?

BERTOLD [*looking*]. That? Well, in the first place, if you don't mind my saying so, it's out of place. Two modern paintings in the midst of all this medieval stuff?

HARALD. You're right, dear boy. And as a matter of fact they weren't there originally. Behind the pictures there are two niches—for two statues they were going to put in—in the style of the period. The niches stayed empty—then they were covered by these two canvases—

LANDOLF [*interrupting and continuing*].—which would certainly be out of place—if they really were paintings!

BERTOLD. They're not paintings? What are they, then?

LANDOLF. If you go and touch them, yes, they're paintings. But for *him* [*he points mysteriously out right, alluding to the* EMPEROR.]—since he does *not* touch them . . .

BERTOLD. He doesn't? What are they, then—for him?

LANDOLF. Well, this is just my interpretation, don't forget. All the same, I think it's pretty good. They're—images. Images—like, um, like images in a mirror, you see? That one there is him [*pointing*], the living image of him, him in this throne room—which is also—as it should be—in the style of the period. What are you so amazed about, may I ask? If we place you in front of a mirror, won't you see *your* living image? Won't you see the "you" of today in the trappings of yesteryear? Well, then, it's as if we had two mirrors here—two living images—in the midst of a world which . . . well, you'll see for yourself, now you live with us, you'll see how this world, too, every part of it, will come to life.

BERTOLD. Now, really, I didn't come here to go mad!

HARALD. Go mad, dear boy? Ts, ts. You're going to have fun!

BERTOLD [*to* LANDOLF]. You certainly have quite a line in philosophy!

LANDOLF. My dear man, you can't go behind the scenes of history—eight hundred years of it—and not bring back a bit of experience!

HARALD. Let's be going, dear boy. We'll fix you up in no time—

LANDOLF. We'll fasten the wires on and have you in full working order: the perfect marionette!

ORDULF. Let's go. [*Takes him by the arm, to lead him off.*]

BERTOLD [*stopping and looking toward the other portrait*]. Just a minute. You haven't told me who *she* is. The Emperor's wife?

HARALD. No, dear boy. The Emperor's wife is called Bertha of Susa.

ORDULF. The Emperor can't stand her. He wants to be young like us. He's planning to get rid of her.

LANDOLF. That's his fiercest enemy: Countess Matilda. Of Tuscany.

BERTOLD. Wait. Wasn't it her castle the Pope was staying in . . .

LANDOLF. At Canossa.

ORDULF. Precisely.

HARALD. Now *do* let's get going!

[*They are all moving over toward the door on the right by which they had entered when the old butler* GIOVANNI, *in modern cutaway, comes in at the left.*]

GIOVANNI [*in a great hurry, and worked up*]. Sss, sss! Franco! Lolo!

HARALD [*stopping and turning*]. Hey! What do *you* want?

BERTOLD [*amazed to see him come into the throne room in his modern coat*]. What's this? *He* comes in *here*?

LANDOLF. A visitor from the twentieth century! Away!

[*He and his two comrades make a joke of running over to threaten him and drive him out.*]

ORDULF. The Pope's ambassador—away with him!

HARALD. Away with the rogue!

GIOVANNI [*defending himself, annoyed*]. Oh, come on, stop this!

ORDULF. No, you're not allowed in here!

HARALD. Get away, old man!

LANDOLF [*to* BERTOLD]. It's witchcraft! He's a demon conjured up by the Great Magician of Rome! Out with your sword! [*And he reaches for his own.*]

GIOVANNI [*shouting*]. Stop this, I say! This is no time for fooling; the Marquis is here, and there's company with him. . . .

LANDOLF [*rubbing his hands*]. Oh, wonderful! Ladies?

ORDULF [*doing the same*]. Old? Young?

GIOVANNI. Two gentlemen.

HARALD. But the ladies; who are they, dear boy?

GIOVANNI. Countess Matilda and her daughter.

LANDOLF [*amazed*]. What? [*Pause*] What's that?

ORDULF [*also amazed*]. The Countess, you say?

GIOVANNI. Yes, yes, the Countess!

HARALD. And the two men, dear boy?

GIOVANNI. I don't know.

HARALD [*to* BERTOLD]. Landolf told you we have form without content in here, but keep your eyes open, dear boy.

ORDULF. The Pope has sent a whole *bevy* of ambassadors! We'll have fun all right.

GIOVANNI. Will you let me speak?

HARALD. Speak! [*Pause*] Speak, dear boy!

GIOVANNI. Well, one of the two men seems to be a doctor.

LANDOLF. Oh, sure, we're used to *them*.

HARALD. Many thanks, Bertold, you bring us luck!

LANDOLF. You'll see how we'll manage *him*.

BERTOLD. I'm walking into a fine old mess, I can see that.

GIOVANNI. Now, listen. They'll be coming into this room.

LANDOLF [*in amazement and consternation*]. What? Is that true? Even she? The Countess will come in here?

HAROLD. This is content—with a vengeance, dear boy.

LANDOLF. This'll be a real tragedy!

BERTOLD [*his curiosity aroused*]. But why? What are you talking about?

ORDULF [*pointing to the portrait*]. The Countess is the woman in the portrait.

LANDOLF. Her daughter is engaged to the Marquis.

HARALD. But what have they come for? That's the question.

ORDULF. If *he* sees her, there'll be fireworks.

LANDOLF. Maybe he won't recognize her anymore.

GIOVANNI. If he wakes up, you'll just have to keep him in there.

ORDULF. Are you joking? How'd we do that?

HARALD. You know what he's like, dear boy!

GIOVANNI. Good heavens, use force if need be! Those are the Marquis's orders. Now get going! Get going!

HARALD. Yes, we'd better go; he may be awake already.

ORDULF. Let's go.

LANDOLF [*leaving with the others, to* GIOVANNI]. You must explain it all later!

GIOVANNI [*shouting after them*]. Lock the door on that side and hide the key! This other door, too. [*He points to the other door at right.*]

[LANDOLF, HARALD, *and* ORDULF *leave by the second door on the right.*]

GIOVANNI [*to the* TWO VALETS]. You must go, too; go on, that way! [*He points to the first door on the right.*] Lock the door and take the key out of the lock!

[*The* TWO VALETS *leave by the first door on the right.* GIOVANNI *goes to the door on the left and opens it for the* MARQUIS CARLO DI NOLLI.]

MARQUIS. You have given the orders properly, Giovanni.

GIOVANNI. Yes, Marquis. Certainly, Marquis.

[THE MARQUIS *goes out again for a moment to bring the others in. First come*
BARON TITO BELCREDI *and* DR. DIONISIO GENONI, *then* COUNTESS MA-
TILDA SPINA *and her daughter* FRIDA. GIOVANNI *bows and goes out. The*
COUNTESS *is about forty-five, still beautiful and shapely, though she too patently
repairs the inevitable ravages of time with a violent if expert makeup which gives
her the haughty head of a Valkyrie. This makeup stands out in high and painful
relief from her mouth, which is very lovely and very sad. Many years a widow,
she now has* BARON TITO BELCREDI *for friend. Neither she nor other people
have ever taken him seriously, or so it appears. What the* BARON *really means to
her, he alone fully knows. He can therefore laugh if she needs to pretend she
doesn't know, can laugh at the laughter of other people, caused, as it is, by the*
COUNTESS's *jests at his expense. Slim, prematurely gray, a little younger than
she, he has a curious, bird-shaped head. He would be very vivacious if his agil-
ity—which makes him a formidable swordsman and is in itself live enough—
were not actually encased in a sleepy, Arab laziness that comes out in his strange
voice, which is rather nasal and drawling.* FRIDA, *the* COUNTESS's *daughter, is
nineteen years old. Having grown sad in the shade to which her imperious and
showy mother relegates her, living in this shade she is also offended by the easy
gossip which the mother provokes to the detriment of them both equally. And yet,
as luck will have it, she is already engaged—to the* MARQUIS CARLO DI NOLLI,
*a stiff young man, very indulgent toward others, yet rigid and shut up in the
small space of what he thinks he can be, of what he thinks he is worth, in the
world, though at bottom even he doesn't know what this worth is. At any rate
his consternation is great at the many responsibilities which he believes weigh
him down. Yes, the others can talk, the others can have their fun, lucky they. He
cannot. Not that he wouldn't like it. Just that he cannot. He is dressed in the
deepest mourning for the death of his mother.* DR. DIONISIO GENONI *has a
fine, satyr's face, insolent and rubicund, with protruding eyes, a short, pointed
beard that shines like silver. He has refined manners and is almost bald. They
enter in a state of consternation, almost afraid, looking with curiosity about the
room—all except the* MARQUIS. *And at first they speak in low voices.*]

BARON. Splendid, it's very splendid!

DOCTOR. Most interesting, how one can see the madness in the room itself,
    in inanimate objects, it really *is* splendid, quite splendid!

COUNTESS [*who has been looking around the room for her portrait, finding it,
    and moving toward it*]. Ah, so here it is! [*Looking at it from a certain
    distance while different feelings arise within her.*] Yes, ye-es . . . why, look
    . . . heavens . . . [*She calls her daughter.*] Frida, Frida. . . . Look. . . .

FRIDA. Ah! Your portrait?

COUNTESS. No, just look, it's not me at all, it's you!

MARQUIS. It's true, isn't it? I told you so.

COUNTESS. I'd never have believed it—to this extent. [*She shakes with a sudden tremor along the spine.*] Heavens, what a strange sensation! [*Then, looking at her daughter*] What's the matter, Frida? [*Slipping an arm about her waist, she pulls her close.*] Come here, don't you see yourself in me—in that picture?

FRIDA [*with a gasp*]. But it's me, why . . .

COUNTESS. Wouldn't you think so? You couldn't miss it, could you? [*Turning to the* BARON] You look, Tito, and *you* tell me!

BARON [*not looking*]. I say it's not you. I know without looking.

COUNTESS. How stupid, he thinks he's paying me a compliment. [*Turning to the* DOCTOR] You tell me, Doctor! [DOCTOR *starts to come over.*]

BARON [*with his back turned, pretending to speak to him secretly*]. Sss! No, Doctor! For heaven's sake, have nothing to do with it!

DOCTOR [*bewildered, smiling*]. But why not, why not?

COUNTESS. Pay no attention to him, just come. He's insufferable.

FRIDA. Don't you know he's a professional fool?

BARON [*to the* DOCTOR, *seeing him go*]. Watch your feet, watch your feet, Doctor, your feet!

DOCTOR [*as above*]. What's wrong with my feet?

BARON. You've got hobnailed boots on!

DOCTOR. What?

BARON. And you're walking toward four little feet of delicate Venetian glass.

DOCTOR [*laughing out loud*]. What nonsense! There's nothing staggering, it seems to me, in the fact that a daughter resembles her mother . . .

BARON. Crash! Now it's over.

COUNTESS [*exaggeratedly angered, coming toward the* BARON]. What do you mean: Crash! What is it? What has he been saying?

DOCTOR [*sincerely*]. Don't you think I'm right?

BARON [*answering the* COUNTESS]. He said there's nothing staggering in it. While *you* are extremely staggered. Why?—if it's all so natural?

COUNTESS [*still more angered*]. You fool! It's *because* it's so natural. Because it's *not* my daughter. [*Pointing to the canvas*] That is *my* portrait. To find my daughter in it instead of myself is a staggering experience. Believe me, I was quite sincerely staggered, I can't let you say I wasn't!

[*After this violent outburst there is a moment of embarrassed silence.*]

FRIDA [*quite annoyed*]. Always the same story: arguments about absolutely nothing.

BARON [*also quiet, almost with his tail between his legs, apologetically*]. I wasn't saying anything of the sort. [*To* FRIDA.] I simply noticed that, from the outset, *you* weren't . . . staggered like your mother. If *you're* staggered, it's merely because the portrait resembles you so strongly.

COUNTESS. Obviously! Because there's no way for her to see herself in *me*—as I was at her age. Whereas I, the girl in the portrait, can perfectly well see myself in her—as she is now.

DOCTOR. True. A portrait stays just as it is. Fixed! It can't move away from the moment when it was made, a distant moment now, and, for the young lady, a moment without memories. Whereas for her mother it brings back many things: movements, gestures, looks, smiles, things that aren't *in* the portrait at all . . .

COUNTESS. Exactly.

DOCTOR [*continuing, turning to her*]. For you, naturally, the same things are to be found in your daughter, too.

COUNTESS. It's so seldom I give way to my feelings, and when I do, *he* has to come and spoil it for me! Just for the pleasure of hurting me!

DOCTOR [*impressed with his own perspicacity, starts up again in a professional tone, turning to the* BARON]. Resemblance, my dear Baron, oftentimes has its roots in intangibles. On these lines, it seems eminently explicable that . . .

BARON [*to interrupt the lecture*]. Someone might find a resemblance between you and me, my dear professor.

MARQUIS. Drop it now, drop it, I beg you. [*He points to the doors on the right, indicating that someone is there who might hear.*] We've been sidetracked too much already, coming . . .

FRIDA. Of course! With him here . . . [*indicating the* BARON]

COUNTESS [*promptly*]. That's why I so much wished he wouldn't come.

BARON. Now you've had a lot of fun at my expense. Don't be ungrateful!

MARQUIS. Tito, please, that's quite enough. The doctor is with us, and we're here for a very serious purpose. You know how much it means to me.

DOCTOR. Precisely. Now let's see if we can't begin by getting certain points quite clear. This portrait of yours, Countess, may I ask how it comes to be here? Was it a gift from you? Did you make him a present of it— I mean in the days—before . . .

COUNTESS. Oh, no. How could I have given him presents in those days? I was just a girl—like Frida now—and not engaged at that. No, no, I let him have it three or four years after the accident. I let him have it because his [*indicating the* MARQUIS] mother urged me to.

DOCTOR. His [*with a gesture toward the doors on the right, the reference being to* EMPEROR HENRY] sister, that is to say?

MARQUIS. Yes, Doctor: my mother was his sister. She died a month ago. It's for her sake we've come here—the payment of a debt to her, you might say. In the normal course of events, she [*indicating* FRIDA] and I would be traveling . . .

DOCTOR. On business of quite another sort, hm?

MARQUIS. Please! My mother died in the firm conviction that her beloved brother's recovery was imminent.

DOCTOR. You couldn't tell me, perhaps, from what evidence she reached this conclusion?

MARQUIS. I believe it was from certain strange things he said to her not long before she died.

DOCTOR. Strange things? Aha! It would be terribly useful to me to know what those things were, by Jove!

MARQUIS. I don't know myself. I only know Mother came home after that last visit extremely upset. It seems he'd shown her a most unusual tenderness, as if he foresaw the coming end. On her deathbed she made me promise never to neglect him, to make sure that people see him, visit him . . .

DOCTOR. I see. Very good. Now, to begin with . . . Oftentimes the most trivial causes lead . . . well, take this portrait . . .

COUNTESS. Heavens, Doctor, how can you attach such overwhelming importance to the portrait? It happened to make a big impression on me for a moment just because I hadn't seen it in so long.

DOCTOR. Just a minute, please, just . . .

BARON. But it's so. It must have been there fifteen years . . .

COUNTESS. More! More than eighteen by now!

DOCTOR. I beg your pardons, but you don't yet know what questions I'm going to ask. I set great store—very great store—by those two portraits. I fancy they were painted before the famous—and most unfortunate—cavalcade, isn't that so?

COUNTESS. Why, of course.

DOCTOR. So it was when he was . . . normal . . . quite . . . sane . . . that's what I'm really getting at.—Was it he who suggested having it painted—to you?

COUNTESS. No, no, Doctor. Lots of us were having them done. I mean, of those who took part in the cavalcade. They were something to remember it by.

BARON. I had one of me done!

COUNTESS. We hardly waited for the costumes to be ready!

BARON. Because, you see, it was proposed to collect them all in the drawing room of the villa that the cavalcade came from. As a memorial. A whole gallery of pictures. But afterward each of us wanted to keep his own picture for himself.

COUNTESS. As for mine, as I told you, I let *him* have it—and without very much regret—because his mother . . . [*indicating the* MARQUIS *again*]

DOCTOR. You don't know if he actually asked for it?

COUNTESS. No, I don't. Perhaps he did. Or perhaps it was his sister—as a loving gesture . . .

DOCTOR. Just one other point: the cavalcade—was it his idea?

BARON [*promptly*]. Oh, no! It was mine!

DOCTOR. Now, please . . .

BARON. The idea was mine, I tell you! After all, there's nothing to boast of in *that*—seeing how it all turned out! It was . . . oh, I remember it well: one evening, early in November, at the club, I was leafing through an illustrated magazine, a German one—just looking at the pictures, you understand, I don't know German—and there was a picture of the German Emperor in . . . what was the university town he'd been a student in?

DOCTOR. Bonn, Bonn.

BARON. Possibly, Bonn. He was on horseback and dressed in one of the strange traditional costumes of the oldest student fraternities. He was followed by a cortege of other students of noble birth, also on horseback and in costume. Well, the idea came to me from that picture. I should have told you some of us at the club had been thinking of possible masquerades for the next carnival. I proposed this . . . historical cavalcade. Historical, in a manner of speaking. It was really a Tower of Babel: each of us was to choose a character, from this century or that, king or emperor or prince, with his lady beside him, queen or empress. All were to be on horseback. With the horses harnessed and dressed up—in the style of the period of course. Well, my proposal was accepted.

DOCTOR. So *he* chose the character of Henry the Fourth?

COUNTESS. Because—thinking of my own name—and, well, not taking the whole thing any too seriously—I said I'd like to be Countess Matilda of Tuscany.

DOCTOR. I don't . . . I don't see the connection . . .

COUNTESS. I didn't understand it myself in the beginning—I just heard him saying, "Then I'll be at your feet at Canossa—like Henry the Fourth." Oh, yes, I knew about Canossa, but to tell the truth I didn't remember much of the story, and it made quite an impression on me when I studied it. I found I was a loyal and zealous friend of the Pope in the fierce struggle he was waging against the German Empire. I now understood why *he* wanted to be next to me in the cavalcade—as the Emperor.

DOCTOR. Ah! You mean because . . .

COUNTESS. . . . because I'd chosen to present his implacable enemy.

DOCTOR. Ah! Because—

BARON. Because he was courting her all the time! So she [*indicating the* COUNTESS] naturally . . .

COUNTESS [*stung, fierily*]. Yes, naturally! I *was* natural in those days . . .

BARON [*pointing to her*]. You see: she couldn't abide him!

COUNTESS. That's not true! I didn't even dislike him. Just the opposite! But with me, if a man wants to be taken seriously—

BARON [*finishing her sentence*].—he gives the clearest proof of his stupidity!

COUNTESS. Don't judge others by yourself, Baron. *He* wasn't stupid.

BARON. But then *I* never asked you to take me seriously.

COUNTESS. Don't I know it! But with him it was no joke. [*Changing her tone and turning to the* DOCTOR.] My dear Doctor: a woman has a sad life, a silly life. And some time or other it's her lot to see a man's eyes fixed upon her, steady and intense and full of—shall we say?—the promise of enduring sentiment! [*She bursts into a harsh laugh.*] What could be funnier? If only men could see their looks of enduring sentiment!—I've always laughed at them. More at *that* time than any other.—And let me tell you something: I can still laugh at them, after more than twenty years.—When I laughed like that at *him*, it was partly from fear, though. Perhaps one could have believed a promise in *those* eyes. It would've been dangerous, that's all.

DOCTOR [*with lively interest and concentration*]. Aha! I'd be interested to know about *that*.—Why dangerous?

COUNTESS [*with levity*]. Because he wasn't like the others. And because I too am . . . I can't deny it . . . I'm a little . . . more than a little, to tell the truth, more than a little [*she searches for a modest word*] intolerant, that's the word. I don't like stuffiness, I don't like people who take life hard.—Anyway, I was too young at that time, you understand? And I was a woman: I couldn't help champing at the bit.—It would have needed *courage,* and I didn't have any.—So *I* laughed at him, too. With remorse. With real self-hatred eventually—my laughter mingled with the laughter of fools, and I knew it. With the laughter of all the fools who made fun of him.

BARON. More or less as they do of me.

COUNTESS. My dear, you make people laugh at your . . . your perpetual affectation of self-abasement—they laughed at him for the opposite reason: it makes a difference, hm?—And, with you, people laugh right in your face!

BARON. Better than behind my back, *I* say.

DOCTOR [*coughing nervously*]. Ahem, yes, um . . . he was already rather . . . strange . . . exalted, as it were—if I've been following you properly?

BARON. Yes. But after a very curious fashion, Doctor.

DOCTOR. Namely?

BARON. Well, I'd say . . . he was damned cold-blooded about it—

COUNTESS. Cold-blooded? What nonsense! This is how it was, Doctor. He was a little strange, it's true, that was because there was so much life in him. It made him eccentric.

BARON. I don't say this . . . exaltation was just an act. Not at all. He was often genuinely exalted. But I could swear, Doctor: he was looking at himself, looking at his own exaltation. And I believe the same is true of every move he made, however spontaneous: he *saw* it. I'll say more: I'm certain it was this that made him suffer. At times he had the funniest fits of rage against himself.

COUNTESS. That is true.

BARON [*to the* COUNTESS]. And why? [*To the* DOCTOR] As I see it, the lucidity that came from acting all the time . . . being another man . . . shattered, yes, shattered at a single blow the ties that bound him to his own feelings. And these feelings seemed—well, not exactly a pretense, no, they were sincere—but he felt he must give them an intellectual status, an intellectual form of expression—to make up for his lack of warmth and spontaneity—so he improvised, exaggerated, let himself go, that's about it, to deafen his own ears, to keep his eyes from seeing himself. He seemed fickle, silly, and sometimes . . . yes, ridiculous, let's face it.

DOCTOR. Was he . . . unsociable?

BARON. Not in the least. He was a regular fellow. He was famous for his *tableaux vivants,* he was always getting up dances, benefit perform-ances, all just for fun, of course. He was an awfully good actor, believe me.

MARQUIS. And he's become a superb and terrifying one—by going mad.

BARON. Even before that. I still remember how—when the accident hap-pened—and he fell from his horse, you know—

DOCTOR. He hit the back of his head, didn't he?

COUNTESS. Oh, what a horror! He was next to me. I saw him between the horse's hooves. The horse reared up—

BARON. At first we'd no idea any great harm was done. There was a stop—a bit of a scrimmage in the cavalcade—people wanted to know what had happened. . . . But he'd been picked up and carried into the villa.

COUNTESS. There was *nothing,* you understand: not a sign of a wound, not one drop of blood.

BARON. We all believed he'd merely fainted—

COUNTESS. —so, about two hours later, when—

BARON [*nervously*].—that's right, he reappeared in the hall of the villa—this is, what I was going to say—

COUNTESS. His face at this moment! I saw the whole thing in a flash.

BARON. No, no, *that's* not true, nobody had the least idea—

COUNTESS. You didn't—you were all behaving like madmen!

BARON. Everyone was performing his own part! As a joke! Oh, it was a real Tower of Babel—

COUNTESS. You can imagine our horror, can't you, Doctor, when we real-ized *he* was playing his part—in earnest?

DOCTOR. Oh, so he too . . .

BARON. Exactly. He entered. Came into the midst of us. We assumed he'd recovered and that he was just acting—like the rest of us . . . only better—he was a fine actor, as I told you—in short, we assumed he was joking.

COUNTESS. Some of the others started fooling with him, jostling, fighting . . . and at a certain point he was hit . . .

BARON. At that instant . . . —he was armed—he drew his imperial sword and bore down on a couple of us. What a moment! Scared the pants off us.

COUNTESS. I shall never forget the scene: all those masked faces, distorted, panic-stricken, turned toward that terrible mask, which was now no mask at all, but the very face of lunacy!

BARON. The Emperor! It was Henry the Fourth himself in a moment of fury!

COUNTESS. His obsession with the masquerade was taking effect, Doctor. He'd been obsessed with it for over a month. And everything he did was an obsession of this sort.

BARON. The things he studied for the purpose! Down to the smallest details . . . minutiae . . .

DOCTOR. Yes, I see. What with the fall, and the blow on the head that caused the damage to his brain, the momentary obsession was perpetuated. Became a fixation, as we say. One can go raving mad, one can become simpleminded . . .

BARON [*to* FRIDA *and the* MARQUIS]. You see the tricks life plays, my dears? [*To the* MARQUIS] You weren't more than four or five. [*To* FRIDA] It seems to your mother that you've taken her place in the portrait though at the time she hadn't even dreamed of bringing you into the world. I have gray hair now. And as for him—[*He clicks finger and thumb.*]—he was hit in the neck—and he's never moved since. He is the Emperor—Henry the Fourth!

DOCTOR [*who has been lost in thought, now takes his hands from before his face as if to focus everyone's attention upon himself, and starts to give his scientific explanation*]. Well, ladies and gentlemen, it all comes down to this . . .

[*But all of a sudden the first door on the right—the one nearest the footlights—opens, and* BERTOLD *emerges, his face very excited.*]

BERTOLD [*rushing in like a man at the end of his tether*]. Excuse me, everybody . . .

[*But he stops directly when he sees the confusion that his entry has created.*]

FRIDA [*with a cry of horror, drawing back.*] My God, it's he!

COUNTESS [*stepping back, upset, with an arm raised so as not to see him*]. It's he. He?

MARQUIS [*promptly*]. No, no, no! Don't be excited!

DOCTOR [*astonished*]. Then who is it?

BARON. A fugitive from the masquerade!

MARQUIS. He's one of the four young fellows we keep here to . . . um, back him up in his lunacy.

BERTOLD. I beg your pardon, Marquis . . .

MARQUIS. So you should! I'd given orders for the doors to be locked! No one was to come in!

BERTOLD. Yes, I know, Marquis. But I can't bear it! I've come to beg off! I want to quit!

MARQUIS. Ah! So you're the one who was to start work this morning?

BERTOLD. Yes, Marquis. But I can't bear it, I tell you—

COUNTESS [*to the* MARQUIS *in lively consternation*]. Then he *isn't* calm—you said he was!

BERTOLD [*promptly*]. That's not it, madam, it isn't him! It's my three comrades. You say they "back him up," Marquis. Back him up! They don't back him up—because it's them that's mad! I come here for the first time, and instead of helping me, Marquis . . .

[LANDOLF *and* HARALD *come to the same door on the right, in haste, anxiously, but stopping at the door.*]

LANDOLF. May we come in?

HARALD. May we, dear Marquis?

MARQUIS. Come in then! But what on earth is the matter? What are you all up to?

FRIDA. O God, I'm going, I'm scared out of my wits! [*She starts to go toward the door on the left.*]

MARQUIS [*who at once holds her back*]. No, no, Frida!

LANDOLF. Marquis, this dumbbell . . . [*indicating* BERTOLD]

BERTOLD [*protesting*]. No: thanks very much, my friends! I'm not staying!

LANDOLF. What do you mean, you're not staying?

HARALD. He's ruined *everything*, Marquis, running in here like this! Ts, ts, ts!

LANDOLF. He's driven him absolutely crazy. We can't keep him in there any longer. He's given orders for this fellow's arrest. Wants to pass judgment on him. From the throne. What's to be done?

MARQUIS. Lock the door of course! Go and lock that door!

[LANDOLF *starts to do so.*]

HARALD. But Ordulf won't be able to hold him all by himself!

LANDOLF [*stopping*]. Marquis, if we could just announce your visit: it would be a distraction for him. Have you gentlemen thought what you'll wear in his presence . . .

MARQUIS. Oh. Yes, we've thought the whole thing out. [*To the* DOCTOR] Doctor, if you think we can make the call at once. . . .

FRIDA. I won't, I won't, Carlo! I'm leaving. You come with me, Mama, please!

DOCTOR. Tell me, Marquis . . . he won't be armed, will he?

MARQUIS. Armed? Of course not, Doctor. [*To* FRIDA] Forgive me, Frida, but these fears of yours are really childish. You wanted to come . . .

FRIDA. I didn't! I didn't at all: it was Mother!

COUNTESS [*firmly*]. Well, I'm ready! So what are we to do?

BARON. Is all this dressing up really necessary?

LANDOLF. Oh, yes, Baron, it's essential! Unhappily, he just sees *us*. . . [*He shows his costume.*] He *mustn't* see you gentlemen in modern dress!

HARALD. He'd think it was some devilish travesty, dear Baron!

MARQUIS. Just as these men seem a travesty to you, to him *we*—in our modern clothes—would seem a travesty.

LANDOLF. And maybe it wouldn't much matter, Marquis, only he'd think it was the work of his mortal enemy!

BARON. The Pope?

LANDOLF. Right. He says he's a pagan.

BARON. The Pope a pagan? Not bad!

LANDOLF. A pagan who conjures up the dead! He accuses him of all the black arts. Lives in constant fear of him.

DOCTOR. Ha! Persecution mania!

HARALD. Oh, he'd be furious, dear sir—

MARQUIS [*to the* BARON]. But you don't have to be there, if I may say so. We'll leave that way. It's enough if the doctor sees him.

DOCTOR. You mean . . . just me?

MARQUIS. They'll be present. [*Indicating the three young men.*]

DOCTOR. It's not that . . . I mean, if the Countess . . .

COUNTESS. That's right: *I* want to be there! I want to see him!

FRIDA. But why, Mother? Come with us, do!

COUNTESS [*imperiously*]. Leave me alone, I came for this! [*To* LANDOLF.] I shall be his mother-in-law, Adelaide.

LANDOLF. Marvelous. Yes. Adelaide, the Empress Bertha's mother. Marvelous! Your ladyship need only put on a cloak—to hide these clothes. And the ducal crown on your head, of course. [*To* HARALD.] Go on, Harald, go on!

HARALD. Just a moment, dear boy, what about this gentleman? [*indicating the* DOCTOR]

DOCTOR. Oh, yes . . . they told me the Bishop, I believe . . . the Bishop of Cluny.

HARALD. You mean the Abbot, dear sir? That'll be simply divine: the Abbot of Cluny!

LANDOLF. He's been here so often before . . .

DOCTOR [*astonished*]. He's been here before?

LANDOLF. Don't be afraid, sir. I only mean it's an easy disguise and . . .

HARALD. And it's been used *often,* dear sir.

DOCTOR. But . . . but . . .

LANDOLF. No, no, he won't remember. It's the clothes he looks at—not the man inside them.

COUNTESS. That'll be just as well. For me, too.

MARQUIS. You and I'll be going, Frida. You come with us, Tito.

BARON. What? Oh. No, no, if she stays, um, [*indicating the* COUNTESS] I'll stay, of course.

COUNTESS. I don't need you in the least, my dear Baron.

BARON. I didn't say you needed me! But you're not the only one who wants to see *him.* Surely I can stay if I want?

LANDOLF [*helping out*]. Yes, um, maybe it's better if there are three!

HARALD. Then the gentleman will surely—

BARON. Yes, I'll need a disguise. Make it an easy one.

LANDOLF [*to* HARALD]. I have it! *He* can be from Cluny, too.

BARON. From Cluny; how do you mean?

LANDOLF. The cassock of a monk from Cluny Abbey. He can be in attendance on the Abbot. [*Still to* HARALD] Now, go, go! [*To* BERTOLD] You go too, and keep out of sight all day today! [*But as soon as he sees him going*] Wait! Bring the clothes he gives you! [*To* HARALD] And you go and announce the arrival of his mother-in-law and the Abbot of Cluny.

HARALD. It shall be done, dear boy.

[HARALD *shepherds* BERTOLD *out by the first door on the right.*]

MARQUIS. Now we can go, Frida.

[*With* FRIDA *he leaves by the door on the left.*]

DOCTOR [*to* LANDOLF]. I take it he should think rather well of me—when I'm the Abbot of Cluny?

LANDOLF. Quite right, you can count on it, sir. The Abbot has always been received with great respect. So have you: *you* needn't worry either, my lady. He hasn't forgotten it was due to the intercession of the two of you that he was admitted to the castle at Canossa and brought before the Pope, who hadn't *wanted* to receive him at all. Kept him waiting in the snow for two days—he almost froze.

BARON. What about me, may I ask?

LANDOLF. You, sir? Oh, yes. You should, um—stand deferentially apart.

COUNTESS [*irritated, very nervous*]. Oh, why didn't you leave?

BARON [*quietly, but nettled*]. You're certainly very worked up over . . .

COUNTESS [*with pride*]. I am as I am! Leave me in peace!

[BERTOLD *returns with the clothes.*]

LANDOLF [*seeing him enter*]. Oh, good, here are the clothes!—This cloak for the Countess.

COUNTESS. Wait, I must take my hat off. [*She does so and gives it to* BERTOLD.]

LANDOLF. Put it over there, Bertold. [*Then to the* COUNTESS, *preparing to place the ducal crown on her head.*] May I, Countess?

COUNTESS. But, heavens, isn't there a mirror here?

LANDOLF. There are mirrors in there. [*He points through the left entrance.*] If your ladyship would prefer to put it on yourself?

COUNTESS. Oh, yes, it'll be much better, give it to me, it won't take a minute.

[*She takes the hat back and goes out with* BERTOLD, *who is carrying the crown and the cloak. In the meantime the* DOCTOR *and the* BARON *put on the monks' cassocks as best they can.*]

BARON. Well, I must say, I never expected to be a Benedictine monk! Think what a heap of money this madness is costing!

DOCTOR [*defensively*]. Oh, well, my dear Baron, lots of other kinds of madness cost . . .

BARON. Surely, if you have a fortune to put into them!

LANDOLF. Yes, indeed. In there we have an entire wardrobe of costumes of the period. Tailored to perfection after ancient models. It's my special job—I commission theatrical costumers, experts. It costs plenty.

[*The* COUNTESS *reenters, wearing cloak and crown.*]

BARON [*immediately, in admiration*]. Ah, magnificent, truly royal!

COUNTESS [*seeing the* BARON *and bursting out laughing*]. Good God, no! Take it off! You're impossible! You look like an ostrich in monk's feathers!

BARON. Well, look at the doctor for that matter!

DOCTOR. Don't be hard on *me*, Countess.

COUNTESS. Oh, you'll do, *you're* all right. [*To the* BARON] But you're ludicrous!

DOCTOR [*to* LANDOLF]. You have many receptions here then?

LANDOLF. It depends. Many times he gives orders for such and such a person to be presented to him. Then we have to hunt up someone who'll serve the purpose. Women, too . . .

COUNTESS. Ah! Women, too?

LANDOLF. At one time there were rather a lot of women.

BARON [*laughing*]. Wonderful! In costume? [*Indicating the* COUNTESS.] Like that?

LANDOLF. Well, you know: any women who'd . . .

BARON. Who'd serve the purpose? I see! [*With innuendo, to the* COUNTESS] Take care, it may get dangerous for you!

[*The second door on the right opens and* HARALD *appears. First he gives a furtive sign to stop all conversation in the room. Then he announces, solemnly*]

HARALD. His Majesty the Emperor!

[*First, the* TWO VALETS *enter, taking up their positions at the foot of the throne. Then, between* ORDULF *and* HARALD, *who hold themselves back a little, deferentially,* EMPEROR HENRY *enters. He is nearly fifty, very pale, and already gray at the back of his head—while on the temples and forehead he seems blond because of very obvious, almost childish hair dye. High on each cheek, in the midst of that tragic pallor, is a patch of red, doll makeup, this too very obvious. Over his regal habit he wears a penitent's sack, as at Canossa. His eyes are characterized by a horrifying, convulsive fixity. At the same time he expresses the attitude of a penitent who wishes to be all humility and repentance. One feels that the humility is as ostentatious as the humiliation is deserved.* ORDULF *carries the imperial crown in both hands,* HARALD *the scepter and eagle and the globe and cross.*]

HENRY [*bowing first to the* COUNTESS, *then to the* DOCTOR]. My Lady . . . My Lord Abbot . . . [*He then looks at the* BARON, *starts to bow to him, too, but turns to* LANDOLF, *who has gone over to his side, and asks, suspiciously, and in an undertone*] Is it Peter Damian?

LANDOLF. No, your Majesty, it's a monk of Cluny: he came with the Abbot.

HENRY [*turns to scrutinize the* BARON *with increasing suspicion and, noting that the latter, hesitant and embarrassed, turns to the* COUNTESS *and the* DOCTOR *as if to take counsel from their eyes, draws himself up very straight and shouts*]. It is the Pope's henchman Father Damian—It's no use, Father, looking at her like that! [*Suddenly turning to the* COUNTESS *as if to ward off a danger*] I swear, my lady, I swear to you, my mind is changed toward your daughter, though I confess that I'd have divorced her if he [*indicates the* BARON] hadn't come to stop me. Oh, yes: there were people prepared to favor such a divorce. The Bishop of Mainz would have arranged it in return for one hundred and twenty farms. [*Steals a look, rather perplexed, at* LANDOLF *and then sud-*

denly says] But at this time I should say nothing against the bishops. [*Humble now, he is in front of the* BARON.] I'm grateful to you, believe me, Peter Damian, I'm glad you stopped me!—My whole life is made up of humiliations! My mother, Adalbert, Tribur, and now Goslar with my young men of the lower aristocracy! [*Of a sudden he changes his tone and speaks like someone who, in a clever parenthesis, runs through a part he is rehearsing.*] But it doesn't matter! Clarity in one's ideas, insight, firmness in behavior, and patience in adversity! [*Then he turns to them all and with contrite gravity says*] I know how to correct my errors, and I abase myself even before you, Peter Damian! [*Bows low to him, and then stays with his back bent, as if under the impulsion of an oblique suspicion. It is new, but it makes him add, almost in spite of himself, in a threatening tone*] Except that it was you who started the obscene rumor about my mother Agnes and Henry, Bishop of Augsburg!

BARON [*since* HENRY *stays bent over, with one finger pointed threateningly at him, places his hands on his breast and then speaks in denial*]. No . . . no, it was not . . .

HENRY [*straightening up*]. You say it wasn't? Sheer infamy! [*Glares at him and then says*] I wouldn't have thought you could! [*Approaches the* DOCTOR *and pulls at his sleeve a little, winking with some cunning.*] It's them! It always is, isn't it, my Lord Abbot?

HARALD [*quietly, whispering, as if prompting the* DOCTOR]. That's it: the rapacious bishops!

DOCTOR [*turned toward* HARALD, *trying to stick to his "part"*]. Oh, them . . . of course, them!

HENRY. They were insatiable! When I was a little child, my Lord Abbot— even an emperor has a childhood—he doesn't know he's an emperor in fact—he's just a kid at play, letting time go by . . . I was six years old and they snatched me from my mother and made use of me against her without my knowing, against her and against the dynasty itself, profaning, robbing, marauding, one greedier than the other— Hanno greedier than Stefan, Stefan greedier than Hanno!

LANDOLF [*in a persuasive undertone, to get his attention*]. Your Majesty . . .

HENRY [*turning of a sudden*]. You're right! At this time I shouldn't speak ill of the bishops.—But this infamous slander against my mother, my Lord Abbot, goes beyond the bounds! [*Melting, as he looks at the* COUNTESS] And I may not even weep for her, my Lady.—I turn to you, you are a mother, you must feel it here. [*Indicates the pit of his stomach*] She came from her convent to seek me out a month ago now. They had told me she was dead. [*Sustained pause, dense with emotion.*

Then with a most mournful smile] I cannot mourn her because if you
are here and I am dressed like this [*shows his sackcloth*] it means I am
twenty-six years old.

HARALD [*almost in an undertone, sweetly, to comfort him*]. It means she is still
alive, your Majesty.

ORDULF [*in the same manner*]. And still in her convent.

HENRY [*turns to look at them*]. True. So I can postpone my grief to another
occasion. [*Almost coquettishly he shows the* COUNTESS *the dye on his
hair.*] Look, I'm still blond . . . [*Then quietly, confidentially*] for you!—
I wouldn't need it, but externals do help. Milestones of time, aren't
they, my Lord Abbot? [*He returns to the* COUNTESS *and, observing her
hair*] Ah, but I see that . . . you too, my Lady . . . [*He winks, makes an
expressive sign with one hand as if to say her hair is false—but without a
hint of scorn, rather with mischievous admiration.*] Heaven keep me from
amazement or disgust!—O vanity of human wishes: we try to ignore
the obscure and fatal power that sets limits to our will! What *I* say
is, if one is born and died—did you wish to be born, Lord Abbot,
did you will your own birth? I didn't—and between birth and death,
both of them independent of our will, so many things happen that
we all wish wouldn't happen. Willy-nilly, we resign ourselves to
them.

DOCTOR [*just to say something while he scrutinizes* HENRY]. It's true, alas!

HENRY. But when we're not resigned, we always start wishing and willing!
A woman wishes to be a man, an old man wishes to be young. . . .
None of us is lying, there's no conscious deception in it, it's simply
this: in entire good faith we are fixed in some fine conception of ourselves, as in a shell or a suit of armor. However, my lord, while you
keep this firm grip on yourself, holding onto your holy cassock with
both hands, something is slipping away from you unnoticed, slither-
ing down your sleeves, gliding off like a serpent. That something is
LIFE, my lord. And when you see your life suddenly taking shape,
coagulating outside you in this way, you are surprised. You despise
yourself, you're furious with yourself. And the remorse, the remorse!
How many times I've seen my own remorse—with a face that was my
own and yet so horrible I couldn't behold it! [*He returns to the*
COUNTESS.] Has this never happened to you, Countess? You can recall being always the same, can you? But, once upon a time, I tell you
. . . how can it be? How *could* you do such a thing? [*He looks her so
sharply in the eyes, she nearly faints.*] Such a thing as . . . precisely . . .
we understand each other. But don't worry, I won't breathe a word to

anyone! And you, Peter Damian, how could you be a friend to *that* man . . .

LANDOLF [*as above*]. Your Majesty . . .

HENRY [*at once*]. No, no, I won't name him, I know it would be too annoying for you. [*Turning on the* BARON, *as if by stealth*] What an opinion, what an opinion you had of him, eh?—All the same, every one of us clings to his idea of himself—like a man who dyes his hair when he grows old. What if the color of the dye in my hair cannot, for you, be that of my real hair? You, Lady, certainly don't dye your hair to deceive others or even yourself. You only deceive—and ever so little at that—your own image in the glass. I do it as a joke. You do it in earnest. But, however much in earnest, you too are in disguise, Lady, and I don't mean the venerable crown that rings your forehead and which I bow before, I don't mean your ducal mantle, I mean you wish to fix a memory in your mind, artificially, the memory of your blond hair as it was when, one day, it pleased you—or of your dark hair if you were dark—the fading image of your youth. With you it's different, isn't it, Peter Damian? You're not interested in *fixing* your memories, are you? For you, to remember what you have been, what you have done, is but to recognize the realities of the past which have lived on inside you, isn't that so? Like a dream. Like a dream! *My* memories are like that too, inexplicable to me as I think them over. . . . Oh, well, don't be amazed, Peter Damian: it'll be the same tomorrow with your life of today! [*Suddenly getting into a rage and seizing his sackcloth*] This sackcloth here! [*With almost fierce joy he begins to take it off while* HARALD *and* ORDULF *at once run up in horror to stop him.*] Oh, God! [*Drawing back and taking off the sackcloth he shouts to them.*] Tomorrow, at Brixen, twenty-seven German and Lombard bishops will sign with me the deposition of the Pope!

ORDULF [*with the other two, imploring him to be silent*]. Your Majesty! In God's name!

HARALD [*motioning to him to put the sackcloth on again*]. Take care, your Majesty!

LANDOLF. The Abbot is here with the Countess Matilda to intercede in your favor! [*Furtively makes urgent signs to the* DOCTOR *to say something at once.*]

DOCTOR [*worried*]. Um, yes, of course . . . we came to intercede . . . sire . . .

HENRY [*repenting at once, almost terrified, lets the three of them put the sackcloth back on for him. He pulls it down over him with convulsive hands*].

Pardon! That's it: pardon, pardon, my Lord Abbot, pardon, Lady!
... I swear to you, I feel the weight of the anathema, I do! [*He bends
down with his head in his hands as if expecting something to fall and crush
him. He stays like this a moment. Then, in a changed voice but in an
unchanged position, he says softly and confidentially to* LANDOLF, HAR-
ALD, *and* ORDULF] I don't know why, but somehow I *can't* be humble
before that man! [*Indicating the* BARON *quasi-secretly*]

LANDOLF [*in an undertone*]. But, your Majesty, why do you persist in believing it's Peter Damian? It isn't at all!

HENRY [*looking at them askance, fearfully*]. It isn't Peter Damian?

HARALD. No, no, it's just a poor monk, your Majesty!

HENRY [*mournfully, with plaintive exasperation*]. Perhaps you, Lady, can
understand me better than the others because you are a woman. This
is a solemn and decisive moment. I could, look you, accept the aid of
the Lombard bishops, capture the Pope, run to Rome, and set up a
pope of my own choosing!—But I do not give way to the temptation,
and believe me, I'm right. I know the drift of the times. I know the
majesty of a man who *can* be what he should be, a pope!—Would you
be inclined to laugh at me in my present situation? You're stupid if
you do. You don't understand the political shrewdness which enjoins
this penitential habit upon me. I tell you that, tomorrow, the roles
could be reversed. And then what would you do? Would you laugh to
see a pope in captive's clothes?—No.—Yet the two cases are the same.
Today I wear the mask of a penitent, tomorrow he wears the mask of
a prisoner. Woe betide the man who knows not how to wear his mask,
whether of pope or emperor!—Perhaps his Holiness is, at present, a
little too cruel, that's true. Think, Lady, how Bertha—your daughter
and my wife—toward whom, I repeat, my heart is changed [*He turns
suddenly on the* BARON *and shouts in his face as if the latter had said him
nay*] changed, CHANGED—because of the affection, the devotion
she was able to show me in that terrible moment! [*He stops, convulsed
by his angry outburst, and makes an effort to hold himself in, a groan of
exasperation in his throat; then, with sweet and mournful humility, he
turns again to the* COUNTESS.] She has come with me, Lady. She is
below, in the courtyard. She insisted on following me as a beggar. And
she is frozen, frozen from two nights in the open, in the snow. You
are her mother. May the bowels of your compassion be moved: with
his aid [*indicating the* DOCTOR] beg the Pope's pardon! Induce him to
receive us!

COUNTESS [*trembling, a thin thread of voice*]. Yes, sire, at once, yes . . .

DOCTOR. Yes, sire, we'll do it!

HENRY. And one more thing, one more! [*He summons them round about him and speaks quietly, as if telling a great secret.*] You see me? I am a penitent, and I swear I'll remain one till the Pope receives me. But it's not enough that he receive me. [*Pause. He starts again.*] You know how he can do anything, literally anything, even to calling up the dead? Now, my Lord Abbot, now, my Lady: my real punishment is [*pointing to himself*]—here—or [*pointing to the picture of himself*] if you like, *there*—for it consists in the fact that I cannot cut myself loose from that piece of magic! When the excommunication is revoked, I want you two to make another request of him who can do everything, namely, that he cut me loose from that picture and let me live! Let me live my poor life, the life I've been excluded from, let me have it intact, entire! One cannot go on being twenty-six forever, Lady! I ask this favor for your daughter, too. So that, well disposed as I am toward her, and so deeply affected by her compassion, I may love her as she deserves. That's all. Just that. I am in your hands. [*He bows.*] My Lady! My Lord Abbot!

[*Still bowing, he starts to withdraw by the door through which he entered. The* BARON, *who had come forward a little to hear the proceedings, now turns to go back again to his place.* HENRY *assumes he wishes to steal the imperial crown which is on the throne. Amid general concern and astonishment,* HENRY *runs over, takes it, hides it under his sackcloth, then, with a cunning smile on his lips and in his eyes, he starts bowing again and disappears. The* COUNTESS *is so deeply disturbed she falls into a chair with a crash, almost fainting.*]

ACT II   Scene 1

Another room in the villa. Antique and austere furniture. On the right, about eighteen inches from the floor, is a raised platform very like a church choir, with a ring of wooden pilasters around it, the ring being broken at the front and sides by two steps. On the platform are a table and six stools of the period, one at the head and two on each side. The main door is at the rear. On the left there are two windows looking out on the garden. On the right there is another door.

It is later in the afternoon of the same day. The COUNTESS, *the* DOCTOR, *and the* BARON *are on stage. They are conversing, but the* COUNTESS *stands gloomily on one side, clearly very irritated by what the other two are saying, though she can't help listening because in her present disturbed state everything interests her in spite of herself—so that she can't concentrate on perfecting the plan which hovers before her mind's eye and beckons and is stronger than she is. The words which she hears the others speak attract her attention because she instinctively feels something like a need to be held fast in the present.*

BARON. Well, my dear Doctor, you *may* be right, but that's my impression.

DOCTOR. I won't gainsay you but I rather think it's only . . . well, yes, an impression.

BARON. But he said it in so many words, my dear Doctor! [*Turning to the* COUNTESS] Didn't he, Countess?

COUNTESS [*interrupted in her thoughts, turning*]. Said what? Oh, yes . . . But not for the reason you think.

DOCTOR. He was referring to the clothes we'd put on. [*To the* COUNTESS] Your cloak, our Benedictine cassocks. The whole thing is childish!

COUNTESS [*in a little burst, indignant, again turning*]. Childish? Doctor, what are you saying?

DOCTOR. On the one hand, it's childish—let me speak, Countess, I beg— and on the other hand, it's much more complicated than you could possibly imagine.

COUNTESS. Not at all. To me, it's crystal-clear.

DOCTOR [*with the expert's pitying smile for the nonexpert*]. All the same! One must take account of that special psychology of madmen according to which, you see, one can be sure that the madman sees, sees right through the disguise we confront him with, sees through it and at the same time accepts it, believes in it, like a child, to whom it is both reality and a game. That's why I said it's all childish. But then it's highly complicated, too—in this respect: that he is, he must be, perfectly aware of being—an image. To himself, I mean. In his own eyes. He is an image. The image in the picture. [*He points out left where the picture is.*]

BARON. He said that!

DOCTOR. Precisely.—Now: to this image, other images have just presented themselves. Ours. The images we created in those clothes. Don't imagine he isn't clever and clear-sighted in his lunacy! On the contrary, he was at once aware of the difference between his sort of image and ours. He knew there was in ours an element of deliberate fiction. So he was suspicious. All madmen are fortified by constant, vigilant suspicion. Not that he could see any further than that. He couldn't see

compassion in the way we adapted our game to his. His own game
seemed the more tragic to us the more he tried to reveal that it was
only a game. Coming before us with paint on his cheeks and temples!
To tell us he'd done it on purpose, as a joke! That's how suspicious he
is! And how defiant!

COUNTESS [*again breaking out*]. No, Doctor, that's not it, that's not it at
all!

DOCTOR. What do you mean, that's not it?

COUNTESS [*positively trembling*]. I am quite sure he recognized me.

DOCTOR. Out of the question, out of the question!

BARON [*at the same time as the* DOCTOR]. Nonsense, nonsense!

COUNTESS [*even more positively, almost convulsed*]. He recognized me, I tell
you. When he came over to talk to me at close quarters, he looked me
in the eyes, deep in the eyes, and recognized me!

BARON. But if he talked of your daughter . . .

COUNTESS. He didn't!—It was me, he was speaking of me!

BARON. Perhaps so, when he said . . .

COUNTESS [*at once, without restraint*]. About my dyed hair? But didn't you
notice how he right away added: "or the memory of your dark hair if
you were dark"?—He remembered perfectly well that in those days I
was dark.

BARON. Nonsense, nonsense!

COUNTESS [*taking no notice of him, turning to the* DOCTOR]. My hair is dark
really, Doctor, like my daughter's. *That* is why he started talking of
her!

BARON. But he doesn't even know your daughter; he's never seen her!

COUNTESS. Exactly! You understand nothing. By my daughter, he meant
me. Me—as I was "in those days"!

BARON. Great heavens, this is catching!

COUNTESS [*quietly, with contempt*]. What's catching? You fool!

BARON. Tell me, were you ever his wife? In his lunacy your daughter is his
wife, Bertha of Susa.

COUNTESS. That's precisely it! Not being dark anymore—as he remembers
me—but like this, blond, I was introduced to him as his wife's
mother.—For him my daughter doesn't exist—he never saw her—
you said so yourself. So how can he know if she's blond or dark?

BARON. Oh, he just happened to say dark, sort of in general, for heaven's
sake. Like anyone who wants to tie down a memory of youth with the
color of a girl's hair—blond, brunette, what have you. As ever, you

go off into foolish fantasies.—Doctor, you say *I* oughtn't to have
come here, but what about *her?*

COUNTESS [*is defeated for a moment by the* BARON's *argument. She has been
lost in thought but now she takes hold of herself, the more excited because
she is unsure of herself*]. No . . . no, he was speaking of me . . . He
talked *to* me, *with* me, *of* me . . .

BARON. Not so bad! He never left *me* for a moment, I couldn't *breathe,* and
you say he was talking with you the whole time? Maybe you think he
was alluding to you when he spoke with "Peter Damian"?

COUNTESS [*defiantly, almost breaking the bounds of decorum*]. Who
knows?—Can you explain to me why, from the very first moment, he
felt an aversion to you, to you in particular?

[*The answer must be almost explicitly expressed in the tone of the query. It is:
"Because he understood that you are my lover." The* BARON *gets the point. Dis-
comfited, he stands there emptily smiling.*]

DOCTOR. May I say the reason could also be that only two persons' arrival
had been announced: the Emperor's mother-in-law, Adelaide and the
Abbot of Cluny. When he discovered a third person who hadn't been
announced, suspicion at once . . .

BARON. Of course: suspicion at once made him see in me an enemy, Peter
Damian.—But if *she's* got it into her head that he recognized her . . .

COUNTESS. There's not the least doubt of it!—His eyes told me, Doctor.
There's a way of looking at someone that leaves no doubt whatsoever,
you know that. Perhaps it was only for an instant, but what more do
you want?

DOCTOR. It's entirely possible he could have a lucid interval . . .

COUNTESS. It's possible—you admit it! But that's not all. His talk seemed
to me full, brim-full, of regret for my youth and his, regret for the
horrible thing that happened to him, the thing that has held him here
in a mask he can't cut from his face. But he'd like to, Doctor. Oh, how
he longs to cut loose!

BARON. Yes: and why? He wants to start loving your daughter. Or even
you. Softened, as you think, by the pity you feel for him.

COUNTESS. Which is great, don't make light of it.

BARON. I won't, my dear Countess. I'm sure a faith healer would consider
the miracle more than likely.

DOCTOR. May *I* speak? I don't perform miracles. I am not a faith healer. I
am a doctor. I've been listening to everything that's been said, and I

must repeat what I've told you already. Every elaborate or, as we say, systemized form of lunacy is characterized by what we call analogical elasticity. In him this elasticity is no longer . . . well, um, elastic. It has worked loose, it's limp. In short, the various elements of his lunacy aren't holding together. Years ago he superimposed a second personality upon himself, but now it's proving next to impossible for him to maintain his equilibrium within it—because (and this is very reassuring) of the attacks this second personality is being subjected to. Sudden recollections are wrenching him free from what has been his state of mind hitherto, a state of mind we call incipient apathy—no, that's not right either, it's really a morbid wallowing in reflective melancholy, accompanied by, yes, considerable cerebral activity. Very reassuring, I say. And now, if by the trick—I should say, the shock treatment—we've planned . . .

COUNTESS [*turning toward the window, in the tone of a querulous invalid*]. How is it the car hasn't come back yet? In three and a half hours . . .

DOCTOR [*stunned*]. What do you say?

COUNTESS. The car, Doctor. It's more than three and a half hours now!

DOCTOR [*taking out his watch and looking at it*]. Yes, more than four, for that matter!

COUNTESS. They could have been here half an hour ago at least, that chauffeur . . .

BARON. Perhaps he couldn't find the dress.

COUNTESS. But I told him exactly where it was. [*She is very impatient.*] And where's Frida?

BARON [*leaning out of the window a little*]. Maybe she's in the garden with Carlo.

DOCTOR. He'll talk the fear out of her!

BARON. It isn't fear, Doctor, don't you believe it: it's just that she's annoyed.

COUNTESS. Do me the favor of not asking her to do this! I know how she is!

DOCTOR. Let's wait. Patiently. Anyhow, it'll only take a moment, and it has to be in the evening.—If, as I was saying, our shock treatment shakes him up till, at a single blow, he breaks the threads that still bind this fiction of his together, threads that are slack enough as it is, if, I say, we give him back what he himself demands—"One cannot go on being twenty-six forever," he said—namely, liberation from this punishment, which even he regards as a punishment, in short, if we can help him regain, all at once, his sense of time, his sense of duration—

BARON [*stepping in*]. He will be cured! [*Then underlining his words with irony.*] We shall have cut him loose from his delusion!

DOCTOR. We can hope he'll start going again—like a clock stopped at a certain hour. Here we stand, so to speak, watch in hand, waiting for that watch to start up. A shake, like this! And now let's hope it'll begin to tell the time again, it's been stopped quite long enough.

[*At this point the* MARQUIS *enters by the main door.*]

COUNTESS. Carlo . . . where's Frida? Isn't she here?

MARQUIS. Yes, Countess. She'll be in at any moment.

DOCTOR. The car got back?

MARQUIS. Yes, Doctor.

COUNTESS. He found the dress, that chauffeur?

MARQUIS. Yes, yes, he found it.

DOCTOR. Well, that's a relief!

COUNTESS [*shuddering*]. Then where is it? Where is it?

MARQUIS [*shrugging his shoulders and smiling sadly with the air of one who lends himself unwillingly to a jest that is out of place*]. You'll see soon enough, Countess. [*Indicating the direction of the main entrance.*] Watch . . .

BERTOLD [*presents himself at the threshold solemnly announcing*] Her Ladyship the Countess Matilda—of Canossa!

[*Magnificent and very lovely,* FRIDA *at once enters. She is dressed in her mother's old dress, that is, as the Countess Matilda of Tuscany, and appears a living version of the dead image we have seen in the throne-room portrait.*]

FRIDA [*as she passes the bowing figure of* BERTOLD, *says to him with contemptuous gravity*]. Of Tuscany, Matilda of Tuscany, please! Canossa is just a castle of mine!

BARON [*admiring her*]. Ah! Well! She looks like someone I know!

COUNTESS. Like me!—God in heaven, do you see?—Stop, Frida!—Do you see? It's my picture come to life!

DOCTOR. Yes, yes . . . to a T, to a T! The portrait!

BARON. No question of that, the portrait! Just look at her: what a girl!

FRIDA. Now don't make me laugh or I'll burst. Heavens, what a wasp waist you had, Mama! I could hardly squeeze myself into it.

COUNTESS [*convulsed, helping to fix the dress*]. Wait . . . keep still . . . Now these pleats . . . Does it really feel so tight?

FRIDA. Stifling! For heaven's sake, let's be quick . . .

DOCTOR. Oh, but we must wait till evening . . .

FRIDA. No, no, I can't! I can't hold out that long!

COUNTESS. But why on earth did you put it on so early?

FRIDA. When I saw it . . . the temptation . . . was irresistible . . .

COUNTESS. At least you could have taken me with you. Or had someone help you . . . It's all crumpled—oh, dear! . . .

FRIDA. I know, Mama, but they're such old creases . . . it'd be hard to get them out.

DOCTOR. It doesn't matter, Countess. The illusion is perfect. [*Then, approaching and asking her to stand in front of her daughter, though without concealing her.*] Pardon me. We place them . . . thus . . . at a certain distance . . . will you stand a little further forward? . . .

BARON. And in this way we learn to appreciate the passage of time!

COUNTESS [*turning slightly to him*]. Twenty years after: isn't it a catastrophe?

BARON. You exaggerate, my dear Countess.

DOCTOR [*highly embarrassed, trying to put matters to rights*]. No, no! I meant . . . I mean, the dress . . . I wanted to see . . .

BARON [*laughing*]. For the dress, Doctor, it's *more* than twenty years: it's eight hundred. An abyss. You want to make him jump across? You'll hit him that hard? From here [*pointing to* FRIDA] to here [*pointing to her mother*]. You'll need a basket to pick up the pieces. My friends, just think for a moment: joking aside, for us it's a matter of twenty years, two dresses, and a disguise. But, for him, if, as you say, Doctor, time is fixed, if he's really living back there with her [*indicating* FRIDA] eight hundred years earlier, I tell you the jump will simply make him dizzy, make his head reel. He'll fall in our midst like a . . . [*The* DOCTOR *shakes a finger in dissent.*] You deny it?

DOCTOR. Yes. Life, my dear Baron, renews itself. *Our* life—here—will at once be real—even to him. It will take hold of him and, at a blow, strip him of his illusion and reveal your eight hundred years as a bare twenty. It will be like certain practical jokes—the leap into space, for example, as the Freemasons do it: you think you're making a tremendous jump, then you find you've taken a single step down.

BARON. Now we're onto something. Doctor: look at Frida and her mother. We say youth goes on ahead. We imagine youth to be in front. But it isn't true, is it, Doctor? We oldsters are ahead, we are in front, we are rightly called "advanced in years," for—time is something we have a lot more *of.*

DOCTOR. Except that the past is all the time receding from us.

BARON. No, no, the point is this. They [*indicating* FRIDA *and the* MAR-
QUIS] have still to do what we have already done, they have still to
grow old, they have still to do more or less the same foolish things . . .
The idea that you start out in life ahead of those who've already
started—this is the great illusion, the great untruth! You are no
sooner born than you start dying. He who started first is therefore
furthest along of all, *he* is ahead, *he* is in front. The youngest of men is
our common father Adam. Behold the Countess Matilda of Tuscany:
[*Shows* FRIDA] She is eight hundred years younger than any of us! [*He
makes a low bow before her.*]

MARQUIS. Please, Tito, this is no laughing matter.

BARON. Oh, if you think I'm joking . . .

MARQUIS. Certainly I do, for heaven's sake . . . ever since you arrived . . .

BARON. What? I've even dressed up as a Benedictine . . .

MARQUIS. Why, yes, for a *serious* purpose . . .

BARON. That's what I'm saying . . . if it's been serious for the others . . .
Frida, now, for example . . . [*Then, turning to the* DOCTOR] Doctor, I
swear I still don't understand what you wish to do.

DOCTOR [*annoyed*]. Give me a chance!—Naturally, with the Countess in
the wrong costume—

BARON. You mean, she too must . . .

DOCTOR. Surely; she must wear a dress exactly like that one [*Indicating*
FRIDA'*s*]. The young lady enters, he sees Matilda of Tuscany, then the
Countess enters, and—

BARON. There'll be two Matildas of Tuscany!

DOCTOR. Two Matildas of Tuscany. Precisely. Such is our shock treatment.
After that, the watch starts going again.

FRIDA [*calling him to one side*]. Doctor, one moment, please!

DOCTOR. Here I am. [*He goes over to* FRIDA *and the* MARQUIS *and is explain-
ing things to them during the following dialogue.*]

BARON [*quietly, to the* COUNTESS]. Good heavens, then . . .

COUNTESS [*turning on him with a firm expression*]. Then what?

BARON. Are you really interested? You'll lend yourself to . . . this sort of
thing?

COUNTESS. I owe it to *him!*

BARON. What you're doing is an insult to me, my dear.

COUNTESS. Who's thinking of *you?*

MARQUIS [*coming forward*]. That's it, yes, that's what we'll do . . . [*Turning
toward* BERTOLD] You! Go and call one of the other three, will you?

BERTOLD. Yes, sir. [*He leaves by the main door.*]

COUNTESS. But first we must pretend to take our leave!

MARQUIS. Exactly. I'm sending for a valet to prepare the leave-taking. [*To the* BARON.] *You* needn't bother, of course, you can just stay here.

BARON [*nodding ironically*]. Of course, *I* needn't bother!

MARQUIS. So as not to arouse his suspicions again, you understand?

BARON. I'm a negligible quantity. Of course.

DOCTOR. His certainty that we've gone away must be absolute. Absolute.

[LANDOLF, *followed by* BERTOLD, *enters by the door on the right.*]

LANDOLF. May we come in, Marquis?

MARQUIS. Yes, come in. Now . . . you're Lolo, are you?

LANDOLF. Lolo or Landolf, as you please, Marquis.

MARQUIS. Good. Now look. The Doctor and the Countess are about to take their leave . . .

LANDOLF. Very good. All we need say is that the Pope has agreed to receive him as a result of their entreaties. He's in his apartment, groaning at the thought of what he's been saying. He's penitent, but quite sure the Pope won't oblige him. Will you come in to him? . . . You must be good enough to put those clothes on again . . .

DOCTOR. Yes, let's be going.

LANDOLF. One moment, Doctor. May I make another suggestion? You should say that Countess Matilda of Tuscany implored the Pope to receive him.

COUNTESS. So he did recognize me!

LANDOLF. No! I beg your pardon, Countess. It's because he so fears Matilda—fears her dislike. The Pope was staying in her castle. It's strange—in the version of the story I know—though doubtless you all know the truth of the matter better than I do—there's nothing about Henry being secretly in love with Matilda, is there?

COUNTESS [*at once*]. Nothing at all! Quite the reverse!

LANDOLF. That's what I thought. But *he* says he loved her—he's always saying so . . . —And now he fears that her indignation on this score will hurt him with the Pope.

BARON. We must make him understand she no longer dislikes him.

LANDOLF. That's it! Precisely!

COUNTESS [*to* LANDOLF]. Yes, yes, quite! [*Then, to the* BARON.] Because, in case you didn't know, it was to the prayers of Matilda and the Abbot of Cluny that the Pope yielded. And let me tell you this, my dear Baron: at that time—the time of the cavalcade, I mean—I was going

to exploit this fact—I was going to show him my heart was no longer
so unfriendly to him as he imagined.

BARON. Well, isn't that marvelous, Countess? You're just following history
. . .

LANDOLF. Yes. So my lady could easily spare herself the trouble of wearing
two disguises and present herself from the start, with the Abbot here
[*indicating the* DOCTOR] in the costume of Matilda of Tuscany.

DOCTOR [*at once, with force*]. No! No! For heaven's sake, not that! That
would spoil everything! His impression of the confrontation must be
instantaneous. A sudden blow. No, Countess, let's be going: you will
again appear as his mother-in-law, Adelaide. And we'll take our leave.
The essential thing is that he know we've gone. Come on now, don't
let's waste any more time, there's still plenty to be done.

[*Exeunt the* DOCTOR, *the* COUNTESS, *and* LANDOLF *by the door on the right.*]

FRIDA. I'm beginning to be terribly afraid, Carlo—

MARQUIS. All over again?

FRIDA. Wouldn't it have been better if I'd seen him before? . . .

MARQUIS. Believe me, Frida, there's nothing to it! All you've got to do is
stand there.

FRIDA. But isn't he raving?

MARQUIS. No, no, he's quite calm.

BARON [*with an ironic affectation of sentimentality*]. He's melancholy, poor
chap. Haven't you heard he loves you?

FRIDA. Thank you, but that's *why* I'm afraid.

BARON. He won't want to hurt you!

MARQUIS. And it'll only be a matter of a moment anyway . . .

FRIDA. Yes. But to be in the dark! With him!

MARQUIS. For one moment. And I'll be at your side. And the others will
be in ambush at the door, ready to run to your assistance. As soon as
he sees your mother, understand? As soon as he sees your mother your
part is finished . . .

BARON. I'm afraid what we're doing is like digging a hole in water.

MARQUIS. Oh, don't start *that* again, Tito! I think the doctor's remedy will
work perfectly!

FRIDA. So do I! I can feel it in me already . . . I'm trembling all over!

BARON. That's all very well, my friends, but madmen—little, alas, as they
know it—are blessed with a certain characteristic which we're forgetting—

MARQUIS [*interrupting, annoyed*]. What characteristic is that?

BARON [*forcibly*]. They do not reason things out!

MARQUIS. What's reasoning got to do with it, for heaven's sake?

BARON. Why, what else is he supposed to do but reason out the situation we're confronting him with—seeing her [*indicating* FRIDA] and her mother at the same time? That's how we planned it, hm?

MARQUIS. Not in the least, it's not a matter of reasoning at all. We're confronting him with . . . "a double image of his own fiction." That's what the doctor said.

BARON [*suddenly taking off*]. I've never understood why they graduate in medicine.

MARQUIS [*stunned*]. Who?

BARON. The psychiatrists.

MARQUIS. Heavens above, what should they graduate in?

FRIDA. They're psychiatrists, aren't they?

BARON. They're psychiatrists, my dear: an exact legal definition! And all they do is talk. The best talker, the best psychiatrist. "Analogical elasticity," "the sense of time, of duration!" They tell you right off the bat they can't work miracles—when a miracle is precisely what we need. Of course, the more they say they're not faith healers, the more people believe they're serious—and don't they know it! They don't work miracles—but they always land on their feet—not bad, huh?

BERTOLD [*who has been spying at the door on the right, looking through the keyhole*]. Here they are! They're coming!

MARQUIS. They are?

BERTOLD. I think he wants to show them out . . . Yes, yes, here he is!

MARQUIS. Let's get out then, get out at once! [*Turning to* BERTOLD *before leaving.*] You stay here!

BERTOLD. I'm to stay?

[*Without answering him, the* MARQUIS, FRIDA, *and the* BARON *make their escape by the main door, leaving* BERTOLD *lost and irresolute. The door on the right opens.* LANDOLF *enters first and at once bows. Then the* COUNTESS *enters with cloak and ducal crown as in Act One, the* DOCTOR *in the cassock of the Abbot of Cluny.* EMPEROR HENRY, *in regal robes, is between them. Behind,* ORDULF *and* HARALD.]

HENRY [*continuing what we suppose him to have been saying in the throne room*]. Now I ask you, how could I possibly be clever, as you now describe me, if I'm also considered obstinate . . .

DOCTOR. Obstinate, sire? Nothing of the sort . . .

HENRY [*smiling, pleased*]. For you, I'm really clever?

DOCTOR. Neither obstinate nor clever, sire, no . . .

HENRY [*stops and exclaims in the tone of someone who wishes, benevolently yet ironically, to observe that matters can't rest here*]. My Lord Abbot, if obstinacy is not a vice that consorts with cleverness, I did hope that in denying it to me you might have conceded me a little cleverness instead. I assure you I could use some! But if you insist on keeping it all for yourself . . .

DOCTOR. I? You think me clever, sire?

HENRY. Oh, no, my Lord, what are you saying? You don't seem very clever to me! [*Cutting this short, so he can turn to the* COUNTESS.] With your permission—a word in confidence with our Empress's lady mother. Here on the threshold. [*He draws her a little on one side and with a great air of secrecy anxiously asks her*] Your daughter is very dear to you, is she?

COUNTESS [*lost*]. Why, of course . . .

HENRY. Would you like me to make amends for the grave wrong I have done her—by offering all my love, all my devotion? Of course you mustn't believe what my enemies say about my debauches.

COUNTESS. I don't believe it, no, I never have . . .

HENRY. So you *would* like it?

COUNTESS [*lost again*]. Like—what?

HENRY. You *would* like me to love your daughter again? [*He looks at her and at once adds in a mysterious tone of mingled admonition and pain*] Don't be friendly to Matilda of Tuscany, please don't!

COUNTESS. But I tell you again she has begged the Pope, she has pleaded with him, as much as we have . . .

HENRY [*at once, quiet, trembling*]. Don't say that, don't say that, in heaven's name, don't you see how it affects me?

COUNTESS [*looks at him, then very quietly indeed as if in confidence*]. You love her still?

HENRY [*dismayed*]. Still? You say *still*? How do you know? No one knows, no one *must* know!!

COUNTESS. But wouldn't *she* know? She who has been on her knees for you?

HENRY [*looks at her for a moment, then says*]. Do you love your daughter? [*A short pause. Turns to the* DOCTOR, *laughingly.*] Ah, my Lord, it was only afterward I realized my wife existed, and that was rather late in the day. . . . Even now, well, I suppose I have a wife, yes, I certainly have a wife, but I assure you I hardly ever give her a thought. It may be a sin, but I don't feel her, I don't feel her in my heart. It's an ex-

traordinary thing but her own mother doesn't feel her in her heart
either. She doesn't mean very much to you, does she, Lady, confess!
[*Turning to the* DOCTOR, *in exasperation*] She talks to me of another
woman, *the* other woman. [*Getting more and more excited*] She *insists*
on talking of her, she insists, I can't understand it!

LANDOLF [*humbly*]. Perhaps, Majesty, you have formed an unfavorable
opinion of Matilda of Tuscany and my Lady would like to remove it?
[*Upset at having allowed himself this remark, he at once adds*] I mean of
course at this particular time . . .

HENRY. *You* maintain that she's my friend?

LANDOLF. At this time, yes, your Majesty!

COUNTESS. Yes, of course, that's the reason . . .

HENRY. I see. So you don't believe I love her. I see, I see. No one ever did
believe it, no one ever dreamed of it, so much the better, let's change
the subject. [*He breaks off, turning to the* DOCTOR, *his face and mind
completely different.*] My Lord Abbot, have you noticed? The Pope will
revoke the excommunication on certain conditions. Have you noticed
that these conditions have nothing, nothing to do with the original
reason he had for excommunicating me? Go tell Pope Gregory I'll
settle accounts with him at Brixen! And you, Lady, should you chance
to meet your daughter—let's say down in the courtyard of your
friend's castle—your friend Matilda of Tuscany—well, what shall I
say? Have her come up. And we'll see if I don't succeed in keeping her
at my side: wife and empress. Many women, before now, have come
here telling me, assuring me, they were she—the wife I knew I had
. . . and, well, sometimes I actually tried—there's nothing shameful in
that, is there?—with one's wife—But every one of them, when she
tried to say she was Bertha, that she came from Susa, I don't know
why, burst out laughing! [*As if in confidence*] We were in bed, understand? I didn't have these clothes on. For that matter, well, she had no
clothes on either . . . heavens, it's natural, isn't it? For a man and a
woman? At those moments we don't think who we are, do we? Our
clothes, on the hook, are—phantoms! [*Changing his tone again, to the*
DOCTOR, *in confidence*] In general, my Lord, I think phantoms are
nothing but slight disorders of the spirit, images we don't succeed in
holding within the bounds of sleep. They come out even in the daytime when we're awake and frighten us. I'm always so afraid when I
see them before me at night. A confused mob of images, alighting
from their horses, laughing! Sometimes I'm afraid of my own blood:
it pulses in my arteries like the dull sound of footsteps in distant
rooms in the silence of the night! But enough! I have kept you far

too long on your feet. Your humble servant, Lady. Your servant, my Lord.

[*He has accompanied them to the threshold of the main door. He takes his leave of them and they bow. Exeunt* MATILDA *and the* DOCTOR. *He shuts the door and at once turns. Another change of expression.*]

The clowns, the clowns, the clowns! Like a color organ: touch it and, look! White, pink, yellow, green. . . . And the other fellow, Peter Damian, ha-ha! He's hit, a bull's-eye. He's scared even to appear before me now!

[*He says this with gay, bursting frenzy, pacing and looking first in this direction, then in that, till of a sudden he sees* BERTOLD, *more than astounded and terror-struck by the sudden change. He stops in front of him and points him out to his three comrades, who also are lost in astonishment.*]

Just look at this idiot here! He stands gaping at me with his mouth open! [*Shaking him by the shoulders.*] Don't you understand? Don't you see how I dress them up, how I fool them, how I like to have them parade before me like terrified clowns! What is there to be terrified by? The fact that I tear off the comic mask and reveal all their trappings as mere disguises? As if it were not I who had forced them to wear the mask in the first place—because it pleased me to play the madman!

LANDOLF ⎫ [*their heads swimming, flabbergasted, looking from one to the*
HARALD   ⎬ *other*]. What? What do you say?
ORDULF   ⎭ Then . . . ?

HENRY [*when they speak, turning at once, and shouting imperiously*]. Enough, then, let's have done with it! The whole thing annoys me! [*Then at once, as if on second thought, he isn't satisfied, he can't believe it.*] God, the effrontery of the woman, coming here, to me, now, her gigolo on her tail . . . Pretending they were doing me a favor, coming out of pity, to keep me within bounds—as if I weren't beyond everything already, beyond this world, beyond life, beyond time! The other fellow, their Peter Damian, wouldn't have permitted such presumption, but *they* would. They would: every day, every minute, they claim that other people are what they would have them be. That isn't presumption, is it? Oh, dear no! It's their way of thinking, their way of seeing, of feeling, every man has his own! You have yours, haven't you? By all means. But what can yours be? That of a flock of sheep: miserable, frail, uncertain . . . They profit by this, they make you swallow their way, so you'll see and feel what they see and feel, or at least so they can kid themselves you will. For what, after all, do they manage to impose on you? Words! Words which each of you understands and repeats in his own fashion. That's the way so-called public opinion is formed! Woe betide the man who, one fine day, finds himself labeled with one of the words that people have been repeating. The word Madman for instance. Or the word—what's another example?—the word Idiot. Tell me something: if someone went around persuading people you are as *he* sees you—went around fixing his own judgment of you in the minds of others—could you stand idly by? "Madman, madman!"—I'm not saying right now that I do it as a joke. Earlier, before I hurt my head falling from a horse . . . [*He stops short, noting their agitation, more than ever upset and astounded.*] You're looking each other over? [*With bitter mimicry he mocks their astonishment.*] Ha? Huh? What's the revelation? Am I or am I not?—I'll tell you: I am! I am mad! [*Becoming terrible*] And so, by God, down on your knees, down on your knees before me! [*One by one he forces them to kneel.*] I order you all to kneel before me! That's it! Now touch the floor three times with your foreheads! Down! That's how everyone should be before madmen! [*At the sight of the four kneeling men, he feels his fierce gaiety evaporate at once. He is indignant now.*] Off your knees, you cattle, get up!—You obeyed me when you might have put a straitjacket on me?—Is a word heavy enough to crush a man with? It's a mere nothing, it's . . . like a fly!—Yet words are heavy enough to crush us all. Oh, the weight of the dead!—Here am I. Can you seriously believe Henry the Fourth is still alive? And yet: I speak and give orders to you, the living! I want you that way!—Do you think this a jest, too—the way the dead continue to take part in life? *Here*, yes, it is a jest. But go outside. Into the living world. Day is dawning. Time lies before you. Break of day. The day that lies before us, you say, will be of our own making. Hm? Of your own making? What about tradition then? Time-honored customs? Come on: speak for yourselves. You will not utter a word that has not been uttered thousands of times before. You think you are living? You are remasticating the life of the dead! [*He is now right in front of* BERTOLD, *who by this time is completely stupefied.*] You don't get it, do you, my boy?—What's your name?

BERTOLD. Me? . . . er . . . Bertold.

HENRY. Bertold? You fool! Between the two of us, what's your name?

BERTOLD. My . . . um . . . real name . . . is Fino . . .

[*No sooner have the other three started to give signs to* BERTOLD, *advising and chiding him, than* HENRY *at once turns to silence them.*]

HENRY. Fino?

BERTOLD. Fino Pagliuca, yes sir.

HENRY [*turning again to the others*]. I've heard the names you use among yourselves so many times. [*To* LANDOLF] You are called Lolo?

LANDOLF. Yes, sir. [*Then, with a burst of joy.*] Heavens! . . . So you . . . ?

HENRY [*at once, very abrupt*]. So what?

LANDOLF [*straightaway growing pale*]. Nothing . . . I mean . . .

HENRY. So I'm not mad anymore? No. You see me, don't you?—It's all a joke on those who believe it. [*To* HARALD] I know your name's Franco . . . [*To* ORDULF] And yours—one second now—

ORDULF. Momo.

HENRY. Momo, that's it! A nice state of affairs, hm?

LANDOLF [*still hesitant*]. Then . . . then . . . heavens.

HENRY [*not changing*]. What? No: not in the least! Let's all have a big, long, lovely laugh about it . . . [*And he bursts out laughing.*]

LANDOLF ⎫ [*looking each other over, uncertain, lost between joy and pain*].
HARALD ⎬ He's cured? It's true? What?
ORDULF ⎭

HENRY. Sh, sh! [*To* BERTOLD.] You don't laugh? Are you still offended? I wasn't addressing you in particular, you know.—*Everybody* finds it convenient, understand? Everybody finds it convenient to believe certain people mad—as an excuse for keeping them locked up. You know why? Because they can't bear to hear what they say. What do I say of these people who've just left? That one is a harlot, another a lecher, another an impostor . . . "It's not true! No one can believe it!"—All the same, they listen to me. Terrified. *Why* do they listen—if what I say is untrue? One simply cannot believe the words of madmen. And yet they listen! Their eyes goggling with terror. Why? You tell me, you tell me why. I am calm, look!

BERTOLD. Well, because . . . maybe they think . . .

HENRY. No, my dear fellow, no! Look at me, look me right in the eyes . . . I don't say it's true, don't worry! Nothing is true! But just look me in the eyes!

BERTOLD. Very well, how's that?

HENRY. There: you see, you see! You, too! You have terror in your eyes!—Because you think I'm mad.—That's the proof! [*He laughs.*]

LANDOLF [*representing all four, plucking up courage, exasperated*]. What's the proof?

HENRY. The distress you're all in because again you think I'm mad!—And, by God, you know it! You believed me: up to now you believed I was mad. Didn't you? [*Looking at them for a moment, he sees the alarm they are in.*] You see this distress? You feel how it can turn into terror? Terror at something that takes the ground from under your feet, that deprives you of the air you breathe? You *do* see it, you *must* feel it! For what does it mean to find yourself face to face with a madman, eh? It means being face to face with one who takes what you have painstakingly constructed within yourself, takes it and shakes it, shakes it down to the very foundations! Your logic—the logic of all these constructions of yours—totters!—Well? Who is it that constructs without logic? The madman! Blessed are the mad—they construct without logic. Or with a logic of their own that floats on air like a feather. They chop and change. Like this today, but tomorrow who knows?— You stick to your guns, they take to their heels. Choppers and changers!—You say: this cannot be! For them, anything can be.—You say it's not true, because—because what?—because it doesn't seem true to [*indicating three of them in turn*] you, you, you, or to a hundred thousand others! Then, my dear friends, we'd have to see what seems true to a hundred thousand others, a hundred thousand who're *not* considered mad. We'd have to see what account *they* can give us of the things they agree on—the fruits of their logic. But this I know: when I was a child, the moon in the pond was . . . true . . . to me. Lots of things were true. People told me about them; I believed; and I was happy. Hold fast to whatever you think true today! Hold fast to whatever you think true tomorrow—even if it's the opposite of what you thought true yesterday! Or woe betide you! Woe betide you if, like me, you are swallowed up by a thought—a thought that will *really* drive you mad. You are with another human being, you're at their side, you look into their eyes—how well I remember doing it, that day—and . . . you might as well be a beggar before some door you must never pass through! Open it if you wish: the man who enters is not you, will never be you, will never carry your world within him, the world you see, the world you touch. You don't know the man. He is another person like *any* other person who, from his own impenetrable world, sees you, touches you . . .

[*A long, sustained pause. The shadows in the room begin to thicken, increasing that sense of distress and deepest consternation which fills the four masqueraders, increasing also the distance between them and the great masquerader, who is lost in the contemplation of a terrible misery which is not his alone but everyone's.*

Then he pulls himself together, and, not feeling their presence around him, starts to look for them, and says]

It's been getting dark in here.

ORDULF [*at once, coming forward*]. Shall I go and get the lamp?

HENRY [*with irony*]. The lamp, yes. . . . Do you think I don't know that as soon as I turn my back and go off to bed, oil lamp in hand, you switch the electric light on! Both here and in the throne room!—I pretend not to see it . . .

ORDULF. Ah! Then you want me to . . .

HENRY. No! It would only blind me.—I want my lamp.

ORDULF. Very well, it'll be here at the door, ready. [*He goes to the center door, opens it, goes out, and returns at once with an ancient oil lamp, the kind you hold by a ring on top.*]

HENRY [*taking the lamp and pointing to the table on the platform*]. There, a little light. Sit there, around the table, all of you. No, not like that! In special attitudes, handsome attitudes! [*To* HARALD.] You, like this. [*Putting him in position. Then to* BERTOLD, *putting him in position, too.*] You, like this. That's right. I'll sit here. [*Turning his head toward one of the windows.*] One should be able to say: "O Moon, shed your light on us! Give us one little ray, a pretty one!" The moon is so good for us, so good! For my part I feel the need of the moon. I often spend my time gazing at her from my window. To look at her, who would think she knows eight hundred years have passed and that this man seated at the window moon-gazing cannot really be the Emperor Henry the Fourth? But look, look at the scene: what a picture! a nocturne! "The Emperor Henry with his trusty councillors." Don't you relish that?

LANDOLF [*quietly to* HARALD *so as not to break the spell*]. You see now? To think that it wasn't true . . .

HENRY. True? What?

LANDOLF [*wavering, as if to apologize*]. Nothing . . . I mean . . . [*pointing to* BERTOLD] he's only just started work here—and I was telling him only this morning what a pity it was . . . with us dressed up like this . . . and with all the other fine clothes in the wardrobe . . . and a room like that one . . . [*Pointing to the throne room*]

HENRY. Well? What's a pity?

LANDOLF. That . . . that we never knew . . .

HENRY. That it was all just playacting, a comedy, a jest?

LANDOLF. Because we thought . . .

HARALD [*coming to his assistance*]. It was all done in earnest, dear sir!

HENRY. And wasn't it? Don't you really think it was?

LANDOLF. Well, sir, if you say . . .

HENRY. I say you are fools. Call it a deception, if you wish. The point is you should have been smart enough to accept this deception—for your own sakes. Not just as a play to enact before me or those who came to visit me from time to time. For your own sakes, for your natural selves, day in, day out, before nobody. [*Taking* BERTOLD *by the arms*] For your own sake, my boy, so you can eat, sleep, within a . . . a piece of fiction that's your own—so you can scratch your back when it itches! [*Turning again to all four*] Feeling alive, really alive in the eleventh century, here, at the court of your Emperor, Henry the Fourth! And, from this vantage point, the vantage point of an age long past, sepulchral, yet colorful, to think that nine centuries down the road of time, down, down, the men of the twentieth century live in the utmost confusion. Their life is all strain, all anxiety to know what will happen to them. To see to what issue the crises will come that keep them in such anguish and turmoil. Whereas—you are history already! With me! What has happened to me may be sad, the situations I've found myself in may have been horrendous, oh, yes, there were bitter struggles, painful vicissitudes . . . BUT they are history! They have stopped changing! They cannot change anymore! You understand? Fixed forever! You can take your ease and marvel at every effect as it follows from every cause in perfect obedience, with perfect logic, at the unfolding of every event—precise and coherent in every particular! The pleasure of history, in fact, the pleasure of history! And how great that is!

LANDOLF. Wonderful!

HENRY. Wonderful! But over with. Now that you know, I can't go through with it. [*He takes the lamp in order to go to bed.*] Nor can you, for that matter. If you've never understood the real reason. It gives me nausea to think of! [*Almost to himself, with violent, contained rage*] By God, I'll make her sorry she came! In a mask of a mother-in-law, pah! With him as Father Abbot!—And they bring me a doctor with them—to study me! Who knows if they don't even hope to cure me? . . . Clowns!—How nice it would be to smack one of them in the face, at least one—*that* one!—A famous swordsman, is he? He'll run me through, will he? We'll see about that. [*He hears a knocking at the center door.*] Who is it?

GIOVANNI's *voice. Deo Gratias!*

HARALD [*delighted at the thought that here's a trick one could still play*]. It's Giovanni the butler. He comes here every evening. As a monk!

ORDULF [*rubbing his hands, lending himself to the jest*]. Yes, let him do his act as usual, sir, let him do his act!

HENRY [*at once severe*]. You fools! Play a prank on a poor old man who's doing this for love of me? Why?

LANDOLF [*to* ORDULF *and* HARALD, *whispering*]. It must be as if it were true, don't you see?

HENRY. Oh, very good—*as if it were true*. Only in that way does the truth cease to be a jest. [*He goes and opens the door and lets* GIOVANNI *in. The latter is dressed as a humble friar with a roll of parchment under his arm.*] Come in, Father, come in! [*Then, taking on a tone of tragic gravity and deep resentment*] All the documents of my life, of my reign, that were favorable to me have been destroyed, deliberately destroyed, by my enemies. All that has escaped destruction is this one—my life, as written by a humble monk who is devoted to me. And you would laugh at him? [*With love in his eyes, he turns again to* GIOVANNI *and invites him to sit at the table.*] Be seated, Father, sit there. With this lamp beside you. [*He places at his side the lamp he is still carrying.*] Now write, write!

GIOVANNI [*unrolls the parchment and prepares to write from dictation*]. Ready, your Majesty!

[*The lights fade, but go up almost at once on*]

Scene 2

[HENRY *is just finishing the dictation.*]

HENRY. ". . . the proclamation of peace issued at Mainz was of benefit to the poor and good while it did harm to the bad and powerful. It brought prosperity to the former, hunger and poverty to the latter." [*Henry's voice is tired. He notices that* GIOVANNI *and the four young men are drowsy. Quietly*] Enough! [*As he rises, the five others are suddenly alert and on their feet.*] No, No! Just stay where you are, I can manage! Good night! [*They continue to watch him as he leaves the room.*]

[*At this point the revolving stage starts to rumble. The throne room set is being brought on.* HENRY *is on the turntable walking in the direction opposite to its*] *movement and at the same speed; hence, in relation to the audience, he is stationary. The rumbling stops; we are in the throne room.**

In the dark, the back wall is hardly visible. The canvases have been removed from the portraits. Within the frames which are now in the two empty niches, in exact imitation of the two portraits, are FRIDA, *dressed as Matilda of Tuscany* [*i.e. as we saw her in Scene 1*] *and the* MARQUIS *dressed as Henry the Fourth.*]

FRIDA [*as soon as she sees* HENRY *has just passed the throne, whispering from her niche like someone who feels she's about to faint with fright*]. Henry!
. . .

HENRY [*stopping at the sound, as if by some treachery he has suddenly received a knife in his back. In his alarm he turns his face toward the back wall and instinctively starts to raise his arms as if in self-defense*]. Who's calling me? [*It is not a question. It is an exclamation which slipped out in a tremor of terror and which asks no answer from the darkness and terrible silence in the room, a darkness and silence which have for him been suddenly filled with the suspicion that he is mad in earnest.*]

FRIDA [*at this act of terror is the more alarmed at what she is to do. She repeats a little more loudly*]. Henry! . . . [*But although she wishes to stick to the part they have assigned her, she stretches her head out a little from the one niche toward the other.*]

[HENRY *gives a mad yell, lets the lamp fall in order to shield his head with his hands, and starts to flee.*]

FRIDA [*jumping from the niche onto the ledge and shouting as if she'd gone mad*]. Henry . . . Henry . . . I'm afraid . . . I'm afraid! . . .

[*The* MARQUIS *jumps onto the ledge and then to the floor, running over to* FRIDA, *who continues to shout convulsively, on the point of fainting. Meanwhile the others rush in from the door on the left: the* DOCTOR, *the* COUNTESS *who is also dressed as Matilda of Tuscany, the* BARON, LANDOLF, HARALD, ORDULF, BERTOLD, GIOVANNI. *One of them suddenly turns on the light: a strange light emanating from small bulbs hidden in the ceiling and arranged in such a fashion that only the upper part of the stage is brightly lit. Without paying attention to* HENRY, *who, after the moment of terror is past (though it continues to vibrate through his whole body), just stays looking on, astonished at the unexpected inrush of people, they anxiously run to support and comfort* FRIDA, *who still trembles and groans and rages in her fiancé's arms. General confusion of voices.*]

---

*These directions are an interpolation by the translator, designed to eliminate the need for a second intermission. In the original, what follows is called Act III.—E. B.

MARQUIS. No, no, Frida . . . *I am here . . . I am with you!*

DOCTOR [*coming up with the others*]. That will do! Nothing more is needed . . .

COUNTESS. He's cured, Frida, look! He's cured, do you see?

MARQUIS [*astonished*]. Cured?

BARON. The whole thing was a joke, don't worry!

FRIDA [*unchanged*]. I'm afraid, I'm afraid.

COUNTESS. Afraid of what? Look at him! It wasn't true, it isn't true!

MARQUIS [*unchanged*]. It isn't true? What are you saying? He's cured?

DOCTOR. It seems so, Marquis. As for myself . . .

BARON. Yes, yes, *they* told us . . .

COUNTESS. He's been cured for some time. He told those four attendants about it.

MARQUIS [*now more indignant than astonished*]. What? Up to a short time ago . . .

BARON. My dear Marquis, he put on an act so he could have a good laugh behind your back, behind the backs of all of us who—in good faith—

MARQUIS. Is it possible? He even deceived his own sister on her deathbed?

HENRY [*who has stayed apart, peering now at one, now at another, as he feels their accusations and their ridicule; for all now believe it has been a cruel jest on his part, and that it is at last unveiled. His flashing eyes have shown that he is pondering a revenge, though up to now his scorn, in tumult within him, has prevented him seeing precisely what it will be. Wounded, he bursts forth at this point with one clear idea: to accept as true the fiction which they have insidiously worked out. He shouts to his nephew*]. Go on talking, go on!

MARQUIS [*stopped by this shout, stunned*]. What, go on?

HENRY. Your sister isn't the only one who's dead.

MARQUIS [*unchanged*]. *My* sister? I'm talking of yours. To the very end you forced her to come here as your mother Agnes!

HENRY [*again having regard to the* MARQUIS's *present disguise*]. *And she wasn't your mother?*

MARQUIS. *My* mother, *my* mother, exactly.

HENRY. To the old man, old and far away, that I am, your mother is dead. But you're newly come down out of that niche! How should *you* know that I've not mourned her in secret—mourned her year in, year out—even in these clothes?

COUNTESS [*in consternation, looking at the others*]. What's he saying?

DOCTOR [*very disturbed, observing him*]. Quiet, for heaven's sake, quiet!

HENRY. What am I saying? I'm asking everyone if Agnes wasn't the Emperor's mother! [*He turns to* FRIDA *as if she were really Matilda of Tus-cany.*] It seems to me, my Lady, you should know!

FRIDA [*still scared, holding on to the* MARQUIS]. I? Oh, no, no!

DOCTOR. Here's the lunacy back again . . . Be careful, everyone!

BARON [*scornfully*]. Lunacy? That's not lunacy, Doctor, it's the same old play acting!

HENRY [*at once*]. I? You have emptied those two niches, and it's *he* that stands here as the Emperor!

BARON. Oh, let's have done with this perpetual jesting!

HENRY. Who says it's jesting?

DOCTOR [*to the* BARON, *loudly*]. Don't excite him, Baron, for the love of God!

BARON [*taking no notice of him, more loudly*]. *They* said so! [*Pointing at the four young men.*] *They* said so!

HENRY [*turns to look at them*]. You said that? You said it was all a jest?

LANDOLF [*timidly, embarrassed*]. No . . . what we said was, you were cured.

BARON. Very well, let's have done! [*To the* COUNTESS.] His appearance [*pointing to the* MARQUIS]—and for that matter yours, Countess—is coming to seem insufferably childish, don't you see that?

COUNTESS. You be quiet! Who cares about clothes if he's really cured?

HENRY. Cured? Yes, I'm cured! [*To the* BARON] Oh, but not to make an end of things all at once as you think! [*Attacking him*] Do you know that for twenty years no one has ever dared to appear before me here like you and this gentleman? [*Indicating the* DOCTOR]

BARON. Of course I know. Only this morning, after all, I myself came in dressed.

HENRY. Dressed as a monk, yes . . .

BARON. And you took me for Peter Damian. And I didn't even laugh, thinking of course . . .

HENRY. That I was mad. It makes you laugh to see her like that—now I'm cured? And yet you might have realized that in my eyes, her present appearance . . . [*He interrupts himself with a burst of scorn and an:* Ach! *He turns at once to the* DOCTOR.] You are a doctor?

DOCTOR. Yes, I . . .

HENRY. And you dressed *her* as Matilda of Tuscany, too? [*Indicating the* COUNTESS] Don't you know, Doctor, that in that moment you risked driving my poor brain back into the night? By heaven, to make the portraits speak, to make them jump, living, from their frames ... [*He contemplates* FRIDA *and the* MARQUIS, *then he looks at the* COUNTESS, *finally he looks at his own costume.*] Oh, quite a coincidence: two couples. Not bad, Doctor, not bad—for a madman... [*With a gesture in the direction of the* BARON] He thinks it's a carnival out of season, does he? [*Turns to look at him*] Then away with my masquerade costume, I'm coming with you, why not?

BARON. Why not indeed?

HENRY. Where shall we go? To the club? White tie and tails? Or home with the Countess—a happy threesome?

BARON. Wherever you like, my dear fellow. I can quite see you wouldn't want to stay here—perpetuating, by yourself, what was after all only the unhappy joke of a carnival day! It's incredible, it's incredible to me that you've been able to do it—even before today—once the effects of the accident were over.

HENRY. Surely, but it was like this, don't you see? After I fell from the horse and was hit on the head, I was *really* mad for quite a time . . .

DOCTOR. Aha! A long time?

HENRY [*very quickly to the* DOCTOR]. Yes, Doctor, a long time: about twelve years. [*Then, at once, turning to the* BARON] Can you imagine how it was, my dear fellow, to see nothing of what happened after that carnival day, what happened for you and not for me—how things changed, how friends betrayed me? Can you imagine having your place taken by others? Maybe . . . let's say . . . in the heart of the woman you loved? Not knowing who had died, who had disappeared! It wasn't such a . . . jest to me as you think!

BARON. Pardon me, but that's not what I meant, I meant afterward!

HENRY. Did you? Afterward? Well, one day . . . [*He stops and turns to the* DOCTOR] A fascinating case, Doctor, study me, study me carefully! [*He shakes from head to foot while speaking.*] One day, all by itself, heaven knows how, the trouble here [*he touches his forehead*] shall we say? stopped. Little by little I opened my eyes again. At first I didn't know if it was sleep or wake. Why yes, I was awake. I touched one thing, then another, I could see clearly again . . . [*He breaks off and makes a gesture toward the* BARON.] I agree with him! away with these clothes, they're a mask, an incubus! Let's open the windows, let in the breath of life! Come on, let's run out of doors! [*Putting the brakes on*] But where? To do what? To have everyone secretly pointing at me and whispering "Emperor Henry!" when I'm no longer like this but out there in the streets with my friends and arm in arm with you?

BARON. Not at all! What are you talking about? What makes you think that?

COUNTESS. Who could conceive of such a thing? An accident is an accident.

HENRY. They all said I was mad—even before—all of them! [*To the* BARON] And you know it! No one was more furious than you if anybody defended me!

BARON. Oh, come, that was only a joke!

HENRY. Look at this hair. [*Shows the hair on his neck*]

BARON. I have gray hair, too.

HENRY. There's a difference: mine went gray here! While I was Emperor! Understand? I never noticed it. I noticed it all at once—one day as I opened my eyes—I was terror-struck! For I realized that my hair wasn't the only thing that was gray, I must be gray all through, decayed, finished! Hungry as a wolf I would arrive at the banquet after it had been cleared away!

BARON. That's all very well, my dear man, but you couldn't expect other people . . .

HENRY [*at once*].—to wait till I was cured. I know. [*Pause.*] Not even those who came up behind and pricked my horse, harnessed and dressed up as he was, with their spurs . . .

MARQUIS [*disturbed*]. What? What was that?

HENRY. Pricked my horse, with their spurs! To make him rear up! Treachery, don't you see? So I'd fall!

COUNTESS [*at once, with horror*]. It's the first I've heard of that!

HENRY. That must have been a joke, too!

COUNTESS. But who was it? Who was behind us?

HENRY. No matter who. All of them! All who went on with the banquet, all who would now leave the scraps, Countess—the scraps of their piddling pity! Whatever leavings of remorse have stuck to their filthy plates they'll give to me! No thanks! [*Turning to the* DOCTOR *on a sudden impulse*] So you see, Doctor: isn't this case absolutely new in the annals of madness? I preferred to stay mad. Everything had been prepared for this new kind of pleasure: to *live* my madness, to live it with the clearest consciousness of it, and so avenge myself on the brutality of a stone which had struck me on the head: to take solitude—*this* solitude—squalid and empty as it seemed when my eyes reopened—to take solitude and straightaway clothe it in all the colors and splendors of that distant carnival day when you—[*he points* FRIDA *out to the* COUNTESS] ah! there you are, Countess!—when you had your day of triumph: to oblige all those who came to see me, to live out, by God, that famous masquerade of long ago which—for you but not for me—was the jest of a single day! To make it last forever—not a jest, no, a reality, the reality of a true madness! So here we were with our masks on—here was the throne room—here were my four privy councillors—traitors, of course! [*He suddenly turns in their direction.*] I'd like to know what you hoped to gain by letting out the fact that I was cured!—Once I'm cured, I don't need *you* anymore, you're fired!—To confide in anyone, now *that,* that is really the act of a madman!—But now it's my turn, and I accuse you! [*He turns to the others.*] Do you know, they thought they and I could play the joke on you now, take *you* in! [*He bursts out laughing. The others manage to laugh, embarrassed, except the* COUNTESS.]

BARON [*to the* MARQUIS]. Just think . . . not bad, hm? . . .

MARQUIS [*to the four young men*]. You?

HENRY. We must forgive them. For me, these clothes [*indicating his own costume*] are a caricature, a voluntary and overt caricature, of that other masquerade, the one that's going on all the time. You take part in it whether you know it or not. If without knowing it you wear the mask of what you think you are, you are still a puppet in this masquerade, though an *in*voluntary one. That's why we must forgive these four young men if they don't yet see these clothes of theirs as in character. [*Again he turns to the* BARON.] You know this? One soon gets used to it. And one walks around like this—[*He does so.*] a tragic character—there's nothing to it—in a room like this!—Look, Doctor. I remember a priest—an Irish priest undoubtedly—good-looking, too—and one November day he was sleeping in the sun in a public park. He'd laid his arm along the back of the seat for support. He was basking in the delight of a golden warmth which to him must have seemed almost like summer. One can be sure that at that moment he didn't know he was a priest anymore, he didn't know where he was. He was dreaming, who knows of what?—A small boy passed. He was carrying a flower he'd plucked, with a long stalk. In passing, he tickled the priest, right here in the neck.—I saw laughter in the priest's eyes as they opened. His whole mouth laughed with the happy laughter of his dream. He'd let himself go, he had escaped. But I must tell you, he soon put himself together again, he soon belonged to his priest's cassock again. He grew rigid. And back into his eyes came the same seriousness that you have seen in mine—for Irish priests defend the seriousness of their Catholic faith with the same zeal I felt for the sacred

rights of hereditary monarchy.—I am cured, gentlemen, for I *know*
I'm playing the madman, I do it quite calmly.—Woe betide you if you
live your madness unquietly, without knowing it, without seeing it!

BARON. So the obvious conclusion is—that *we* are the madmen!

HENRY [*with a little outburst that he manages to check*]. If you were not
mad—you and she—would you have come?

BARON. Actually, I came here believing the madman to be you.

HENRY [*loudly of a sudden, indicating the* COUNTESS]. And she?

BARON. She? I don't know. I see that she seems bewitched by what you
have to say, fascinated by this conscious madness of yours! [*He turns
to her.*] Dressed as you are, I'm sure you could stay here and live it out,
Countess . . .

COUNTESS. You are impertinent!

HENRY [*at once, placating her*]. Don't mind him, don't mind him. He's
determined to provoke me—though that was just what the doctor
told him not to do. [*Turning to the* BARON] Do you think I'll trouble
myself any more about what happened between me and you—about
the part you played in my misfortune with her [*indicates the* COUNT-
ESS, *then turns to her, indicating the* BARON]—the part he is now playing in *your* life?—My life is like this! Yours is not!—The life you have
grown old in—I have not lived at all! [*To the* COUNTESS] Is that what
you wanted to say, to prove, to me? You were even prepared to take
the doctor's advice and dress like that? Well done, Doctor, I say again.
Two pictures: "Before and After: what we were then, and what we are
today!"—But I'm not mad in your way, Doctor. I well know he [*indicating the* MARQUIS] can't be me because *I* am Henry the Fourth.
I've been Henry the Fourth for twenty years, understand? Fixed in
this eternity of masquerade! [*Indicating the* COUNTESS] She has lived
them, she has enjoyed them, the twenty years, and she's become—a
woman I can't recognize. For I know her thus [*indicating* FRIDA *and
going over to her*]—in my eyes, this is she, forever . . . You seem like a
child that I can frighten as I will. [*To* FRIDA] You've been badly frightened, haven't you, my child, by the joke they persuaded you to play?
They didn't understand that, to me, it could hardly be the joke they
intended, it could only be this terrible prodigy: a dream come alive—
in you! More alive than ever! For there [*pointing to the niche*] you were
an image. They have made you a living creature. You are mine, mine,
mine! And by right! [*He takes her in his arms, laughing like a madman
while the others are scared out of their wits and shout. But, when they try
to tear* FRIDA *from his arms, he becomes terrible and shouts to his four*

young men.] Hold them back, hold them back, I order you to hold them back!

[*Stunned, yet fascinated, the four young men automatically set about holding back the* MARQUIS, *the* DOCTOR, *and the* BARON.]

BARON [*liberates himself at once and rushes toward* HENRY]. Leave her alone! You are *not* mad!

HENRY [*drawing the sword, swift as lightning, from the side of* LANDOLF, *who is next to him*]. Not mad? We'll see about that! [*And he wounds him in the belly.*]

[*A general yell of horror. The* MARQUIS *and* BERTOLD *run to support the* BARON.]

MARQUIS. He's wounded you?

BERTOLD. He's wounded him! He's wounded him!

DOCTOR. I told you so!

FRIDA. God, God!

MARQUIS. Frida, come here!

COUNTESS. He's mad, he's mad!

MARQUIS. Hold him!

BARON [*while they carry him out by the door on the left, fiercely protesting*]. No! He's not mad! He's not mad! He's not mad!

[*They are shouting as they leave by the door on the left. And they keep on shouting until, amid the general din, is heard a more piercing shout from the* COUNTESS. *Then silence.*]

HENRY [*is left on stage with* LANDOLF, HARALD, *and* ORDULF. *His eyes are starting from his head. He is thunderstruck at the life of the fiction he himself created. In a single moment it has driven him to crime.*] This time . . . we've no choice. [*Calls them around him as if to defend himself.*] We're here . . . forever!

The Man with the Flower in his Mouth

CHARACTERS

The Man with the Flower in his Mouth
A Peaceful Customer
Toward the end, at the points indicated, a Woman is seen at the corner,
   clad in black, and wearing an old hat with drooping feathers.

At the back, we see the trees of an avenue and electric lights showing through the leaves. On both sides, the last houses of a street which leads into this avenue. Among the houses on the left, a cheap all-night café, with chairs and little tables on the sidewalk. In front of the houses on the right, a streetlamp, lit. On the left, where the street meets the avenue, there is another lamp affixed to the corner house; it too is lit. At intervals, the vibrant notes of a mandolin are heard in the distance.

When the curtain rises, the MAN WITH THE FLOWER IN HIS MOUTH *is sitting at a table and looking in silence at the* PEACEFUL CUSTOMER *who is at the next table, sucking a mint frappé through a straw.*

MAN. Well, what I was just going to say. . . . Here you are, a law-abiding sort of man. . . . You missed your train?

CUSTOMER. By one minute. I get to the station and see the damn thing just pulling out.

MAN. You could have run after it.

CUSTOMER. Sure—but for those damn packages. I looked like an old pack-horse covered with luggage. Isn't that silly? But you know how women are. Errands, errands, errands! You're never through. God! You know how long it took me to get my fingers on the strings of all those packages—when I climbed out of the cab? Three solid minutes. Two packages to each finger.

MAN. What a sight! Know what *I'd* have done? Left 'em in the cab.

CUSTOMER. How about my wife? And my daughters? And all the other women?

MAN. They'd squawk. I'd enjoy that.

CUSTOMER. You don't seem to know how women carry on when they get out in the country.

MAN. I know exactly how they carry on. [*Pause*] They tell you they won't need a thing, they can live on nothing.

CUSTOMER. Worse, they pretend they live there to *save* money. They go out to one of those villages*—the uglier and filthier the better—and then insist on wearing all their fanciest get-ups! Women! But I suppose it's their vocation. "If you're going into town, could you get me one of these—and one of those—and would it trouble you *too* much to get me . . . " Would it trouble you *too* much! "And since you'll be right next door to . . . " Now really, darling, how do you expect me to get all that done in three hours? "Why not? Can't you take a cab?" And

---

*The scene is rather obviously laid in Rome. The villages where "commuters" live are some ten miles out.—E. B.

the hell of it is—figuring on those three hours—I didn't bring the keys to our house here in town.

MAN. Quite a thing. So?

CUSTOMER. I left my pile of packages at the station—in the parcel room. Then I went to a restaurant for supper. Then I went to the theater— to get rid of my bad temper. The heat nearly killed me. Coming out, I say: "And now, what? It's after midnight. There isn't a train till four. All that fuss for a couple of hours of sleep? Not worth the price of the ticket." So here I am. Open all night, isn't it?

MAN. All night. [*Pause*] So you left your packages in the parcel room?

CUSTOMER. Why do you ask? Don't you think they're safe? They were tied up good and . . .

MAN. Oh, sure, sure! [*Pause*] I feel *sure* they're safe. I know how well these salesmen wrap their stuff. They make quite a specialty of it. [*Pause*] I can see their hands now. What hands! They take a good big piece of paper, double thickness, sort of a reddish color, wavy lines on it—a pleasure just to look at it!—so smooth, you could press it against your cheek and feel how cool and delicate it is. . . . They roll it out on the counter and then place your cloth in the middle of it with *such* agil- ity—fine cloth too, neatly folded. They raise one edge of the paper with the back of the hand, lower the other one, and bring the two edges together in an elegant fold—*that's* just thrown in for good mea- sure. . . . Then they fold the corners down in a triangle with its apex turned in like this. Then they reach out with one hand for the box of string, instinctively pull off just exactly enough, and tie up the parcel so quickly you haven't even time to admire their . . . virtuosity—the little loop is ready for your finger!

CUSTOMER. Anyone can see you've given a lot of attention to this matter.

MAN. Have I! My dear man, I spend whole days at it. What's more, I can spend a solid hour at a single store window. I lose myself in it. I seem to *be* that piece of silk, I'd *like* to be that piece of silk, that bit of braid, that ribbon—red or blue—that the salesgirls are measuring with their tape and—you've seen what they do with it before they wrap it up?— they twist it round the thumb and little finger of their left hand in a figure eight! [*Pause*] I look at the shoppers as they come out of the store with their bundle on their finger—or in their hand—or under their arm. I watch them pass. My eyes follow them till they're out of sight. I imagine, oh, I imagine so many, many things, you've no idea, how could you have? [*Pause. Then, darkly, as to himself*] All the same, it helps.

CUSTOMER. What helps?

MAN. Latching on—to life. With the imagination. Like a creeper around the bars of a gate. [*Pause*] Giving it no rest—my imagination, I mean—clinging, clinging with my imagination to the lives of others—all the time. Not people I know, of course. I couldn't do that. That'd be annoying, it'd nauseate me if *they* knew. No. Just strangers. With them my imagination can work freely. Not capriciously, though. Oh no, I take account of the smallest things I can find out about them. You've no idea how my imagination functions. I work my way *in*. In! I get to see this man's house—or that man's, I live in it, I feel I belong there. And I begin to notice—you know how a house, any old house, has its own air, how there's something special about the air in it? Your house? Mine? Of course, in your own house, you don't notice it any more, it's *your* air, the air of *your* life, isn't it? Uh huh. I see you agree—

CUSTOMER. I only meant . . . well, I was thinking what a good time you must have imagining all this!

MAN [*annoyed, after thinking a moment*].Good time? I had a—!

CUSTOMER. Good time, yes. I can just see you—

MAN. Tell me something. Did you ever consult an eminent physician?

CUSTOMER. Me? Why should I? I'm not sick!

MAN. Just a moment. I ask because I'd like to know if you ever saw a fine doctor's waiting room—full of patients waiting their turn?

CUSTOMER. Well, yes. I once had to take my little girl. She's nervous.

MAN. OK. You needn't tell me. It's the waiting rooms. . . . [*Pause*] Have you ever given them much attention? The old-fashioned couch with dark covers, the upholstered table chairs that don't match as a rule . . . the armchairs? Stuff bought at sales and auctions, coming together there by accident, for the convenience of the patients. It doesn't belong to the house. The doctor has quite another sort of room for himself, for his wife, his wife's friends . . . lavish . . . lovely . . . If you took one of the chairs from the drawing room and put it in the waiting room, why, it'd stick out like a sore thumb. Not that the waiting room isn't just right—nothing special of course but quite proper, quite respectable . . . I'd like to know if you—when you went with your little girl—if you took a good look at the chair you sat in?

CUSTOMER. Well, um, no, I guess I didn't.

MAN. Of course not. You weren't sick . . . [*Pause*] But often even the sick don't notice. They're all taken up with their sickness. [*Pause*] How many times they sit, some of them, staring at their finger which is making meaningless markings on the polished arm of the chair. They're thinking—so they don't see. [*Pause*] And what an impression you get when you get out of the doctor's office and cross the waiting room and see the chair you'd been sitting in awaiting sentence on the as yet unknown sickness just a short time before! Now, there's another patient on it and *he's* hugging his secret sickness too. Or it's empty— oh, how *impassive* it looks!—waiting for Mr. X to come and sit on it. [*Pause*] What were we saying? Oh, yes. The pleasure of imagining things. And I suddenly thought of a chair in one of those waiting rooms. Why?

CUSTOMER. Yes, it certainly . . .

MAN. You don't see the connection? Neither do I. [*Pause*] You recall an image, you recall another image, they're unrelated, and yet—they're *not* unrelated—for you. Oh, no, they have their reasons, they stem from *your* experience. Of course you have to pretend they don't. When you talk, you have to forget them. Most often they're so illogical, these . . . analogies. [*Pause*] The connection could be this, maybe. Listen. Do you think those chairs get any pleasure from imagining which patient will sit on them next? What sickness lurks inside him? Where he'll go, what he'll do after this visit? Of course they don't. And it's the same with me! I get no pleasure from it. There are those poor chairs and here am I. *They* open their arms to the doctor's patients, *I* open mine to . . . this person or that. You for instance. And yet I get no pleasure—no pleasure at all—from the train you missed, the family waiting for that train in the country, your other little troubles. . . .

CUSTOMER. I've plenty, you know that?

MAN. You should thank God they're little. [*Pause*] Some people have big troubles, my dear sir. [*Pause*] As I was saying, I feel the need to latch on—by the skin of my . . . imagination—to the lives of others. Yet I get no pleasure from this. It doesn't even interest me. Quite the reverse, quite. . . . One wants to see what their troubles are just to prove to oneself that life is idiotic and stupid! So that one won't mind being through with it! [*With dark rage*] Proving that to yourself takes quite a bit of doing, huh? You need evidence, you need a hundred and one instances, and—you—must—be—*implacable!* Because, well, because, my dear sir, there's something—we don't know what it's made of, but it exists—and we all feel it, we feel it like a pain in the throat— it's the hunger for life! A hunger that is never appeased—that never *can* be appeased—because life—life as we live it from moment to moment—is so hungry itself, hungry *for* itself, we never get to taste it even! The taste of life, the flavor and savor of life, is all in the past, we carry it inside us. Or rather it's always at a distance from us. We're tied to it only by a slender thread, the rope of memory. Yes, memory ties us to . . . what? that idiocy, these irritations, those silly illusions, mad pursuits like . . . yes. . . . What today is idiocy, what today is an irritation, even what today is a misfortune, a grave misfortune, look! Four years pass, five years, ten, and who knows what savor or flavor it will have, what tears will be shed over it, how—it—will—*taste!* Life, life! You only have to think of giving it up—especially if it's a matter of days—[*At this point the head of the* WOMAN IN BLACK *is seen at the corner.*] Look! See that? At the corner! See that woman, that shadow of a woman? She's hiding now.

CUSTOMER. What? Who was it?

MAN. You didn't see? She's hiding now.

CUSTOMER. A woman?

MAN. My wife.

CUSTOMER. Ah! Your wife? [*Pause*]

MAN. She keeps an eye on me. Oh, sometimes I could just go over and kick her! It wouldn't do any good, though. She's as stubborn as a lost dog: the more you kick it, the closer it sticks to you. [*Pause*] What that woman is suffering on my account you could not imagine. She doesn't eat. Doesn't sleep any more. Just follows me around. Night and day. At a distance. She *might* brush her clothes once in a while—and that old shoe of a hat. She isn't a woman any more. Just—a rag doll. Her hair's going gray, yes, the white dust has settled on her temples forever, and she's only thirty-four. [*Pause*] She annoys me. You wouldn't believe how much she annoys me. Sometimes I grab hold of her and shake her. "You're an idiot!" I shout. She takes it. She stands there looking at me. Oh, that look! It makes my fingers itch. I feel like strangling her! Nothing happens, of course. She just waits till I'm a short way off. Then she starts following me again. [*The* WOMAN IN BLACK *again sticks her head out.*] Look! There's her head again!

CUSTOMER. Poor woman.

MAN. Poor woman? You know what she wants? She wants me to stay and take it easy at home—all cozy and quiet—and let her be nice to me, look after me, show me wifely tenderness . . . Home! The rooms in perfect order, the furniture elegant and neat, silence reigns. . . . It used to, anyway. Silence—measured by the tick-tocking of the dining-room clock! [*Pause*] That's what she wants! I just want you to see the absurdity of it! Isn't it absurd? It's worse: it's cruel, it's macabre! Don't you see? Think of Messina. Or Avezzano. Suppose they knew an earthquake was coming. Do you think those cities could just sit? You think they could just sit calmly in the moonlight waiting for it? Carefully preserving the lovely lines of their streets and the spaciousness of their piazzas? Not daring to deviate one inch from the plans of the City Planning Commission? You're crazy. Those cities would drop everything and take to their heels! Every house, every stone, would take to its heels! [*Wheeling on the* CUSTOMER] You agree?

CUSTOMER [*frightened*].Well . . .

MAN. Well, just suppose the people knew? The citizens of Avezzano and Messina. Would they calmly get undressed and go to bed? Fold their clothes and put their shoes outside the door? Creep down under the bedclothes and enjoy the nice clean feeling of freshly laundered sheets? Knowing that—in a few hours—they would be dead?—You think they might?

CUSTOMER. Maybe your wife—

MAN. Let me finish. [*Starting over*] If death, my dear sir, if death were some strange, filthy insect that just . . . settled on you, as it were, took you unawares, shall we say . . . You're walking along. All of a sudden a passerby stops you, and, with finger and thumb cautiously extended, says: "Excuse me, sir, excuse me, honored sir, but death has settled on you!" And with finger and thumb cautiously extended, he takes it and throws it in the gutter. Wouldn't that be wonderful? But death is not an insect. It has settled on many walkers in the city—however far away their thoughts may be, however carefree they may feel. They don't see it. They're thinking what they'll be doing tomorrow. But I [*he gets up*] . . . look, my dear sir, come here [*he gets the* CUSTOMER *up and takes him under the lighted lamp*] under the lamp. Come over here. I'll show you something. Look! Under this side of my mustache. See that little knob? Royal purple? Know what they call it? It has such a poetic name. It suggests something soft and sweet. Like a caramel. Epitelioma. [*The "O" is stressed.*] Try it, isn't it soft and sweet? Epitelioma. Understand? Death passed my way. He stuck this . . . flower in my mouth and said: "Keep it, old chap. I'll stop by again in eight months—or maybe ten." [*Pause*] Now tell me. *You* tell *me*. Can I just sit quietly at home as that unhappy girl wishes me to—with this flower in my mouth? [*Pause*] I yell at her. "So you want me to kiss you, do you?" "Yes, yes, kiss me!" You know what she did? A couple of weeks ago she took a pin and cut herself—here—on the lip—then she took hold of my head and tried to kiss me, tried to kiss me on the mouth. She said she wanted to die with me. [*Pause*] She's insane. [*Angrily*] I'm not home! Ever! What I want is to stand at store windows admiring the virtuosity of salesmen! Because, you see, if ever, for one second, I am not occupied, if ever I'm *empty*—know what I mean?— why, I might take a life and think nothing of it, I might destroy the life in someone . . . someone I don't even know, I'd take a gun and kill someone—like you maybe—someone who's missed his train. [*He laughs.*] Of course, I'm only joking. [*Pause*] I'll go now. [*Pause*] It'd be myself I'd kill. [*Pause*] At this time of year, there's a certain kind of apricot, it's good. . . . How do *you* eat them? Skin and all? You cut them in exact halves, you take hold with finger and thumb, length- wise, like this . . . then! [*He swallows.*] How succulent! Pure delight! Like a woman's lips! [*He laughs. Pause*] I wish to send my best wishes to your good lady and her daughters in your country home. [*Pause*] I imagine them . . . I imagine them dressed in white and light blue in the middle of a lovely green meadow under the shade of . . . [*Pause*] Will you do me a favor when you arrive, tomorrow morning? As I figure it, your village is a certain distance from the station. It is dawn. You will be on foot. The first tuft of grass you see by the roadside— count the number of blades, will you? Just count the blades of grass. The number will be the number of days I have to live. [*Pause*] One last request: pick a big tuft! [*He laughs*] Then: Good night!

He walks away humming through closed lips the tune which the mandolin is playing in the distance. He is approaching the corner on the right. But at a certain point—remembering his wife—he turns and sneaks off in the opposite direction. The CUSTOMER *follows with his eyes—more or less dumbfounded.*

Translator's Notes

The little play can readily be converted into a monologue in the following manner:

The Woman can simply be cut out.

The Customer's lines can be either omitted or given to the Man in changed form as follows. Three dots indicate a jump forward to the next change:

Man: Well, here you are, a law-abiding sort of man—. As you say, you miss your train, see the damn thing just pulling out. But for those packages, you could have run after it. Your wife sends you shopping . . . I'd have left the packages in the cab and grabbed my train! Hm? Yes, I know your wife would have squawked. What of it? I like to hear the women squawk. Let me get your story straight. You live in the country. You commute. And your wife sends you shopping. Now you've missed your train, there isn't another till 4:00 A.M., so you figure it isn't worth leaving town at all, you may as well spend the night at this café. You left your packages in the parcel room. They're safe there, too. I know how those salesmen wrap their stuff. They make a specialty of it. [*Pause.*] I can see their hands . . . ready for your finger! I've given a lot of attention to this matter. I spend whole days at it. What's more . . . it helps. Latching on—to life. With the imagination . . . I see you agree—You're thinking what a good time I must have imagining all this. Good time! Tell me something. Did you ever consult an eminent physician? Did you ever see a fine doctor's waiting room full of patients waiting their turn? Yes? Well, you needn't tell me. It's the waiting room—. . . took a good look at the chair you sat in? Of course not. You weren't . . . Why? You don't see the connection? . . . your other little troubles . . . And thank God they're little . . . She's hiding now. You didn't see? A woman, yes. My wife. She keeps an eye on me . . . There's her head again! You know what she wants? She wants . . . You agree? Well, suppose just the people . . . You think they might? Let me finish. If death . . .

About the time and place. The place, as noted above, is Rome. The time? Around 1920. The story on which the play is based first appeared in 1918 under the title "Caffè Notturno" (All Night Café). The play was first performed in 1923; first published in 1926.